qmail

Other resources from O'Reilly

Related titles
Sendmail
sendmail Cookbook
Essential System
    Administration
TCP/IP Network
    Administration

Exim: The Mail Transfer
    Agent
Postfix: The Definitive Guide
Programming Internet Email
Internet Core Protocols: The
    Definitive Guide

oreilly.com
oreilly.com is more than a complete catalog of O'Reilly books. You'll also find links to news, events, articles, weblogs, sample chapters, and code examples.

oreillynet.com is the essential portal for developers interested in open and emerging technologies, including new platforms, programming languages, and operating systems.

Conferences
O'Reilly & Associates brings diverse innovators together to nurture the ideas that spark revolutionary industries. We specialize in documenting the latest tools and systems, translating the innovator's knowledge into useful skills for those in the trenches. Visit *conferences.oreilly.com* for our upcoming events.

Safari Bookshelf (*safari.oreilly.com*) is the premier online reference library for programmers and IT professionals. Conduct searches across more than 1,000 books. Subscribers can zero in on answers to time-critical questions in a matter of seconds. Read the books on your Bookshelf from cover to cover or simply flip to the page you need. Try it today with a free trial.

qmail

John R. Levine

O'REILLY®

Beijing · Cambridge · Farnham · Köln · Paris · Sebastopol · Taipei · Tokyo

qmail
by John R. Levine

Copyright © 2004 O'Reilly Media, Inc. All rights reserved.
Printed in the United States of America.

Published by O'Reilly Media, Inc., 1005 Gravenstein Highway North, Sebastopol, CA 95472.

Editor:	Simon St.Laurent
Production Editor:	Sarah Sherman
Cover Designer:	Emma Colby
Interior Designer:	David Futato

Printing History:

March 2004:	First Edition.

 This book uses RepKover™, a durable and flexible lay-flat binding.

ISBN: 1-56592-628-5
[M]

Table of Contents

Part II. Advanced Qmail

Preface

Since its release in 1998, qmail has quietly become one of the most widely used applications on the Internet. It's powerful enough to handle mail for systems with millions of users, including Yahoo Mail and VSNL (the largest ISP in India), while being compact enough to work on even the smallest PC Unix and Linux systems. Its component design makes it easy to extend and customize while keeping its key functions secure.

Qmail's design is rather different from its best-known predecessor, sendmail. People who are familiar with sendmail often have trouble recasting their problems and solutions in qmail terms. In this book, I try first to help the reader establish a qmail frame of mind, then show how the pieces of qmail work, and finally show how qmail can deal with some more complex mailing tasks such as handling mail for multiple domains, mailing lists, and gateways to other services.

What's Inside?

This book is organized into two sections, consisting of the following chapters.

Part I: Introduction to Qmail

Chapter 1, *Internet Email*, provides an overview of Internet email and the terminology used to describe it.

Chapter 2, *How Qmail Works*, outlines how qmail works, and gives a description of its basic parts and the philosophy behind its design and use.

Chapter 3, *Installing Qmail*, covers the basics of downloading, configuring and installing qmail, and other essential packages.

Chapter 4, *Getting Comfortable with Qmail*, finishes the job of configuring and starting qmail.

Chapter 5, *Moving from Sendmail to Qmail*, addresses issues encountered when converting an existing sendmail system and its configuration files to qmail.

Chapter 6, *Handling Locally Generated Mail*, looks at the issues involved in accepting mail from users on the qmail host and other systems, including cleaning up the sloppily formatted mail that most user mail programs send.

Chapter 7, *Accepting Mail from Other Hosts*, describes the processing of incoming mail, various tricks to let users identify themselves as local users when roaming away from the local network, and adding cryptographic security to mail transfers.

Chapter 8, *Delivering and Routing Local Mail*, covers sorting, reading, and otherwise dealing with local mailboxes.

Chapter 9, *Filtering and Rejecting Spam and Viruses*, covers anti-virus and anti-spam techniques, both those that can be built into qmail and ways to call external filters like Spamassassin.

Part II: Advanced Qmail

Chapter 10, *Local Mail Delivery*, defines the way that qmail delivers mail to local addresses.

Chapter 11, *Remote Mail Delivery*, defines the way that qmail delivers mail to remote addresses.

Chapter 12, *Virtual Domains*, describes qmail's simple but powerful abilities to handle domains with their own sets of addresses, including building mail gateways to other services, and special routing for selected mail destinations.

Chapter 13, *POP and IMAP Servers and POP Toasters*, covers POP and IMAP, the standard ways that users pick up mail from PC mail programs, as well as "POP toasters," dedicated POP servers with many mailboxes.

Chapter 14, *Mailing Lists*, details qmail's built-in mailing list features, the companion ezmlm mailing list manager, and offers some advice on connecting qmail to other mailing list managers such as mailman and majordomo.

Chapter 15, *The Users Database*, describes qmail's built-in database of local mail addresses and subaddresses.

Chapter 16, *Logging, Analysis, and Tuning*, describes log analysis tools and offers rules of thumb for tuning qmail for best performance.

Chapter 17, *Many Qmails Make Light Work*, covers applications with multiple copies of qmail on one computer, copies of qmail cooperating on many computers, and the mini-qmail package to run a mail hub serving many small client systems.

Chapter 18, *A Compendium of Tips and Tricks*, shows many problems and solves them.

Style Conventions

This book uses the following typographical conventions:

Italic

> Indicates the names of files, databases, directories, hostnames, domain names, usernames, email addresses, sendmail feature names, Unix utilities, programs, and it is used to emphasize new terms when they are first introduced.

`Constant width`

> Indicates configuration files, commands and variables, m4 macros and built-in commands, and Unix command-line options. It is used to show the contents of files and the output from commands. Keywords are also in `constant width`.

`Constant width bold`

> Used in examples to show commands or text that you would type.

`Constant width italic`

> Used in examples and text to show variables for which a context-specific substitution should be made. (The variable `filename`, for example, would be replaced by some actual filename.)

Examples and Patches

The examples from this book and the author's source code patches for qmail and related packages are freely downloadable from the author's web site at:

> *http://qmail.gurus.com*

Comments and Questions

We have verified the information in this book to the best of our ability, but you may find that features have changed (or even that we have made mistakes!). Please let us know about any errors you find, as well as your suggestions for future editions, by writing to:

> O'Reilly Media, Inc.
> 1005 Gravenstein Highway North
> Sebastopol, CA 95472
> (800) 998-9938 (in the United States or Canada)
> (707) 829-0515 (international or local)
> (707) 829-0104 (fax)

We have a web page for this book, where we list errata, examples, or any additional information. You can access this page at:

> *http://www.oreilly.com/catalog/qmail*

To comment or ask technical questions about this book, send email to:

> *bookquestions@oreilly.com*

You can sign up for one or more of our mailing lists at:

> *http://elists.oreilly.com*

For more information about our books, conferences, software, Resource Centers, and the O'Reilly Network, see our web site at:

> *http://www.oreilly.com*

You may also write to the author directly at:

> *qmail@gurus.com*

Acknowledgments

I wish to thank my reviewers, Mark Delany and Russell Nelson, for careful reading of the manuscript and many suggestions to improve it. I particularly thank my editor Simon St.Laurent and the staff at O'Reilly for believing my assurances that this book would in fact be finished, despite mounting evidence to the contrary.

## PART I

Introduction to Qmail

The first nine chapters provide an introduction to Internet email and qmail. They describe installing and configuring qmail, including advice on setting up a qmail system as a mail hub, converting an existing system from sendmail, and filtering out viruses and spam from incoming mail:

Chapter 1, *Internet Email*

Chapter 2, *How Qmail Works*

Chapter 3, *Installing Qmail*

Chapter 4, *Getting Comfortable with Qmail*

Chapter 5, *Moving from Sendmail to Qmail*

Chapter 6, *Handling Locally Generated Mail*

Chapter 7, *Accepting Mail from Other Hosts*

Chapter 8, *Delivering and Routing Local Mail*

Chapter 9, *Filtering and Rejecting Spam and Viruses*

Internet Email

Despite being one of the oldest applications on the Internet, email remains the Net's "killer application" for most users. For users' email to be sent and delivered, two kinds of programs have to work together, a *mail user agent* (MUA)* that a person uses to send and read mail, and a *mail transfer agent* (MTA) that moves the mail from server to server. Qmail is a modern MTA for Unix and Unix-like systems.

Before diving into the details of qmail, it's a good idea to closely examine some of the basics of Internet email that apply to all MUAs and MTAs. Common terms like *envelope* and *mailbox* have special meanings in Internet mail parlance, and both the structure of mail messages and the path that messages take through the mail system are carefully defined. The essential documents are RFC 2821, which defines the Simple Mail Transfer Protocol (SMTP) used to move mail from one place to another, and RFC 2822, which defines the format of mail messages. These RFCs were published in April 2001, updating the original RFCs 821 and 822 published in 1982. (All RFCs are available online at *http://www.rfc-editor.org.*)

For many years, the only widely used MTA for Unix and Unix-like systems was the venerable sendmail, which has been around in one form or another for 20 years. As a result, many people assume that whatever sendmail does is correct, even when it disagrees with the RFCs or has unfortunate consequences. So even if you're familiar with sendmail (indeed, especially if you're familiar with sendmail), at least skim this chapter so we all can agree on our terminology.

Mail Basics

The Internet's SMTP mail delivers a message from a sender to one or more recipients. The sender and recipients are usually people, but may also be mailing lists or

---

* Popular MUAs include pine and mutt on Unix systems, and Eudora, Netscape, Outlook, and Outlook Express on PCs and Macs.

other software agents. From the point of view of the mail system, the sender and each recipient are addresses. The message is a sequence of lines of text. (RFC 2821 uses the word "mailbox" as a synonym for "address" and "content" for the message.)

Addresses

All email addresses have the simple form *local-part@domain*. The domain, the part after the at-sign, indirectly identifies a host to which mail should be delivered (although the host rarely has the same name as the domain). The local-part, the part before the at-sign, identifies a mailbox within that domain.

The set of valid domains is maintained by the Internet's Domain Name System (DNS). Every domain is a sequence of names separated by dots, such as *example. com*. The names in email domains consist of letters, digits, and hyphens. (If current efforts to internationalize domain names ever settle down, the set of valid characters will probably become larger.)

The local-part is interpreted only by the host that handles the address's domain. In principle, the mailbox can contain any characters other than an at-sign and angle brackets, but in practice, it is usually limited to letters, digits, and a small set of punctuation such as dots, hyphens, and underscores. Upper- and lowercase letters are equivalent in domains. It's up to the receiving mail host whether upper- and low-ercase are equivalent in local parts, although most mail software including qmail treats them as equivalent.

Addresses appear in two different contexts: "envelope" data that is part of an SMTP transaction defined by RFC 2821, or in the header of a message defined by RFC 2822. In an SMTP envelope, addresses are always enclosed in angle brackets and do not use quoting characters or permit comments. In message headers, the address syntax is considerably more flexible. An address like *"Fred.Smith"@example.com* (*Fred Smith*) is valid in message headers but not in SMTP. (The form *Fred.Smith@example.com* is valid in either.)*

Envelopes

Every message handled by SMTP has an *envelope* containing the addresses of the sender and recipients). Often the envelope addresses match the addresses in the To: and From: headers in the message, but they don't have to match. There are plenty of legitimate reasons why they might not.

The envelope sender address is primarily used as the place to send failure reports (usually called bounce messages) if message can't be delivered. If the sender address

---

* Sendmail has often confused the two address contexts and has accepted message header formats in SMTP, both causing and masking a variety of bugs.

is null (usually written in angle brackets as <>), any failure reports are discarded. Bounce messages are sent with null envelope senders to avoid mail loops if the bounce message can't be delivered. The sender address doesn't affect normal mail delivery.

The envelope recipient address(es) control where a message is to be delivered. Usually a message starts out with the envelope recipients matching the ones on the To: and Cc: lines, but as a message is routed through the network, the addresses change. If, for example, a message is sent to *able@example.com* and *baker@domain.com*, the copy sent to the host handling example.com will only have able's address in the envelope and the one sent to the host handling domain.com will only have baker's address. In many cases a user will have a different internal than external address—for example, mail to *john.q.public@example.com* is delivered to *jqpublic@example.com*, in which case the envelope recipient address is changed at the place where the mail is received for the original address and readdressed to the new one.

Messages

An Internet email message has a well specified format defined in RFC 2822. The message consists of lines of text, each ended by a carriage-return line-feed pair. All of the text must be seven-bit ASCII. (The 8BITMIME extension to SMTP permits characters with the high bit as well but still doesn't permit arbitrary binary data. If you want to send binary material as email, you must encode it using MIME encodings.)

The first part of the message is the *header*. Each header line starts with a tag that says what kind of header it is, followed by a colon, usually some whitespace, and then the contents of the header line. If a header is too long to fit on one line, it can be split into multiple lines. The second and subsequent lines start with whitespace to identify them as continuations. Every message must have From: and Date: header lines, and most have other headers such as To:, Cc:, Subject:, and Received:. The contents of some headers (such as Date:) are in a strictly defined format, while the contents of others (such as Subject:) are entirely arbitrary.

Some mail programs are more careful than others to create correct headers. (Many, for example, put invalid time zones in Date: headers.) Qmail is quite careful when it creates headers at the time a new message is injected into the mail system, but doesn't look at or change message headers on messages that are transported through the system. The only change it makes to existing messages is to add Received: and Delivered-To: headers at the top, to chronicle the message's path through the system.

The headers are separated from the body of the message by an empty line. The body can contain any arbitrary text, subject to a rarely enforced limit of 998 characters per line. The message must end with CR/LF, that is, no partial line at the end.

Lines

Every line in a message must end with CR/LF, the two hex bytes 0D 0A. This simple sounding requirement has caused a remarkable amount of confusion and difficulty over the years. Different computer operating systems use different conventions for line endings. Some use CR/LF, including all of Microsoft's systems and a string of predecessors from CP/M to the 1960s era TOPS-10. Unix and Unix-like systems use LF. Macintoshes use CR, just to be different.

Regardless of the local line-ending convention, messages sent and received via SMTP have to use CR/LF, and the MTA has to translate from local to CR/LF when sending mail and back from CR/LF to local when receiving mail. Unfortunately, a common bug in some MTAs has been to forget to make this translation, typically sending bare LFs rather than CR/LF. Furthermore, RFC 822 said nothing about what a bare CR or LF in a mail message means. Some MTAs (sendmail, notably) treat a bare LF the same as CR/LF. Others treat it as any other data character. Qmail rejects incoming SMTP mail containing a bare CR or LF on the theory that it's impossible to tell what the sender's intent was, and RFC 2822 agrees with qmail that a bare CR or LF is forbidden. (It's easy enough to tweak qmail's SMTP daemon to accept bare LF, of course, if you really want to. See Chapter 6.)

Mailstore

The *mailstore* is the place where messages live between the time that qmail or another MTA delivers them and the user picks them up. Often, it's also the place where the user saves messages after reading them.

I divide mailstores into two varieties: transparent and opaque. A transparent mailstore is one that an MUA can directly access as files, while an opaque one requires a network protocol to access. (As you might expect, there's considerable overlap between the two, with an MUA running on the system where the mail is stored using a user's mailstore as transparent and one running on a PC elsewhere using the same mailstore as opaque.)

A mailstore has several jobs beyond receiving messages. It must:

* Maintain a little per-message status information, such as whether a message is read, answered, or deleted
* Make it possible to group messages into multiple folders
* Make it possible to delete messages and move them from folder to folder

Transparent Mailstore

Unix systems have had a variety of mailstore file formats over the years. The oldest and still most popular is *mbox*, a format invented in two minutes in the 1970s for an early Unix mail program, and largely unchanged since then. An mbox is just a text file with the messages one after another. Each message is preceded by a From line and followed by a blank line. The From line looks like this:

```
From fred@example.com Wed Oct 06 19:10:49 1999
```

The address is usually (but not always) the envelope sender of the following message, and the timestamp is the time the message was added to the mailbox. Although it's easy to add a new message to an mbox, it's difficult to manipulate messages in the middle of a mailbox, and sharing a mailbox reliably between two processes is very tricky due to problems with file locking on disks shared over a network. Mboxes have been surprisingly durable considering their nearly accidental origins and their drawbacks, discussed in more detail in Chapter 10.

The MH mail system, developed at the RAND corporation in the 1980s, used a more sophisticated mailstore that made each mailbox a directory, with each message a separate file in the directory. Separate files made it easier to move messages around within mailboxes but still didn't solve the locking problems.

Qmail introduced *Maildir*, a mailbox format that uses three directories per mailbox to avoid any need for locking beyond what the operating system provides. Maildirs are covered in detail in Chapter 10.

Opaque Mailstore

Opaque mailstores became popular when PCs started to gain dial access to the Internet, and users started running mail programs on the PCs rather than using Telnet to connect to shared servers and running mail programs there. The two popular opaque schemes are Post Office Protocol (POP3 for Version 3), and Internet Message Access Protocol, (IMAP4, pronounced eye-map, for Version 4).

POP3

POP3 is by far the most popular scheme used to deliver mail to PC clients. It is a fairly simple scheme that lets client systems download mail messages from servers. A client program connects to the POP server, sends user and password information, and then usually downloads all the waiting mail and deletes it from the server. It is possible for the client to leave the mail on the server, for people who check their mail from multiple places and want to receive all the mail on their primary computer even if they've peeked at it from somewhere else. POP3 can also assign unique ID strings (UIDs) to messages so that client programs can check to see which messages on the server haven't been seen before. (Despite these features, IMAP is usually better suited for people who read mail from more than one place.)

Qmail comes with a POP3 server that uses Maildirs for its internal mailstore. You can also use Qualcomm's popular *qpopper* that uses mbox mailboxes or the POP server from the Courier mail package that uses Maildirs. See Chapter 13.

IMAP4

IMAP is a scheme that lets client software manipulate messages and mailboxes on the mail server. It is much more powerful than POP at the cost of being much more complex as well. The client can tell the IMAP server to copy messages in either direction between client and server, create folders, move messages among folders, search for text strings in messages and mailboxes, and just about any other function that a mail client could possibly do to a message or mailbox.

The goal of IMAP is to allow client programs to manipulate mailboxes on the server just as though they were on the client system. This makes it possible for users to leave all their mail on the server so that they see a consistent view of their mail no matter from where they check it.

Qmail does not come with an IMAP server, but several IMAP servers work with qmail. The original IMAP server from the University of Washington uses mbox mailboxes, while the Courier IMAP server, part of the Courier MTA package, and the newer binc IMAP server use Maildirs.

The Structure of Internet Mail

Now that we've seen all the pieces of Internet mail, let's put them together and watch the typical path of a message as it's sent from one person to another.

First the sender runs a MUA, such as Pine or Eudora, and creates the message. Then a click of the Send button (or the equivalent) starts it on its way by passing it to the MTA (most likely qmail if you're reading this book), a process known as submitting the message. If the MUA is running on the same computer as the MTA, the MUA submits the message by running the MTA's injection component with the message as an input file. If the MUA is running on a separate computer, such as a Windows PC, the MUA makes a network connection to the computer running the MTA, and transfers the message using SMTP or a minor variant of SMTP called SUBMIT that's specifically intended for host-to-host message submission.

Either way, the MTA receives the message envelope with the sender and recipient addresses and the message text. Typically the MTA fixes up the header lines in the submitted message so that they comply with RFC 2822, then looks at the domain parts of each recipient address. If the domain is one that the MTA handles locally, the MTA can deliver the message immediately. In the more common case that it's not, the MTA has to send the message over the Net.

To figure out where to send the message, the MTA consults the DNS. Every domain that receives mail has an MX (Mail eXchanger) record in DNS identifying the host that receives mail for the domain.* Once the MTA has found the MX host for a domain, it opens an SMTP connection to the MX host and sends the message to it. In some cases, the MX host uses SMTP to forward the message again if, for example, the MX host is a firewall that passes mail between MTAs on a private network and the rest of the Internet.

Eventually the message arrives at a host where the MTA knows how to deliver mail to the recipient domain. Then the MTA looks at the local part of the recipient address to figure out where to deliver the mail. In the simple case that the address is a user mailbox, the MTA either deposits the message directly into the mailstore or, more likely, calls a local delivery agent program to deliver the mail. (On Unix, a popular local delivery agent is *procmail*, which does mail sorting and filtering as well as delivery.) Depending on the MUA that the recipient user has, the MUA may read the message directly from a transparent mailstore on the mail server, or use POP or IMAP to read the mail on a client PC.

A domain can have more than one MX record in its DNS. Each MX record contains a numeric value known as the *preference* or *distance* along with the name of a host. Sending systems try the MX host with the lowest distance first, and if that MX host can't be contacted, successively higher distances until one answers or it runs out of MXes. If there are several MX hosts at the same distance, it tries them all in any order before going on to hosts at a higher distance. If the sending host can't contact any of the MXes, it holds onto the message and retries later.

When the Internet was less reliable, *backup MXes* with a higher distance than the main MX were useful to receive mail for a domain when the main MX was unavailable, and then send it to the main MX when it came back. Now, backup MXes are only marginally useful, because sending hosts retry mail for at least a few days before giving up. They wait until the main MX is available and then deliver the mail. Multiple MXes at the same distance are still quite useful for busy domains. Large ISPs often have a dozen or more MXes to share the incoming mail load.

---

* Well, they're supposed to at least. For backward compatibility with pre-1980 mail systems, if a domain has no MX record but does have an A record containing a numeric IP address, the mail system uses that instead.

## CHAPTER 2

How Qmail Works

People who are familiar with other mail transfer agents (MTAs), notably sendmail, rarely receive satisfactory results from qmail. Qmail was designed and written in a very different way from most other mail programs, so approaches used to solve problems with other programs don't work with qmail and vice versa.

Small Programs Work Together

Earlier MTAs were written as large monolithic programs. Sendmail, for example, is one large executable program that listens for incoming SMTP connections, accepts locally generated mail, queues mail, attempts outgoing SMTP deliveries, performs local deliveries, interprets *.forward* files, retries mail that for which earlier delivery attempts failed, and about 50 other functions. While this means that all of these functions can share utility routines and it's easy for one function to call on another or pass a message to another, it also means that sendmail is a large program (300 KB of code on my system, not including any libraries it uses) that is slow to start up and expensive to fork, and bugs anywhere in the code can potentially make any of the functions misbehave or fail. Other monolithic MTAs, such as smail and exim, share these problems.

Qmail, on the other hand, is about 10 small programs, none with as much as 30 KB of code, working together. This design approach offers many advantages.

Each Program Does One Thing

Each of qmail's programs performs a single function. For example, *qmail-lspawn* spawns (starts up) local deliveries, and *qmail-clean* deletes the queue files of messages that have been completely processed. The various programs use documented protocols to communicate, which makes it easier both to debug them and to substitute one version of a program for another.

For example, on a local area network (LAN) with several workstations, the most common mail setup is for one server to handle all of the incoming mail and deliveries. All the other workstations use that server as a "smarthost" and immediately forward locally generated mail to the smarthost. In this arrangement, each workstation traditionally has a complete implementation of the MTA, with configuration files set to forward mail to the smarthost. Note that about 90% of the MTA's function is present but not used, and strange bugs often surface when the configuration files on the workstations get out of sync with each other. The optional QMQP package makes it possible to install a tiny "mini-qmail" package on the workstations, with the only configuration being the address of the smarthost. In a regular qmail installation, the program *qmail-queue* takes a message and creates a queue entry so the message can be processed and delivered. Several other programs call *qmail-queue*, including *qmail-smtpd*, which receives incoming mail via SMTP, and *qmail-inject*, which receives locally generated mail. QMQP replaces *qmail-queue* with a small program that immediately forwards incoming mail to the smarthost. There's no need to install the queueing and delivery part of qmail on the workstations, but to the programs that call *qmail-queue*, mail works the same as it always did.

The Principle of Least Privilege

Most monolithic MTAs have to run as the super-user to open the "privileged" port 25 for SMTP service and deliver mail to user mailboxes that are not world-writable. Qmail uses the *principle of least privilege*, which means it runs only the program that starts local mail deliveries, *qmail-lspawn*, as root. All of the other programs run as nonprivileged user IDs. Different parts of qmail use different IDs—for example, only the parts that change the mail queue run as the user that can write to the queue directories. This offers an extra level of resistance to accidental or deliberate errors.

Qmail also offers the very useful ability to delegate management of a virtual domain to a Unix user in a simple and secure way. The user can manage all the addresses in the domain by adjusting his own files as needed without ever having to bother the system manager or run super-user privileged programs.

Program Wrapping

Qmail makes extensive use of *program wrapping* to allow users and administrators to add and modify features.* A wrapper program runs a second program, modifying the second program's action in some way. The syntax for wrapper programs is:

```
wrapper wrapargs program progargs
```

---

* There's no standard name for this clever software design. Some people call it program chaining, and some people call it Bernstein chaining or a djb pipeline because Dan Bernstein is one of its best-known users.

That is, first come any arguments the wrapper takes, then the name of the program to run.

For example, when qmail runs a program for local delivery, it does not normally insert a mailbox separator line at the beginning of the message, but some programs, such as the procmail mail sorting package, require that line. The *preline* wrapper program provides the needed line:

```
| preline procmail arguments
```

That is, *preline* runs the program given as its argument, inserting a separator line ahead of the input.

In some cases, multiple wrappers can be cascaded, with several setup programs running each other in turn to create the environment for a main program. For example, the qmail POP3 daemon is implemented in three parts. The outermost, *qmail-popup* reads the username and password from the client. It then runs *checkpassword*, which validates the username and password, and changes to the directory that contains the mail. Finally, it then runs *qmail-pop3d*, which runs the rest of the POP3 session. By substituting different versions of *checkpassword*, it's easy to handle mail-only users, addresses in virtual domains, or any other local mailbox and password conventions.

No New Languages

Qmail tries very hard not to create new configuration or command languages, in reaction to the baffling complexity of the sendmail configuration-file language. Instead, qmail uses standard Unix features wherever possible. We saw program wrapping, previously, as one way to make programs configurable. The other way is to use the standard Unix shell. Rather than put a lot of options into the syntax of *.qmail* files, which control local deliveries, qmail builds in only the two most common options: delivery to a mailbox and forwarding to a fixed address. For anything else, you put shell commands in the *.qmail* file, generally using a few small helper programs such as *forward*, which sends a message to the address(es) given as arguments. This has proven in practice to be very flexible, and it's usually possible to express complex delivery rules in a few lines of shell script.

Configuration Files

Rather than put all of the configuration information into one huge file, qmail splits it up into multiple small files. The global configuration information goes into files in */var/qmail/control*, while per-user delivery instructions go into files in each user's home directory.

Most of the files are simple lines of text, such as */var/qmail/localhosts*, which lists the hostnames that should be treated as local to the system on which qmail is running, one per line. As a concession to efficiency, files that could potentially become large, such as the list of virtual domains, are compiled into CDB files that use a hashing technique to permit programs to look up any entry with one or two disk reads. Each file contains only one kind of information, so there's no need for a language to define file sections or subsections.

What Does a Mail Transfer Agent (MTA) Do?

The Internet model of email delivery divides the process into several separate stages and the software into several parts. The two important kinds of software are the Mail User Agent (MUA) and the Mail Transfer Agent (MTA). The MUA is the program that permits a user to send and receive mail. Familiar mail programs such as Pine, Elm, and Gnus on Unix and Eudora, Pegasus, Outlook, and Netscape or Mozilla on PCs are all MUAs. Each MUA has a rather complex user interface, and has many features, such as composing and reading mail, moving mail among mailboxes, and selecting the order in which to read mail. But an MUA doesn't deliver mail to other users; for that it hands its messages to an MTA.

In the first stage of mail delivery, the message is *submitted* or *injected* to the MTA. Usually the message comes from an MUA, but it can just as well come from another program, such as a mailing list manager. The MTA examines the address(es) to which each message is sent, and either attempts to deliver the message locally if the address is local to the current host, or attempts to identify a host to which it can relay the message, relaying the message to that host. (If that last sentence sounds a little vague, it's deliberately so, because there are many different ways that mail relaying happens.) Each of these steps could fail—a local address might not exist, it might exist but the MTA might be temporarily or permanently unable to deliver the message to it, the MTA might be temporarily or permanently unable to identify a relay host, or the MTA might be able to identify a relay host, but temporarily or permanently unable to relay messages to it. In case of permanent failure, the MTA sends a failure report back to the message's sender. In case of temporary failure, the MTA hangs on to the message and retries until either the delivery succeeds or eventually the MTA treats the failure as permanent.

Although the basic idea of an MTA is simple, the details can be complex, particularly the details of handling errors. Fortunately, qmail handles most of the details automatically, so administrators and users don't have to.

The Pieces of Qmail

Qmail consists of five daemons that run continuously, and about ten other programs run either from those daemons or from other commands, as shown in Figure 2-1.

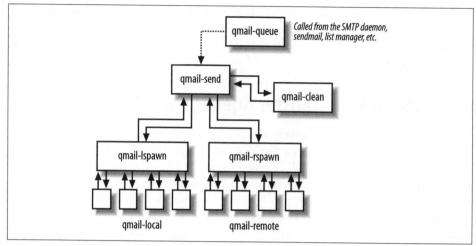

Figure 2-1. How the qmail daemons connect to each other

The primary daemon is *qmail-send*, which manages the message queue and dispatches messages for delivery. It is connected to two other daemons, *qmail-lspawn* and *qmail-rspawn*, which dispatch local and remote deliveries, respectively, using *qmail-local* and *qmail-remote*.

Once a message has been completely processed, with all deliveries having either succeeded or permanently failed, *qmail-send* notifies *qmail-clean* to remove the files for the message. The fifth daemon, *tcpserver* is discussed next.

A Message's Path Through Qmail

A message enters qmail either from another program within the system or via incoming SMTP. Regardless of where the mail originates, the originating program runs *qmail-queue*, which copies the message to a file in the queue directory, copies the envelope sender and recipient to a second file, and notifies *qmail-send*. For locally originating mail, *qmail-queue* is generally called from *qmail-inject*, or *newinject*, which adds missing header lines and cleans up address fields. (It's entirely legitimate for programs to call *qmail-queue* directly if they create messages with all needed headers. Mailing list managers such as Majordomo2 do for efficiency.) Most often, *qmail-inject* is run from *sendmail*, a small program that interprets its arguments like the legacy sendmail and calls *qmail-inject*. It's a useful shim to maintain compatibility with the many applications that call sendmail directly to send mail.

For mail arriving from remote systems, *tcpserver* runs as a daemon listening for incoming connections on the SMTP port. Each time a connection arrives, it runs *qmail-smtpd*, which receives a message via SMTP and calls *qmail-queue* to queue the message.

Regardless of where the message originates, *qmail-queue* writes the message to a temporary file in the *queue/todo* directory, putting a new Received: line at the top, and also saves the envelope sender and recipient addresses to files. Then it notifies *qmail-send* by writing a byte to a "trigger" socket file.

qmail-send takes the message out of *queue/todo*, and analyzes each recipient address to see if it's local, remote, or virtual.

For local addresses, it notifies *qmail-lspawn* to run *qmail-local* to do the local deliveries. For each local delivery, *qmail-local* sets up the context of the user that controls the delivery address (user id, group id, home directory, and a few environment variables) and then performs the actions listed in the address's *.qmail* file. Depending on the contents of the *.qmail* file, the local delivery may store the message into a mailbox, provide a different address to which to deliver the message, run a program to handle the message, or any combination of the three. Qmail doesn't provide any other built-in facilities for local deliveries, instead using separate programs run from *.qmail* files.

For each remote address, *qmail-send* notifies *qmail-rspawn* to run *qmail-remote* to do the remote deliveries. Every remote address is delivered through a separate SMTP session, even if there are several addresses in the same domain. (This is one of the most controversial features of qmail. See Chapter 11 for some ways you can merge multiple deliveries together and why you probably don't want to.)

For virtual addresses, *qmail-send* rewrites each virtual address as a modified local address, using the information from the *virtualdomains* files. (See Chapter 12.) Once it's translated a virtual address to the corresponding local address, the message is delivered the same as to any other local address.

For each delivery, local or remote, the spawn program writes back status reports to *qmail-send*. Each delivery can succeed, fail temporarily, or fail permanently. A delivery that fails temporarily is retried later until the message is "too old," by default a week, but usually configured to be less. A delivery that fails permanently, or that fails temporarily but is too old, produces a bounce report that is mailed back to the message's envelope sender.

Once all of a message's addresses have succeeded or failed, *qmail-send* notifies *qmail-clean* to remove the message's files from the queue, and qmail is done with it.

CHAPTER 3

Installing Qmail

Qmail probably doesn't come preinstalled on your machine. It probably isn't even shipped in source form with your machine. You must go to the FTP server, download it, configure it, compile it, test it, and install it. If this sounds like a huge amount of work, it's not—some of these steps can be a single command.

Where to Find Qmail

The official place to get qmail is through Dan Bernstein's web and FTP server at *http://cr.yp.to*. (The *.to* domain is actually the island nation of Tonga, but they'll sell a "vanity" address to anyone willing to pay, and Dan's professional interests center around cryptography.) An alternate address is *http://pobox.com/~djb/qmail.html*.

Both URLs are currently redirected to Dan's FTP server, *koobera.math.uic.edu*, at the Math department of University of Illinois at Chicago. For the rest of this book, we'll nickname that site *koobera*. The actual name of the site is subject to change at any time, which is the whole point behind using cr.yp.to and pobox.com.

If you use a web browser or a graphical FTP program to open an FTP connection to koobera, the list of files you receive may be scrambled. Dan uses an FTP server of his own creation, publicfile, which is good and bad. It's good because it's a typical Dan Bernstein program: small, secure, and fast. It's bad because most web browsers and visual FTP programs don't know how to parse the server's listing format.

Visual FTP programs without special support for anonftpd's file format (EPLF, Easily Parsed Listing Format) cannot give you a listing of files. The standard command-line FTP that comes with BSD, Linux, and most versions of Unix has no such troubles, nor does the FTP distributed with versions of Windows, because neither attempts to parse the listing. The current version of squid, a popular proxy server, has support for EPLF, so if you're accessing the Net through a squid FTP proxy, you should have no troubles.

Once you've made sure you can contact the FTP server, make a directory where you're going to download and build your software such as */var/src* or */usr/local/src*, and FTP a copy of qmail there. Use `gunzip` and `tar` or `pax` to unpack it into a subdirectory.

Copyright

Dan Bernstein reserves most rights when he distributes qmail. Copyright law lets him prohibit anyone from making copies (except within fair use, which includes actually loading the software from disk into memory, memory into cache, cache into processor, and disk onto backup media and back again). Dan has given users several permissions, however. You can redistribute the source to any of qmail 1.00, 1.01, 1.02, and 1.03. This source must be unmodified, in the original *.tar.gz* format, and match a certain checksum provided by Dan.

In addition to redistributing unmodified source, you can also redistribute certain derived works. An executable that is equivalent to that which a user would create through the documented install process is also redistributable. In practice, this means that you can download, compile, patch, install, and use qmail any way you want. The one thing you can't do is to distribute modified versions of qmail. That's why all of the user modifications are distributed as patches relative to the distributed 1.03, rather than as modified versions of qmail itself.[*]

Netqmail

Three well-known members of the qmail user community, Charles Cazabon, Russell Nelson, and Dave Sill, made a package called netqmail 1.05 that includes qmail 1.03, a small set of recommended patches, and a script to create a patched version of qmail ready to build. It also contains a few recommended patches for other packages often used with qmail. For people installing qmail from scratch, netqmail is the best place to start. It's on the web at *http://www.qmail.org/netqmail*.

To use netqmail, download and unpack it, which will create a directory called *netqmail-1.05*. Go into that directory and run *./collate.sh* to unpack qmail 1.03 and apply the patches. Once you've done that, there will be a second *netqmail-1.05* directory within the first one containing a patched set of sources ready to build as we describe in this chapter.

---

[*] Disclaimer: this description undoubtedly has a different legal import than Dan's permissions. Read Dan's license before you make any decisions about redistributing qmail yourself.

Should I Upgrade?

For better or worse, there's never been a good answer to that question. The best answer that I can offer is that in qmail 1.02 a user could crash the copy of *qmail-smtpd* she was running, by issuing a:

```
rcpt to: <>
```

However, this would only cause the user's copy to crash. Nobody else would be affected.

A good answer might be "because there's a bug that prevents X from working." This has never happened. Another good answer might be "because there's a security hole that endangers the security of your machine." This has also never happened.

The only way to answer your question is to examine the *CHANGES* file that comes with qmail. If you see a change there that affects you, then you should consider upgrading your version of qmail. Otherwise, the wise maxim "If it's not broken, don't fix it" applies.

The most important reason to upgrade is that if you're running the same version as most other qmail users, it's easier to ask them specific questions, pass patches and configuration tricks around, and otherwise be part of the qmail community. For most people, this is the best reason to stay in sync with new versions. I assume that you're using Version 1.03, the most recent as of the time this book was published, or netqmail 1.05, which is 1.03 with some recommended patches.

Other Software You Should Fetch

As long as you're accessing koobera, there's some other software you should fetch. I'm going to leave the version number out of the package name. Look for the current version when you're downloading.

Unpack most of these packages the same way you do qmail, with gunzip and tar or pax, each into its own subdirectory of your download directory. Starting with Version 0.75 of daemontools and, presumably, new versions of other packages, Dan has invented a new installation setup described at the end of this chapter.

ucspi-tcp
> A package for servers that respond to incoming TCP connections, as an alternative to the old *inetd* daemon. It used to be optional, but its *tcpserver* is now the only supported way to run qmail's SMTP daemon. If your system has the newer *xinetd*, it's possible to run qmail's SMTP daemon from it, although I don't recommend it. See *http://www.barriebremner.com/qmailxinetd.html*.

checkpassword
> If you're using qmail's built-in POP3 server, you want Dan's *checkpassword* program, which validates user logins as well. Even if you're installing an alternative checkpassword, it's nice to have Dan's checkpassword installed for testing.

dot-forward

For compatibility with sendmail's *.forward* file. It interprets the contents of a *.forward* file, and forwards the mail or deliver, it to a mailbox as needed.

fastforward

For compatibility with sendmail's */etc/aliases* file and handling large tables of forwarding addresses. It converts an aliases-format file into a CDB (Constant Data Base—another of Dan's packages) and forwards by a CDB lookup, which is fast and efficient. If you have more than a thousand aliases, you'll probably want this package.

serialmail

To deliver mail on-demand. Qmail's queue is designed to deliver mail to hosts that should always be available. Its queuing and scheduling policy presumes that domains' MX hosts are usually able to receive mail at any time other than relatively short downtimes. If this is not the case for any reason, then serialmail should be used to deliver mail when the host is able to receive it. Serialmail is also useful to single-thread deliveries to recipient hosts that can't handle parallel deliveries.

mess822

Contains *ofmipd*, the Old-Fashioned Mail Injection Protocol (OFMIP) daemon. SMTP isn't supposed to fix up mail that it transfers (a rule too widely ignored by sendmail and other MTAs). OFMIP is just like SMTP, except that *ofmipd* rewrites any hostnames or headers in messages it handles into standard compliant form. Mail sent by your users using desktop mail clients should be accepted using *ofmipd*.

Creating the Users and Groups

Qmail uses a set of user ids and group ids to control access to various qmail facilities. Because Dan doesn't trust the system libraries (history is on his side), he doesn't make system calls to determine these uids. Instead, the uids are compiled into various programs. That means that the qmail users must exist prior to compiling the programs.

Some versions of Unix and Linux are distributed with the qmail users and groups already defined. If your */etc/passwd* (or equivalent) contains entries for alias, qmaild, qmaill, qmailp, qmailq, qmailr, and qmails, and your */etc/group* contains entries for qmail and nofiles, you're all set and can skip ahead to "Configuring and making the software." Otherwise you must create the users and groups yourself. There are several ways to do this.

The adduser Script

Some Unices have a program called *useradd* or *adduser* to create users and groups. Often, use of this program is mandatory, because the machine uses shadow passwords. To be safe, use the program when it exists. The *INSTALL.ids* file has the necessary commands. Copy that file to */tmp/mu*, locate the right set of commands, delete everything else, delete the pretend root prompt characters in front of the commands, save it to a file, and run that file using sh /tmp/mu.

Adding by Hand

Some Unices let you create groups by editing the */etc/group* file and users by editing the */etc/passwd* file, the latter typically through the *vipw* program. Edit */etc/group* and add the following two lines:

```
qmail:*:2107:
nofiles:*:2108:
```

Make sure that 2107 and 2108 are unique group id numbers. If you have to change them, also change them in the user information in the next section.

Always edit */etc/passwd* using the *vipw* program, if it exists. It ensures that your shadow password database (if you're using one) is kept up to date. It also locks the password file against other programs changing it. If you have no *vipw* program, then go ahead and edit with your favorite text editor.

Add the following set of lines to */etc/passwd*:

```
alias:*:7790:2108::/var/qmail/alias:/bin/true
qmaild:*:7791:2108::/var/qmail/:/bin/true
qmaill:*:7792:2108::/var/qmail/:/bin/true
qmailp:*:7793:2108::/var/qmail/:/bin/true
qmailq:*:7794:2107::/var/qmail/:/bin/true
qmailr:*:7795:2107::/var/qmail/:/bin/true
qmails:*:7796:2107::/var/qmail/:/bin/true
```

Verify that 7790 through 7796 are unique user id numbers. If they're already in use, pick some other unused numbers. The exact id numbers don't matter so long as they're all different from each other and different from every other user on the system.

Nofiles Group Really Has No Files

The Unix "groups" concept makes it convenient to allow access to some files and deny it to others. One commonly overlooked possibility is that some users do not need to have *any* group permissions. The Unix kernel requires that each user belong to at least one group. However, obtain the effect of "no group" by a user-level discipline.

Qmail creates a group that no files ever use. This group is called nofiles, naturally enough. Qmail uses this group for users who do not need group permissions. Users alias, qmaild, qmaill, and qmailp have no need to read or write files other than some very specific ones, and each owns the files it needs to write. Some Unices have a "nogroup" or "nobody" group; however, these cannot be used by a process and so cannot be used by qmail.

On most Unix systems, audit your system to see if any files are owned by "nofiles" using the following find command:

```
find / -group nofiles
```

Configuring and Making the Software

The vast majority of the qmail configuration occurs at runtime. There are, however, a few configuration options that can only be changed at compile time. These options are, as you might expect, not often changed. If you're reading this book front to back, skip this section and come back to it later, because most of the compile-time options won't make any sense to you.

These configuration options are each in a separate file in the qmail source directory, the first line or lines of which are the value. Lines beyond those have an explanation of the meaning of the value.

conf-break

Qmail permits users to have subaddresses, which qmail calls extensions. For example, *nelson-qmail-book@crynwr.com* has an extension of "qmail-book" if the break character is a dash. By default it is a dash character, but some sysadmins may wish to use a plus or equals character for compatibility with other software. (Sendmail uses a plus sign.[*])

conf-cc

The compiler is not set in the makefile, as is typical for a Unix program. The makefile actually uses a generic *compile* script. This script is created by the makefile. It combines *conf-cc* with some more information. If your C compiler needs special optimization flags, this is the place to put them.

---

[*] One potential cause of confusion is the difference between the break character and the character that separates the parts of extensions. *conf-break* specifies the break between the username and the extension. Extensions are also split into parts; however, they are always split at a dash character. So, if you set your break character to a plus, then *nelson+list-qmail* will be matched by *~nelson/.qmail-list-default* if there's no better match. See Chapter 7 on local delivery for more information.

conf-groups

The first two lines of this file list the names of the groups that qmail uses. They are used in the building process to get the group id (gid) for the install process. The first is the name of the group that several qmail users use to share information through group permissions. The second is the name of the group used by the other qmail users who don't need to use group permissions. Don't change this unless your system already has groups called qmail or nofile that conflict with qmail's use of them.

conf-ld

The first line of this file is the command used to link *.o* files into an executable. The most common change is to replace the –s flag it contains with –g to preserve symbols for debugging. If your linker supports static shared libraries, which start up faster than the more usual dynamic shared libraries, this is where you put the flags or command to use them.

conf-patrn

Qmail refuses to deliver mail to insecure accounts. If a user allows anyone to modify files in his home directory, anyone can modify his *.qmail* files. And that means that anyone can execute any command as the user. So, giving away write permission gives away everything.

An insecure account is identified by excess write permissions on the user's home directory and on the user's *.qmail* files. The excess write permissions are given as an octal number in the first line of this file. The default (002) is that other-write permission cannot be given. A stricter value would be 022, which disallows group-write in addition.*

conf-qmail

Qmail installs all its files (configuration, manpages, binaries, and mail queue) under a single directory, */var/qmail*. This is advantageous because qmail is not a special program (for example, it needs to be located at */usr/lib/sendmail*, or to own the queue at */var/spool/mqueue*).

This directory (by default, */var/qmail*) must be a local directory, not mounted via a network filesystem. Don't change it unless you have a very good reason to do so. The most likely reason to do this is to create two copies of qmail to run in parallel, as described in Chapter 17.

---

* The Red Hat Linux *useradd* program creates a separate group for each user. In this context, group-write permissions are not a security hole, so using a conf-patrn of 022 rather than 002 just causes extra work without improving security.

conf-spawn

This is one of the few static limits in qmail. It's imposed by the underlying operating system. A program can wait only for so many children at one time, and this number is the limit. It's set to 120 for portability reasons. You would need to increase it only if you need a concurrencylocal or concurrencyremote higher than 120, and if your operating system also allows it. (This number has to be less than half the number of file descriptors that a select( ) system call can wait for. On many Unix-like systems, it's possible to increase this limit at compile time. See Chapter 16.)

conf-split

The qmail queue is split into a number of hashed subdirectories, with one message in each of the subdirectories. The default of 23 is chosen so that the typical queue doesn't make the subdirectories too large. If your queue isn't typical (because, say, you run a big ISP or send mail to many customers) and has more than 10,000 messages in it, you might want to increase this number to a larger prime value. See Chapter 16.

conf-users

The first eight lines of this file list the names of the users that qmail uses. They are used in the building process to get the user ID (uid) for the install process. The first one (usually alias) is the user qmail uses when no other user matches. The second (qmaild) is used for the SMTP daemon. The third (qmaill) is used to log information. The fourth (root) is used to own binaries and documentation. The fifth (qmailp) is used to map a username into a uid/gid/homedir combination. The sixth (qmailq) is used to own files in the queue. The seventh (qmailr) is used to make remote connections as an SMTP client. The eighth (qmails) is used to schedule messages for delivery from the queue and generate bounce messages. Don't change this file.

Build Using make

To build qmail, simply run *make*. There's no separate configuration program as in some other packages. A number of portability problems are solved by Dan's inclusion of his own library functions. His library is the same from host to host and so are the calls to the library.

Because qmail uses less of the C library, qmail is less vulnerable to security holes in the C library. Unfortunately, some functions cannot be rewritten, because they require internal knowledge about the OS. For example, to read a directory, some versions of Unix require read( ) to be called and others require an internal interface routine to be called; there's no alternative to readdir( ).

If the Build Fails

There are only three reasons why the build might fail. First, because you didn't create the qmail users listed previously; seond, because a necessary external program—such as *make*, *cc*, or *nroff*—isn't present; or third, your platform isn't close enough to Unix to support qmail.

If your build fails with complaints about *errno*, you've tripped over a compatibility problem between qmail and recent versions of the C library. See the sidebar "Building with Recent GLIBC and Fixing the errno Problem" later in this chapter for the simple fix.

Building the Other Packages

You must build at least the ucspi package, which includes *tcpserver*, to get qmail going. Fortunately, Dan's other packages are even easier to set up than qmail, because none of them depend on user IDs. For each package, just unzip and unpack the downloaded tar file into a work directory and type make. Normally all of the files in each package are installed under */usr/local*, with programs in */usr/local/bin*. If that's not where you want them before you make the package, edit the file *conf-home* and put the installation directory on the first line of the file.

Starting with daemontools 0.75, Dan has developed an extremely automatic and somewhat incompatible system to install his programs, described at *http://cr.yp.to/daemontools/install.html*. All of the packages are built in the directory */package*, which you have to create, most likely as a symlink to a directory on a disk with more space than your root partition. (I link it to */usr/package*.) Packages are built in */package*, with commands symlinked into the new directory */command*. For backward compatibility it also links them into */usr/local/bin*. Documentation, if any, goes into */doc*. See *http://cr.yp.to/unix.html* for more details.

To install daemontools, FTP the package (or copy it if you've already FTP'ed it somewhere else) into */package* and unpack it, at which point the files will be in */package/admin/daemontools-0.76* (or whatever the current package name and version are). Then chdir to *admin/daemontools-0.76* and, as super-user, run the script *package/install*, which builds and installs the whole thing, building the commands in *commands* and symlinking them into */command* and */usr/local/bin*.

Finally, it creates */service* and arranges to start *svscan* at boot time. It adds lines to */etc/inittab* if it exists, otherwise to */etc/rc.local* to run *svscanboot* at boot time to startup *svscan*. If you have */etc/inittab*, the build process pokes the init process to start *svscan* for you; if not, it suggests that you reboot. Rather than rebooting, run the command it just added to *rc.local*:

```
csh -cf '/command/svscanboot &'
```

If your system has a daemon command to run programs unattached to any terminal, use it:

```
daemon /command/svscanboot
```

Installing Qmail

First become the super-user. Change to the directory where you built qmail, and type make setup. This makes all of the directories and installs all of the qmail files into */var/qmail*. Now type make check, which checks to make sure that all of the required files and directories are present. Assuming it reports success, qmail is installed and ready to go.

Installing Other Programs

To install the other programs, notably the ucspi package, change to the directory where you built each package and type make setup to install the files into */usr/local* (or if you changed *conf-home*, into the home directory you selected). For daemontools and other packages using the new */package* scheme, the build process already installed them.

Patching Qmail

Dan's license for qmail forbids the distribution of modified versions of qmail, so many people offer add-ons and patches that you can apply to qmail yourself. Add-ons are distributed as installable packages that you download and install like any other package, but patches are distributed as text files of differences between the original and the patched version of qmail, as created by the *diff* utility. You don't need any patches to get qmail going (other than the errno patch for recent Linux versions), but because so many useful changes are distributed as patches, nearly everyone uses a few of them, so you should be prepared to use them.

The *patch* program, distributed with most Unix-like systems, reads the patch files and applies the changes. If your system doesn't have it, it's available for download from the Free Software Foundation at *http://www.fsf.org/software/patch/patch.html*. To apply a patch to a package, be sure the source code for the package is stored in a subdirectory of the current directory with the package's usual name (such as *qmail-1.03*), then feed the patch file to patch:

```
$ patch < some-patch.txt
```

patch produces a chatty report of its progress. Patch files invariably contain context diffs, so *patch* warns you if the file you're patching appears not to match the one on which the patch is based. You must look at the rejected patches in the source directory with filenames like *filename.rej* and figure out where the patches should go. Occasionally when you're applying multiple patches to the same set of files, the patches can collide, but for the most part, the useful patches to qmail apply without trouble. Once a patch is applied, rebuild and reinstall the package from the patched source code.

If you're installing the recommended netqmail package, you've already patched the source. Netqmail includes a patch file called *netqmail-1.05.patch* that is automatically applied by *./collate.sh*.If you want to try patching qmail, a good patch to start with is the QMAILQUEUE patch, available at *http://www.qmail.org/qmailqueue-patch*. (Netqmail users needn't bother, because it's already applied.) It's quite small but very useful. Once you've applied the patch, any qmail component that calls *qmail-queue* to queue a mail message checks the QMAILQUEUE environment variable and if it's set, uses it as the name of a program to run instead. This makes it easy to insert filters of various sorts into qmail's processing without having to add special code to individual programs.

Now that you've built and installed qmail, daemontools, and perhaps other add-on packages, the next chapter tells you how to start it all up.

Building with Recent GLIBC and Fixing the errno Problem

If your system uses the GNU GLIBC Version 2.3.1 or newer, qmail won't compile without some small patches. This problem affects most recent versions of Linux. The qmail source code defines *errno*, the place where system calls put error codes, to be an int variable, but in these libraries it's not, it's a macro.

In the source file *errno.h*, replace the line that declares errno with this:

```
#include <errno.h>
```

In the source files *dns.c* and *cdb_seek.c*, find any lines that declare *errno* or *h_errno* and delete them so that the system *errno* is used instead. Then recompile.

The netqmail package available at *http://www.qmail.org/netqmail* includes the errno patch for qmail and, in its *other-patches* subdirectory, the errno patch for four other packages.

## CHAPTER 4

Getting Comfortable with Qmail

This chapter guides you through the basics of running qmail and delivering mail to users on your qmail host. It's quite possible to run qmail in parallel with your old mail system, which is usually a good idea during a transition, so you can do everything in this chapter while leaving your old mail system in place.

Mailboxes, Local Delivery, and Logging

Before you start up qmail, you must make a few configuration decisions. None of these are irrevocable, but if you know what you want, it's easier to set them that way at first than to change them later.

Mailbox Format

Qmail supports two mailbox formats: the traditional mbox and Dan's newer Maildir. I won't belabor the difference here (see Chapter 10 for more details) other than to note that mbox stores all its messages in a single file and is supported by all existing Unix mail software, while Maildir stores each message in a separate file in a directory, and is supported by a reasonable set of software (including procmail, the mutt MUA, and several POP and IMAP servers) but not as many as mboxes. If you're converting from an existing mail system that uses mboxes, it's easier to keep using mboxes, but if you're starting from scratch, go with Maildirs.

Local Delivery

If you use mbox files, qmail normally puts the incoming mailboxes in users' home directories. That is, for user fred, the mailbox would be *~fred/Mailbox*. Older mail programs often put all of the mailboxes into */var/mail*. For both security and disk management reasons, it's better to put the mail in the user's home directory with his or her other files, but if you have existing mailboxes in */var/mail*, it's not hard to persuade qmail to continue delivering mail there.

If you're converting from an older MTA, you can either set up qmail to deliver into the same mailboxes as the old MTA or, if you're feeling cautious, set qmail to deliver into Maildirs or home directory mboxes while the old MTA still delivers to /var/mail. (The disadvantage is that once you're happy with qmail, you have to convert and merge the old mailboxes. See "Creating Addresses and Mailboxes" later in this chapter.)

Logging

The traditional way to make log files is with the system syslog facility. It turns out that syslog is a serious resource hog and on a busy system can lose messages. On a small system this doesn't matter, but on a busy mail host, it sucks up significant resources that otherwise could be devoted to something more useful. Dan Bernstein wrote a logging program called *multilog*, part of the daemontools package, which is far faster and more reliable than syslog, but not particularly compatible with it. If you're sure that syslog won't be a bottleneck, go ahead and use it, but if you might eventually want to use *multilog*, you're better off starting with it because switching a running system is a pain in the neck.

An Excursion into Daemon Management

A daemon is a program that runs in the background (that is, without interacting with a user) and is useful. On Unix systems, there are two kinds of daemons: the ones that run continuously and the ones that run on demand. Familiar Unix examples of continuous ones include named, the DNS server, and httpd, the Apache web server, while on-demand ones include servers for network services, such as *telnet* and *ftp*, and cleanup scripts run once a day or once a week. The on-demand ones are all started from continuous servers such as *cron* for time-based services, and *inetd* or *tcpserver* (the qmail replacement for *inetd*) for network services.

The daemontools package provides a consistent way to run continuous daemons, optionally (but almost invariably) also arranging to collect log information that the daemons produce. The two key programs are *supervise*, which controls a single daemon, and *svscan*, a "superdaemon," which controls multiple copies of *supervise* and connects each daemon with its logger.

For each daemon to be controlled, *supervise* uses a directory containing information about the daemon. The only file that you must create in that directory is *run*, the program to run. Although it can be a link to the daemon, it's usually a short shell script that sets up the environment and then exec's the daemon. The *supervise* program creates a subdirectory also called *supervise*, where it stores info about what it's doing. Once *supervise* is running, you can use the *svc* program to stop and start the daemon, and send signals to it. (This consistent way to signal daemons is one of *supervise*'s greatest strengths.)

To run *supervise*, follow these two steps: create */service*, which you do with a regular mkdir command as the super-user, and start *svscan*, which I cover in the next section. Once *svscan* is running, it looks at */service* and starts a *supervise* process in each of its subdirectories. Every five seconds it looks again and creates new processes for any new subdirectories. If a subdirectory has a sub-subdirectory called *log*, *svscan* arranges to log the output of the program. In this case, it starts a pair of processes connected by a pipe, equivalent to:

```
supervise subdir | supervise subdir/log
```

The *log* subdirectory contains a *run* file that invariably runs *multilog* to write the output into a rotating set of log files.

Starting a Daemon

One of the least standardized aspects of Unix and Unix-like systems is the way that you start daemons at system boot time. Even if you use *supervise* as I recommend, you still must start the *svscan* daemon to get everything else going. Here are some hints to start *svscan*. If you ignore my advice and run daemons directly, start each of them the way I recommend you start *svscan*.

Versions 0.75 and later of daemontools include a startup script for *svscan* called *svscanboot*, and the daemontools installation process tries, usually successfully, to edit a call to that program into your system startup scripts. It sets up the environment and runs *svscan*, piping its output into a new program called *readproctitle* that copies anything it reads on top of its program arguments, which means that any error messages from *svscan* will show up in ps listings in the arguments to *readproctitle*. This kludge makes it possible to see what's wrong if *svscan* has trouble starting up or starting *supervise* for any of the directories under */service*:

Single rc file

Solaris and some versions of BSD put all of the startup commands in a file called */etc/rc*, usually with local modifications in */etc/rc.local*. If the daemontools installation hasn't already done so, add this line to either of those files:

```
/command/svscanboot
```

If it's convenient to reboot your system, do so. If not, just run *svscanboot* from a root shell prompt, detaching it from the terminal:

```
# daemon /command/svscanboot     # if you have the "daemon" command
# csh -cf '/command/svscanboot &' # if not
```

Either way, check with ps to be sure that *svscan* is running.

SysV /etc/inittab

System V and its derivatives and clones, including most versions of Linux, start daemons from a file called */etc/inittab*. If the daemontools installation hasn't already done so, add this line to the end of it:

```
SV:123456:respawn:/command/svscanboot
```

Then, to tell the *system* to rescan *inittab*, type:

```
kill -HUP 1
```

Again, check with ps to be sure that *svscan* is running.

Setting Up the Qmail Configuration Files

The final hurdle before starting up qmail is to create a minimal set of configuration files. The qmail distribution includes a script called *config* that makes a set of configuration files that's usually nearly right. I suggest you run the *config* script, then look at the files to see what it did and fix the files up as needed. All of the configuration files are in */var/qmail/control*. The ones you need to create include:

me

> The name of this host, e.g., mail.example.com. This provides the default to use for many other configuration files.

defaulthost

> The hostname to add to unqualified addresses in submitted mail. If your email addresses are of the form mailbox@example.com, this would contain example. com, so that mail to, say, fred is rewritten to fred@example.com. (Note that this rewriting happens only to locally submitted mail sent via *qmail-inject*, not to mail that arrives via SMTP.)

defaultdomain

> The domain to add to unqualified domains in submitted mail addresses, usually your base domain, such as example.com. This would rewrite fred@duluth to fred@duluth.example.com. (This rewriting also happens only in locally submitted mail.)

locals

> Domain names to be delivered locally, one per line. Mail to any domain listed in *locals* is delivered by treating the mailbox part as a local address. This usually contains the name of the host and the name of the domain used for user mailboxes, such as example.com and mail.example.com. Do *not* list virtual domains (domains hosted on this machine but with their own separate sets of mailboxes) in *locals*. I discuss them later.

rcpthosts

> Domains for which this host should accept mail via SMTP. This generally contains all of the domains in *locals*, as well as any virtual domains and any domains for which this host is a backup mail server. If *rcpthosts* does not exist, qmail accepts and delivers mail for any domain, a severe misconfiguration known as an "open relay," which will be hijacked by spammers. Be sure your *rcpthosts* file exists before starting qmail. If you haven't defined any virtual domains, just copy *locals* to *rcpthosts*.

There are over 20 more control files, but the rest can be left for later.

Starting and Stopping Qmail

Starting qmail is easy in principle. You run *qmail-start* and it starts the four communicating daemons that qmail needs. Two details complicate the situation: the default delivery instructions, and connecting the daemons to whatever you want to use for logging.

Because the daemontools package of which *supervise* is a part wasn't written until after qmail 1.03 was released, all of the provided startup files use *splogger* to send the log information to syslog. I find daemontools greatly preferable, so I primarily discuss how to set up qmail using *supervise*.

Choosing a Startup File

Qmail 1.03 comes with a selection of startup files you can use, either directly or as a starting point for a customized startup file of your own. You can find the startup files in */var/qmail/boot*. None of them are usable directly with daemontools, but they're useful as templates. The differences among them only affect what happens when mail is delivered to a user who has no *.qmail* file, because the only difference is the string to use as a default *.qmail*. They include:

binm1
> Default delivery using */usr/libexec/mail.local*, the 4.4BSD mail delivery agent, which puts mail in */var/spool/mail*

binm1+df
> Same as *binm1*, also providing dot-forward emulation

binm2
> Default delivery using */bin/mail* with SVR4 flags, which also puts mail in */var/spool/mail*

binm2+df
> Same as *binm2*, also providing dot-forward emulation

binm3
> Default delivery using */bin/mail* with flags for older versions of Unix; puts mail in */var/spool/mail*

binm3+df
> Same as *binm3*, also providing dot-forward emulation

home
> Default delivery using qmail's internal *qmail-local*, which puts mail in the user's Mailbox

home+df
> Same as *home*, also providing dot-forward emulation

proc

Default delivery using procmail, which puts mail wherever procmail puts it, usually */var/spool/mail* unless you patch procmail as I describe later

proc+df

Same as *proc*, also providing dot-forward emulation

Which flavor of startup depends mostly on your existing mail configuration. If you use procmail, keep using it. If you have a lot of users with *.forward* files, use a dot-forward version. (If you only have a few *.forward* files, it's easier to hand-translate them into *.qmail* files.) I don't recommend using any of the old mail delivery programs unless you really, really want to keep delivering mail in */var/mail*. For testing and usually for production, I suggest either plain home-directory mailbox delivery or procmail.

Assuming that you've installed and started daemontools as suggested earlier in this chapter, you now must create a pair of *supervise* directories for qmail. I use */var/qmail/supervise/qmail-send* and */var/qmail/supervise/qmail-send/log* to be consistent with the widely used qmail setup instructions at *http://www.lifewithqmail.org*. Create them like this (as the super-user, which is why the following command lines start with a # prompt):

```
# mkdir /var/qmail/supervise/qmail-send
# mkdir /var/qmail/supervise/qmail-send/log
# chown root /var/qmail/supervise/qmail-send /var/qmail/supervise/qmail-send/log

# mkdir /var/qmail/supervise/qmail-send/log/main
# chown qmaill /var/qmail/supervise/qmail-send/log/main
```

The *log* directory contains a subdirectory *main* that contains the actual logs. It belongs to qmaill, the qmail log pseudo-user.

Then create *run* files in both the main qmail and log directories, as in Example 4-1.

Example 4-1. qmail run

```
1. #!/bin/sh
2.
3. limit open 1000
4. limit maxproc 100
5.
6. exec env - PATH="/var/qmail/bin:$PATH" \
7.   qmail-start ./Mailbox
```

The two `limit` commands on lines 3 and 4 ensure that qmail can run many deliveries in parallel. Set maxproc to be larger than the number of parallel remote deliveries permitted. (By default the number of deliveries is 20, but you'll probably want to increase it unless you have a very slow or overloaded network connection, or handle a very small amount of mail.) Also set open, the per process open-file limit, to be at least twice the greater of the number of simultaneous local or remote deliveries permitted, because *qmail-lspawn* and *qmail-rspawn* use two pipes per delivery subprocess. Then the exec env command on line 6 clears out the environment, sets PATH to a known value, and runs *qmail-start*. The argument to *qmail-start* is copied from the example in */var/qmail/boot/home* to default deliveries to *Mailbox* in a user's home directory. (You can copy the startup command from one of the other example files, such as *boot/proc*.)

Also create *log/run* to start up the logging process, as in Example 4-2.

Example 4-2. qmail log/run

```
1. #!/bin/sh
2.   exec setuidgid qmaill \
3.     multilog t s4000000 ./main
```

The setuidgid command switches to the qmail log pseudo-user, then runs multilog to store qmail's output into rotating log files. The arguments say to prefix each line with a time stamp, and to create log files of up to 4 MB in the subdirectory *main*.

Supervise starts the *run* scripts directly, so they need to be executable:

```
# chmod +x /var/qmail/supervise/qmail-send/run
# chmod +x /var/qmail/supervise/qmail-send/log/run
```

Be sure the initial #!/bin/sh line is present in each of the scripts so they are self-running.

Fire 'er Up

Once you've created the *run* files, it's time to start qmail:

```
# ln -s /var/qmail/supervise/qmail-send /service
```

Assuming you have *svscan* running, within a few seconds of making the line, qmail will start. Look at the log file */var/qmail/supervise/qmail-send/log/main/current* to be sure. It should contain a line similar to this:

```
status: local 0/10 remote 0/20
```

Now try telling qmail to send some local mail:

```
$ /var/qmail/bin/qmail-inject
To: me

my first qmail message
^D
```

(Use your own username instead of *me*, of course.) The log file should now contain lines logging the local delivery:

```
new msg 175283
info msg 175283: bytes 230 from <fred@example.com> qp 5524 uid 100
starting delivery 1: msg 175283 to local fred@example.com
status: local 1/10 remote 0/20
delivery 2: success: did_0+0+1/
status: local 0/10 remote 0/20
end msg 175283
```

Your file *Mailbox* should contain the message. If not, the log should contain evidence of the problem, which is usually files or directories not created with the correct owner or permissions.

Now try a message to a nonexistent address:

```
$ /var/qmail/bin/qmail-inject
To: baduser

oops
^D
```

In this case, qmail attempts to deliver the message, then finds it can't and sends back a failure notice, which should end up in your mailbox. The log should look like this:

```
new msg 175283
info msg 175283: bytes 212 from <fred@example.com> qp 5690 uid 100
starting delivery 1: msg 175283 to local baduser@example.com
status: local 1/10 remote 0/20
delivery 1: failure: Sorry,_no_mailbox_here_by_that_name._(#5.1.1)/
status: local 0/10 remote 0/20
bounce msg 175283 qp 5695
end msg 175283
new msg 175284
info msg 175284: bytes 746 from <> qp 5695 uid 124
starting delivery 2: msg 175284 to local fred@example.com
status: local 1/10 remote 0/20
delivery 2: success: did_0+0+1/
status: local 0/10 remote 0/20
end msg 175284
```

Finally, try a test message to a mailbox on a remote system. If you don't have a remote mailbox handy, use the author's autoresponder at *qmail@gurus.com*. (It will send a response message telling you how clever you were to write to it, with a blurb for my books.)

```
$ /var/qmail/bin/qmail-inject
To: qmail@gurus.com

boing
^D
```

The logs show the remote delivery, including the IP address of the remote system and the remote system's response:

```
new msg 175283
info msg 175283: bytes 223 from <me@example.com> qp 6808 uid 100
starting delivery 3: msg 175283 to remote qmail@gurus.com
status: local 0/10 remote 1/20
delivery 3: success: 208.31.42.43_accepted_message./Remote_host_said:_250_ok_
993021663_qp_16918/
status: local 0/10 remote 0/20
end msg 175283
```

If all three of these tests work, you have correctly installed qmail. Congratulations!

Stopping Qmail

When you're running qmail for real, you'll almost never want to stop it, but when debugging, just tell *supervise* to stop qmail and mark it as down:

```
# svc -td /service/qmail-send
```

If there are deliveries in progress, qmail will wait for them to finish or time out. Then it exits. Use svc -u to bring qmail back up.

Incoming Mail

Next, install the SMTP daemon to receive incoming mail. If you have another mail system already running, set up qmail's SMTP daemon for testing on a different port than the standard port 25.

Configuration Files

The SMTP daemon only needs one configuration file to run: */var/qmail/rcpthosts*. For simple applications, *rcpthosts* can contain the same list of domains as *locals*. It is very important that you set up *rcpthosts* before starting your SMTP daemon. If you don't, your mail system will be an "open relay," which will transmit mail from anywhere to anywhere and be abused by spammers and blacklisted.

A little later we'll also be setting up a control file to tell the daemon what IP addresses are assigned to local users allowed to relay mail.

Setting Up the Daemons

Setting up SMTP involves three layers of daemons. *Supervise* runs *tcpserver*, which waits for incoming network connections. Each time a remote system connects, *tcpserver* starts a copy of *qmail-smtpd*, which collects the incoming message and passes it to *qmail-queue* for delivery. To run it under *supervise*, create a pair of directories, and call them */var/qmail/supervise/qmail-smtpd* and */var/qmail/supervise/qmail-smtpd/log*:

```
# mkdir /var/qmail/supervise/qmail-smtpd
# mkdir /var/qmail/supervise/qmail-smtpd/log
# chown root /var/qmail/supervise/qmail-smtpd  /var/qmail/supervise/qmail-smtpd/log

# mkdir /var/qmail/supervise/qmail-smtpd/log/main
# chown qmaill /var/qmail/supervise/qmail-smtpd/log/main
```

The *run* script eventually becomes rather complex as you add code to handle local versus remote users, spam filters, and the like, but this is adequate to start (see Example 4-3).

Example 4-3. Running the SMTP daemon

```
1. #!/bin/sh
2. limit datasize 3m
3. exec tcpserver \
4.    -u000 -g000 -v -p -R \
5.      0 26 \
6.        /var/qmail/bin/qmail-smtpd 2>&1
```

The limit command on line 2 defends against a denial-of-service attack in which the attacker feeds the SMTP daemon a gargantuan message that fills up all of memory and crashes the machine. Then the tcpserver command on line 3 accepts SMTP connections and runs *qmail-smtpd* for each one. The -u and -g flags on line 4 set the user and group numbers; substitute the values on your system for qmaild. The -v flag does verbose logging (recommended, it's not that verbose) and -p does "paranoid" validation of deduced hostnames of remote systems. The -R flag means to not try to collect *ident* information from the remote host. (Ident information is rarely useful and a failed ident request can stall the daemon startup for 25 seconds.) On line 5, host number 0 means to accept connections on any IP address assigned to this machine, and 26 means to use port 26 rather than standard SMTP port 25, which allows you to run the daemon for testing without interfering with an existing MTA on port 25. (If there's no other MTA running, you might as well use port 25.) Finally, line 6 has the command for *tcpserver* to run once a connection is open. At the end, 2>&1 combines any output to standard error with the regular output so both appear in the log files.

The *log/run* file is the same as the one for qmail logging:

```
1. #!/bin/sh
2.    exec setuidgid qmaill \
3.        multilog t s4000000 ./main
```

Once you have all the files created, symlink the *smtpservice* directory so *svscan* starts it up:

```
# chown +x /var/qmail/supervise/qmail-smtpd/run
# chown +x /var/qmail/supervise/qmail-smtpd/log/run

# ln -s /var/qmail/supervise/qmail-smtpd /service
```

If you look at *log/current*, you should see this:

```
tcpserver: status: 0/40
```

Now try sending yourself some mail, using Telnet to talk to the SMTP server:

```
$ telnet localhost 26
Trying 127.0.0.1...
Connected to localhost.example.com.
Escape character is '^]'.
220 example.com ESMTP
helo localhost
250 tom.example.com
mail from:<me@example.com>
```

```
250 ok
rcpt to:<me@example.com>
250 ok
data
354 go ahead
Subject: a message

hi
.
250 ok 993620568 qp 5602
quit
221 example.com
Connection closed by foreign host.
```

The log file for the SMTP daemon in */service/qmail-smtpd/log/main/current* should show the connection to the daemon:

```
tcpserver: status: 1/40
tcpserver: pid 5582 from 127.0.0.1
tcpserver: ok 5582 localhost:127.0.0.1:26 localhost:127.0.0.1::54044
tcpserver: end 5582 status 0
tcpserver: status: 0/40
```

Check the qmail log in */service/qmail-send/log/main/current* to be sure the message has been delivered:

```
new msg 175297
info msg 175297: bytes 198 from <me@example.com> qp 5845 uid 120
starting delivery 1: msg 175297 to local me@example.com
status: local 1/10 remote 0/20
delivery 1: success: did_0+0+1/
status: local 0/10 remote 0/20
end msg 175297
```

(The numbers vary somewhat; qmail uses the inode number of the spool file as the msg number.)

If this works, you now have a working mail system. If not, the qmail and tcpserver logs should give you hints about what's wrong. The most likely problems are missing directories or configuration files, or incorrect file modes. Also be sure you just didn't make a typing error while telnetting to the SMTP port.

If you want to stop the SMTP daemon, use svc -td just as you did to stop qmail. It's perfectly OK for the SMTP daemon to be running while qmail isn't. In this case, incoming mail is queued but won't be delivered until qmail is started.

Once you believe that qmail works, kill any other mail daemon listening on port 25, change port 26 to 25 in the *run* file, and restart the daemon with svc -t to start receiving mail on the standard port. The rest of the examples in this chapter use port 25 rather than port 26, on the assumption that qmail is now your production mail system, but for testing, they all work equally well on port 26.

Make Some Mail Aliases

Every mail system on the Internet should define a few standard addresses, such as postmaster, webmaster, and mailer-daemon. (The last is the return address in the From: line of bounce messages.) To define an address, just create a *.qmail* file for the address in the home directory of the alias user:

```
# echo fred > /var/qmail/alias/.qmail-postmaster
# echo fred > /var/qmail/alias/.qmail-mailer-daemon
```

(If your login name isn't fred, adjust these examples appropriately.)

Now try using qmail to send mail to postmaster and check that it lands in your mailbox. On a busy system, postmaster gets a lot of mail and you'll probably want to use procmail (discussed later) to sort it to some place other than your personal mailbox.

Relaying for Local Users

Your qmail system most likely is a mail hub for a bunch of PCs or workstations. You want to accept mail destined for any address from your users so they can use your mail hub as a "smart host," but for security reasons, you want to accept only mail destined for your own network from elsewhere. Setting up relay control involves two steps: defining the list of locally handled domains for which you'll accept mail from outside and defining the addresses of hosts that are allowed to relay. A third step is to treat mail from local PCs as "injected" mail that must have its headers validated and completed. (As opposed to mail that's relayed from other systems that should already have valid headers, but I save that for later in this chapter.)

You should have already put the list of locally handled domains into */var/qmail/rcpthosts*. (If not, do so now.)

Arranging for your users to relay is a little more complicated, because *tcpserver* and *qmail-smtpd* provide a general scheme that permits mail to be treated differently depending on what IP address it is received from. You create a file of IP address ranges and environment variables to set and compile it into a CDB database that *tcpserver* reads. When it receives a connection from an IP address in the database, it passes the corresponding environment variable to *qmail-smtpd*. For relay control, the relevant variable is RELAYCLIENT. If it's set, *qmail-smtpd* permits mail to any address, not just the ones in relayhosts, and appends the contents of RELAYCLIENT to each envelope recipient address.

Different people have different preferences for the location of the TCP rules file. I prefer to keep them with the rest of the qmail files in a directory called */var/qmail/rules*, so create a file called */var/qmail/rules/smtprules.txt* with contents like this (the # lines are comments):

```
# allow relay from this host
127.:allow,RELAYCLIENT=""
```

```
# allow relay from other hosts on this network
172.16.42.:allow,RELAYCLIENT=""
172.16.15.1-127.:allow,RELAYCLIENT=""

# otherwise, allow connections but no relay
:allow
```

The first line says to accept connections from any address starting with 127, that is, the loopback pseudo-network used for connections from the qmail host to itself, and to create an empty RELAYCLIENT variable. This permits any SMTP connection from the host that qmail is running on to relay. The second and third lines permit relay from any address in 172.16.42.x, and in the range 172.16.15.1 through 172.16.15.127. Replace these lines with ones listing the IP range(s) of your own network. You can have as many lines as you want; more lines don't make the lookup any slower once the file is compiled into a CDB. The last line is the default, and permits connections from anywhere else, but without setting any variables.

Now you must compile the rules into a CDB file, using *tcprules*. Although it's not hard to run *tcprules* by hand, it's a pain to do it every time you update your *smtprules* file (which you will, to block IP addresses that send a lot of spam). It's easy to automate the process using a *Makefile* to rebuild the CDB, as in Example 4-4.

Example 4-4. Makefile to rebuild the rules file for the SMTP listener

```
default: smtprules.cdb

smtprules.cdb: smtprules.txt
    cat $> | /usr/local/bin/tcprules $@ $@.$$$$
```

(The odd looking $@.$$$$ is the temporary name of the new CDB, the real name with the PID of the make process added to ensure uniqueness.) Finally, tell *tcpserver* to look at the rules file. Edit */var/qmail/supervise/qmail-smtpd/run* and add an –x flag to the *tcpserver* line, as in Example 4-5.

Example 4-5. Running the SMTP listener

```
1. #!/bin/sh
2. limit datasize 2m
3. exec  \
4.    tcpserver -u000 -g000 -v -p -R    \
5.    -x/var/qmail/rules/smtprules.cdb 0 25  \
6.    /var/qmail/bin/qmail-smtpd 2>&1
```

You're all set. Finally, use svc -t /service/supervise/qmail-smtpd to restart *tcpserver* with the new arguments.

To test this, send mail from a computer on the local network to an address somewhere else (such as a Hotmail account), and check the logs to verify that it's accepted and mailed back out.

Procmail and Qmail

If you do any sorting or filtering of incoming mail, you should install the popular procmail mail filtering package. Although procmail's filter definition language is terse to the point of obscurity, it's very powerful and easy to use once you get the hang of it. In the past, procmail's default mailbox location was in */var/mail*, and it didn't support Maildirs. Recent versions of procmail work well with qmail. Version 3.14 added support for Maildirs, and it's now easy to compile procmail to put the default mailbox in qmail's preferred place.

The source for procmail is available at *http://www.procmail.org*. Download it to a local work directory and unpack it. To make its default delivery be to *Mailbox*, edit the file *src/authenticate.c*. Around line 47 find the definition of MAILSPOOLHOME, remove the comment characters at the start of the line, and change the file name to *Mailbox*:

```
#define MAILSPOOLHOME "/Mailbox"
```

Or to make the default delivery to a user's Maildir, type:

```
#define MAILSPOOLHOME "/Maildir/"
```

(Note the slash after the directory name, which tells procmail that it's a Maildir rather than an mbox.)

Then make and install procmail as described in its *INSTALL* file. The procmail installation recommends that you install procmail as set-uid to root. When working with qmail, it does *not* need set-uid to work correctly, and I recommend that you don't do this. When used as the mail delivery agent for sendmail, procmail needs set-uid to run as the id of the delivered-to user. Qmail switches to the correct user ID before running procmail, as it does for any delivery agent, so procmail doesn't need to do so. Installing as set-uid won't cause any immediate problems, but it will pose a possible security problem should there turn out to be lurking bugs in procmail.

To use procmail as your default delivery agent, use this in your qmail *run* file:

```
exec env - PATH="/var/qmail/bin:$PATH" \
       qmail-start '|preline procmail'
```

(The preline command is a qmail component that inserts a From line that procmail needs at the front of the message.) Alternatively, to make procmail the delivery agent for an individual user, put the procmail command into the user's *.qmail* file:

```
|preline procmail
```

Sendmail systems often pass the address extension as an argument to procmail so it can be used as $1 in scripts. That's easy enough to do in *.qmail-default*:

```
|preline procmail -a "$EXT"
```

Procmail makes most environment variables available in its rule files anyway, so if you're not converting from sendmail, just use $EXT in your scripts.

It's frequently advantageous to use different procmail filter definitions for different qmail subaddresses. For example, if you are user fred and use the address fred-lists for your mailing list mail, *.qmail-lists* could contain this:

```
|preline procmail procmaillists
```

to use *procmaillists* to sort list mail.

Creating Addresses and Mailboxes

With the setup so far, every user in */etc/passwd* automatically has a mailbox with the same name as the login name.* If you're using mbox mailboxes, each mailbox is created the first time a message is delivered to it. If you're using Maildirs, you must create the Maildirs yourself using `maildirmake`. If all of your home directories are stored in */usr/home* or */home*, it's easy enough to give everyone a Maildir. Run a script like this as root to create them:

```
cd /home
for u in *
do
    maildirmake $u/Maildir
    chown -R $u/Maildir
done
```

The `chown` is important so that each user owns his own Maildir.

If you have more than two or three mailboxes to create, use the convert-and-create script from *http://www.qmail.org/*. It creates Maildirs for every user with a mailbox, and copies the mail from */var/mail* mboxes into the new Maildirs.

Once you've created Maildirs for all of your existing users, creating them for new users is considerably easier. Just add a line or two to your system's *adduser* script to create the Maildir as it creates the rest of the new user's files. On Linux systems, use `maildirmake` to create */etc/skel/Maildir*, a prototype that gives every subsequent new user a Maildir.

Reading Your Mail

If you use mbox mailboxes, the only additional change you may have to make is to tell your mail program (and your shell if it's one that reports new mail) that the mailbox is in *~/Mailbox* rather than in */var/mail*. Most mail programs check the shell variable $MAIL. For testing, change the MAIL variable at your shell prompt:

```
% setenv MAIL ~/Mailbox    (in csh)
$ export MAIL=~/Mailbox    (ksh and bash)
$ export MAIL=$HOME/Mailbox (in sh)
```

---

* That's not quite true; for security reasons qmail won't deliver mail to the root user.

Once you're committed to qmail and your mail is in */var/mail*, you want to copy everyone's mailbox to their home directory, using the convert-and-create script mentioned previously. Then, find the place in */etc/profile* or */etc/cshrc* that sets MAIL and change it to refer to the new mailbox location.

If you use Maildirs, your options are simpler. The only mail program with built-in Maildir support is mutt. On qmail.org there are some patches for pine to handle Maildirs, and a version of movemail for GNU Emacs users. If you use something else, you can use the scripts distributed with qmail such as *elq* or *pinq* that copy mail from a Maildir into an mbox and then run elm or pine. Honestly, if a user normally uses a mail program that expects mbox mailboxes, it's easier to tell qmail to use mboxes than to tell the program to use Maildirs.

An alternative that makes Maildirs available to most mail clients is to use an IMAP server such as Courier that handles Maildirs (see Chapter 13). The IMAP server can retrieve mail from the Maildir and from any number of Maildir-format subfolders. You can set up pine or Mozilla to use IMAP to deal with the Maildir folders, and use its built-in mbox support to handle mboxes directly as files. This has the added advantage that you can check your mail using any IMAP client from other computers if you're away from your usual computer.

Configuring Qmail's Control Files

Qmail is controlled by a large set of control files stored in */var/qmail/control*. Unlike some other MTAs that group everything into one huge file that they have to parse to figure out what's what, qmail puts each different kind of information into a separate file, so that each file needs little or no parsing. All files are lines of plain text (although a few files are compiled into CDB databases before use). Some, noted below, allow comment lines with a # at the beginning of the line. In files where each line contains multiple fields, the fields are separated by colons.

Most of the control files are optional, and qmail uses a reasonable default in most cases if a file isn't present. The only files that are absolutely essential are *me*, which contains the hostname of the local host, and *rcpthosts*, which lists the names of the domains for which this host accepts mail.

Here's a list of all the control files in alphabetical order, noting which component uses each one. Many of the optional patches introduce new control files, which are discussed during the description of the patch.

badmailfrom (qmail-smtpd)

> Envelope addresses not allowed to send mail. If the envelope From address on an incoming message matches an entry in badmailfrom, the SMTP daemon will reject every recipient address. Entries may be either email addresses, or *@dom. ain* to reject every address in a domain. This is a primitive form of spam filtering. These days, it's mostly useful to block quickly a mailbomb or flood of rejection messages.

bouncefrom (qmail-send)
> Default: MAILER-DAEMON. The mailbox of the return address to put in bounce messages. I've never found any reason to change it.

bouncehost (qmail-send)
> Default: me. The domain of the return address to put in bounce messages. I've never found any need to change it, although it's possible that if your mail host is mail.example.com, you might want to have the bounces come from example.com.

concurrencylocal (qmail-send)
> Default: 10. The maximum number of simultaneous local deliveries. Unless you have very slow delivery programs, the default is adequate for all but very large systems. Keep in mind that if you have slow delivery programs, it is quite possible to have all 10 or however many running as the same user, so be sure that the per-user process limit is high enough to permit them all to run.

concurrencyremote (qmail-send)
> Default: 20. The maximum number of simultaneous remote deliveries. The default is adequate for small systems, but too low for large systems or systems that host mailing lists. You should adjust it so that qmail uses as much of your outgoing bandwidth as you want it to. In the distributed version of qmail, you can increase this up to 120, which is enough for a moderately busy system with mailing lists sharing a T1 with other services. See Chapter 16 for advice on increasing it past 120 on large systems.

defaultdomain (qmail-inject)
> Default: the literal string defaultdomain. The domain to add to unqualified host names (names with no dot) on outgoing mail. That is, if someone injects a message with a sender or recipient address of fred@bad and this file contains

example.com, the address is rewritten as fred@bad.example.com. You invariably want to set this to the local domain. Note that only mail injected via *qmail-inject* has its header addresses rewritten. Addresses in mail that arrives via SMTP or is injected directly via qmail-queue aren't modified.

defaulthost (qmail-inject)

Default: me. Similar to defaultdomain; the domain to add to addresses in outgoing mail that have no domain at all. If defaulthost doesn't contain a dot, defaultdomain is added, too. Set this to the name of the local domain.

databytes (qmail-smtpd)

Default: 0, meaning no limit. The maximum message size to accept via SMTP. I usually set it to about 1/10 the size of the typical amount of free space on the partition where the qmail queue resides, to keep a single bloated incoming message from causing qmail to run out of disk space. The DATABYTES environment variable overrides the control file, so if there are certain systems from which you want to accept huge messages, you can put entries into the SMTP rules file to permit that. For example:

```
# allow 50 megabyte powerpoints from the boss
209.58.173.10:allow,DATABYTES="50000000"

# allow 20 meg outgoing mail from nearby hosts
172.16.15.1-127.:allow,RELAYCLIENT="",DATABYTES="20000000"
```

doublebouncehost (qmail-send)

Default: me. The domain to which to send double-bounce messages. There's rarely any reason to change it.

doublebounceto (qmail-send)

Default: postmaster. The mailbox to which to send double-bounce messages, that is, they go to *doublebounceto@doublebouncehost*. You can also send these messages to a special mailbox that you examine rarely, or because these days there are vast numbers of double bounces caused by spam with fake return addresses, you can set it to nobody or some other address that just throws them away.

envnoathost (qmail-send)

Default: me. The domain to add to envelope recipient addresses with no domain. This value is used by *qmail-send*, while defaultdomain is used by *qmail-inject*, so in practice this value is used to fix up mail received by SMTP. The default value is fine, unless you receive a lot of spam with bare addresses, in which case you can set it to something like invalid to make incoming mail with no domain bounce.

helohost (qmail-remote)

Default: me. The domain to use in the HELO command of outgoing SMTP sessions. The default is fine.

idhost (qmail-inject)

Default: me. The domain to use when creating Message-ID: lines in outgoing mail. The default is fine. If you want to do something special with message ID's, you can provide them yourself on mail you send, in which case qmail won't alter them.

localiphost (qmail-smtpd)

Default: me. When *qmail-smtpd* sees incoming mail to an address using a dotted quad rather than a domain name, like fred@[10.11.12.99], and the IP address is one on this host, it substitutes in localiphost. The default is usually fine unless you want to change it to the local mail domain.

locals (qmail-send)

Default: me. Domains to treat as local. Any addresses in domains listed in this file are considered to be local and are routed using the local delivery rules. All local domains are equivalent; if foo.org and bar.com both appear in *locals*, the addresses fred@foo.org and fred@bar.com are handled identically.* This file always includes the name of the local host (the same as what's in me) and generally includes the local domain as well and any other domains that may have been used for the same set of addresses. For example, the *locals* file on my mail server tom.iecc.com also includes iecc.com (the current local domain), iecc.cambridge. ma.us (its old name), and iecc.us (a trendy vanity equivalent.)

Note that local domains are not the same as virtual domains, nor are they the same as the SMTP recipient domains listed in *rcpthosts*.

me (qmail-send)

Default: none; this file is required. The name of the current host. This should be the same as what the hostname command returns.

morercpthosts (qmail-smtpd and qmail-newmrh)

Default: none. More domains for which this host accepts SMTP mail. The contents of this file are compiled into *morercpthosts.cdb* by *qmail-newmrh*. The SMTP daemon consults the cdb file after it checks *rcpthosts*. If a host accepts mail for more than about 50 domains, Dan suggests that you put the 50 busiest into *rcpthosts* and the rest into *morercpthosts*.

percenthack (qmail-send)

Default: none. The "percent hack" is a primitive form of source routing introduced by sendmail in the early 1980s. If you send mail to *user%in.side@out.side*, the mail would be sent to *out.side*, where the address would be rewritten to *user@in.side* and sent along to *in.side*. In the past 20 years, most of the connectivity problems that require source routing have been solved, and for the ones that remain there are better tools such as smtproutes (described later), so the

---

* A very perverse user could test $HOST in a delivery rule in a *.qmail* file to tell two local domains apart, but I don't think I've ever seen anyone do so.

percent hack is obsolete. If for some reason you absolutely need it (you have an ancient mission-critical program for which all the source code has been lost that sends mail using the percent hack, perhaps) any addresses in domains listed in *percenthack* are scanned for percent signs and rewritten. In the previous example, *out.side* would have to be listed there.

If a domain listed in *percenthack* is also listed in *rcpthosts*, your system is an open relay, because spammers can send mail anywhere through your system by putting the actual target address in percent form inside an address in the listed domain. Yes, spammers actually do so. The solution is simple: don't do it.

plusdomain (qmail-inject)

Default: me. If the domain part of an address in an injected message ends with a plus sign, the contents of *plusdomain* are appended to the end. In environments with many subdomains of a single main domain, say east.bigcorp.com, west.bigcorp.com, and south.bigcorp.com, this lets people abbreviate addresses to fred@south+. No longer widely used.

qmqpservers (qmail-qmqpc)

Default: none. A list of servers to which messages can be queued using QMQP. See Chapter 17.

queuelifetime (qmail-send)

Default: 604800 seconds (a week). How long to keep trying to deliver a message. More precisely, if qmail tries to send a message and the attempt fails with a temporary error, the error is treated as permanent if the message is older than *queuelifetime*, in which case the message bounces.

The default time of a week is reasonable, but you might want to decrease it to three or four days if you'd rather know sooner that a message isn't getting through, at the risk that the destination host might have come back to life if you'd waited longer.

rcpthosts (qmail-smtpd)

Default: every domain. The list of domains for which this host accepts SMTP mail. It is *extremely important* that this file exist. If it doesn't, qmail will accept mail destined for anywhere and will be an "open relay," and a magnet for spammers.

If you receive mail for more than 50 domains, see *morercpthosts*.

smtpgreeting (qmail-smtpd)

Default: me. When another hosts connects via SMTP to send you mail, the greeting string to send. The default is fine.

smtproutes (qmail-remote)

Default: none. Explicit routes to use to deliver outgoing mail, overriding MX data. Each line is of one of these forms:

```
domain:relay
domain:relay:port
```

domain is the domain in the destination email address, *relay* is the name of the host to which to deliver the mail, and the optional *port* is the port number if not the standard port 25.

The *domain* can use wildcards; if it starts with a dot, it matches any target domain that ends with that domain. If the *domain* is empty, it matches all addresses, providing "smarthost" routing to send all mail to a single smarthost for delivery. If *relay* is empty, qmail uses the standard MX lookup, letting you override a broader wildcard or smarthost route.

Most systems can get by without *smtproutes*, but there are three situations where it can come in handy. The first is a smarthost, mentioned previously, if your computer is on a dialup, DSL, or cable modem, and the smarthost is your ISP's outgoing mail server. The second is to temporarily patch around broken MX records or mail relays. The third is to route mail for private domains within your network.

timeoutconnect (qmail-remote)
> Default: 60 seconds. How long to wait for a remote server to accept the initial connection to send mail. Unless you need to exchange mail with extremely slow and overloaded remote servers, don't change it.

timeoutremote (qmail-remote)
> Default: 1200 seconds. Once a remote server is connected, how long to wait for each response before giving up. The default of 20 minutes is extremely conservative, and can lead to all of your remote sending slots being tied up while waiting for somnolent remote hosts to time out. Unless you communicate with extraordinarily slow and overloaded remote servers, you can drop it to a minute.

timeoutsmtpd (qmail-smtpd)
> Default: 1200 seconds. How long *qmail-smtpd* waits for each response from a remote client before timing out and giving up. As with *timeoutremote*, you can decrease this to a minute unless you have some really slow remote clients.

virtualdomains (qmail-send)
> Default: none. The list of virtual users and domains for which this system receives mail. If you don't handle any virtual domains, you don't need this file.
>
> The virtual domain scheme works by taking the mailbox in the virtual domain, prepending a string and a hyphen to create a local address, and redelivering the mail to the local address. The virtual domain file lists the prepend string to use for each virtual user and domain. (See Chapter 12.) Each line is of one of these forms:
>
> ```
> user@dom.ain:string (1)
> dom.ain:string (2)
> .domain:string (3)
> domain: (4)
> :string (5)
> ```

Form (1) controls mail to a specific address. Forms (2) and (3) control mail to any address in a domain or in subdomains of a domain, respectively. Form (4), with an empty prepend, is used to create an exception to a domain that would otherwise be handled by a line of form (3) or (5) and means to handle the domain normally, not as a virtual domain. Form (5) is a catchall and controls all domains not listed in *locals* or elsewhere in *virtualdomains*.

If a domain erroneously appears both in *locals* and *virtualdomains*, the listing in *locals* takes precedence. Don't do that.

Using ~alias

Although qmail automatically handles deliveries to most users with entries in the Unix password file (or qmail's adjusted version of it; see Chapter 15), any useful mail setup also needs to deliver mail to addresses unrelated to entries in the password file. Qmail handles this in a simple, elegant way with the alias pseudo-user. As part of the installation process, create a user called alias and set its home directory to */var/qmail/ alias*. When qmail is running, if mail arrives for a local mailbox that isn't in the normal list of users, qmail prepends alias- to the address and retries the delivery. This makes any address not otherwise handled in effect a subaddress of alias, so you can handle addresses by putting *.qmail* files into *~alias*. For example, if you have a user robert and want mail addressed to bob to be forwarded to him, create *~alias/.qmail-bob* and in it put &robert. Since qmail handles deliveries using the *.qmail* files in *~alias* the same way that it handles any other deliveries, you have all of the same options delivering to nonuser addresses that you do to user addresses.

Because qmail doesn't deliver to root and other users that have a 0 user ID or that don't own their home directories, you should arrange to send root's mail to the system manager by creating *~alias/.qmail-root*. Also create *.qmail-postmaster*, *.qmail-abuse*, *.qmail-webmaster*, and any other role addresses that you want to support.

The final default delivery is, not surprisingly, found in *~alias/.qmail-default*. If that file doesn't exist, unknown addresses bounce, often just what you want. The most common thing to put in that file is a line to run the *fastforward* program (see the next section) to take delivery instructions from a file of addresses, roughly as sendmail does. You can also implement other default delivery rules. For example, if you want to make mail to subaddresses of *~alias* users default to the base address, so mail to fred-foop is delivered to fred if it's not otherwise handled, put a line like this in your default delivery file. (It appears wrapped here, but it has to be on one long line in the file.)

```
| case "$DEFAULT" in *-*) forward "${DEFAULT%%-*}" ;; *) bouncesaying
"Sorry, no mailbox here by that name. (#5.1.1)" ;; esac
```

This says that if an address contains a hyphen, strip off the hyphen and everything after it and redeliver it. Otherwise bounce the message. The bouncesaying command lets you provide your own failure message, but a simple exit 100 would do the trick as well, telling qmail to bounce.

fastforward and /etc/aliases

Sendmail and other MTAs use configuration files such as *letc/aliases* that contain lists of mailboxes and forwarding instructions. While qmail doesn't have a built-in feature to do that, the add-on *fastforward* package (available at *http://cr.yp.to/ fastforward.html* provides both a mostly compatible way to handle existing *letc/alias* files) and a more general scheme to handle files with forwarding instructions and mailing lists.

Installing fastforward

You can download and install the *fastforward* package the same way you install Dan's other programs, as described in Chapter 3. This section describes *fastforward* Version 0.51.

Using fastforward

The central program in the *fastforward* package is *fastforward* itself. It's designed to be run from a *.qmail* file. When run, it gets the recipient address from $RECIPIENT or optionally $DEFAULT@$HOST, looks up the address in a delivery database, and if it finds the address, follows the delivery instructions for the address.

fastforward takes its instructions from a CDB-format file. There are two ways to create the file: using newaliases to create *letc/aliases.cdb* from *letc/aliases*, which is in sendmail format, or using *setforward* to create a CDB from an arbitrary file, which is in a different, more flexible format. All of *fastforward*'s CDB files have the same format, regardless of which program created them.

The CDB file can refer to *mailing list* files of addresses; the difference is that the CDB file contains addresses and delivery instructions, while a mailing list file just contains a list of addresses and other mailing list files, for use within a delivery instruction. Mailing list files can be created by *newinclude*, which reads input containing a list of addresses in a format similar to the one sendmail uses for *:include:* files, or by *setmaillist*, which reads input in a more flexible format. Mailing list files created by either program have the same format, so you can use the input format that is more convenient. Compiled mailing list files have the extension *.bin*. In this section, I describe *letc/alias* compatibility and leave the rest for the sections on virtual domains (Chapter 12) and mailing lists (Chapter 14).

The most common way to use *fastforward* is to call it from *~alias/.qmail-default* so it can take a crack at any addresses not handled otherwise:

```
| fastforward /etc/aliases.cdb
```

Or you can also combine it with other default rules. For example, to use *fastforward* and then redeliver mail to subaddresses to the base address of the subaddress:

```
| fastforward -p /etc/aliases.cdb
| case "$DEFAULT" in *-*) forward "${DEFAULT%%-*}" ;; *) bouncesaying "Sorry, no
mailbox here by that
name. (#5.1.1)" ;; esac
```

The -p flag says to "pass through," that is, exit 99 if an address is found or exit 0 if not, so qmail goes on to the next line in the *.qmail* file if *fastforward* didn't deliver it. (In the absence of -p, *fastforward* exits 0 if it forwards the message and 100 otherwise to bounce the mail.)

Alias File Format

The format of */etc/alias* is a sequence of forwarding instructions. The most common instruction forwards an address to one or more other addresses:

```
bob: robert
ted: edward, edwin, eduardo
fred@example.com: frederick
fred@bad.example.com: nobody
@good.example.com: mary
```

Mail to ted is forwarded to edward, edwin, and eduardo. This form is useful for role accounts that are handled by several people or tiny mailing lists that change rarely. If there are multiple names in *localhosts* for this host, distinguish addresses by putting the domain of the address, and forward all addresses in a domain by using @domain. (This feature is more often used to handle addresses in virtual domains; see Chapter 12.) As a concession to sendmail compatibility, addresses can have comments and can be quoted as they are in To: and From: lines. Any line that starts with # is a comment, and any line can be continued by starting continuation lines with whitespace:

```
bell: |ringthebell
klaxon: "|ringthebell --reallyloud"
```

Any address that starts with a vertical bar is treated as a command for program delivery. If the command contains whitespace or at-signs, it has to be quoted. *fastforward* runs the program as whatever user it's running as, which is alias if it's called from *~alias/.qmail-default*. (To run a program as another user, it has to be called from a *.qmail* file belonging to that user. See Chapter 15.) The program is run as:

```
preline sh -c command
```

so that the message starts with a sendmail-style From line.

```
cephalopods: :include:/usr/fred/cephalopods
owner-cephalopods: fred
```

Any address that starts with *:include:* refers to the contents of a mailing list file. The mailing list file must have been compiled by *newinclude* or *setmaillist*, so in the previous example, *fastforward* looks for */usr/fred/cephalopods.bin*, and the delivery is deferred if the file isn't available. If there is an entry for both listname and owner-listname, any forwarded mail to listname has its envelope sender changed to owner-listname so bounces will go back to the owner of the list.

Note that mailing list files are read by *fastforward* when they're needed, not by *newaliases*. This means that, in the previous example, the addresses on the list belong to user fred, who can update the list file and rerun *newinclude* as needed. Mailing list files can refer to other mailing list files, but for security reasons (and unlike sendmail), they cannot contain program deliveries. This is not much of a problem in practice. In the previous example, if Fred wanted to, say, fax list messages to someone using a fax program, he could add an address fred-squidfax to the mailing list, then create *~fred/.qmail-squidfax* with whatever program deliveries he wants, running as fred, not as alias.

fastforward lives up to its name when doing list deliveries, and it can dispatch messages to huge lists very quickly. Nonetheless, if you have a large list with hundreds or thousands of recipients, it's better to use a mailing list manager like ezmlm (Chapter 14) to provide automated bounce handling, and a partly or fully automated subscribe and unsubscribe service for list members.

CHAPTER 5

Moving from Sendmail to Qmail

More often than not, a site that plans to run qmail is already running some other mail software on a Unix-ish server, and more often than not, that software is sendmail. This chapter walks through the steps involved in moving a mail system from sendmail to qmail.

Running Sendmail and Qmail in Parallel

Users tend to be upset when they can't access their email, so it's rarely possible to shut down the old mail system, spend a day getting the new system installed and tested, then turn the mail back on. Fortunately, you don't have to. It's easy to run sendmail and qmail in parallel on the same machine, delivering mail into the same mailboxes, until you're satisfied qmail is working properly, and then shut sendmail down.

Any MTA receives mail through two routes: local and remote. On Unix systems, local mail is injected via the *sendmail* program, and remote mail is injected via SMTP. When you're running qmail and sendmail in parallel, as long as */usr/lib/sendmail* is a link to sendmail, local mail will go to sendmail, and as long as sendmail is listening on port 25, remote mail will also go to sendmail. While you're testing, put qmail's version of sendmail somewhere else, say */var/qmail/bin/sendmail*, and run qmail's SMTP daemon on port 26.

Once you're happy with your qmail installation, move the original */usr/lib/sendmail* to */usr/lib/sendmail.old* (and similarly for any other links to it such as */usr/sbin/sendmail*) and link the qmail version in its place. That will start routing local mail to qmail.

For remote mail, kill the sendmail daemon, and restart the qmail SMTP daemon running on port 25. That will start routing remote mail to qmail. Because sendmail probably still has some mail to flush out, restart the sendmail daemon but without the -bd flag that makes it listen on port 25. A typical command would be sendmail -q30m to keep retrying failed deliveries every 30 minutes. After a few days, or when the sendmail queue is empty, you can shut sendmail down for good.

Sendmail Switching Systems

Some versions of BSD and Linux have their own schemes to handle multiple mail systems with different versions of sendmail by providing a layer of indirection between the sendmail program that other applications call and the actual program provided by the mail package. These schemes don't do anything that the direct approach can't also do, but they document the setup better and are more likely to survive system upgrades, so you should use them when you can.

NetBSD and FreeBSD use a program called *mailwrapper*, which is installed where sendmail would usually go. It consults a file called */etc/mail/mailer.conf,* which has the names of the actual programs to run when sendmail is called under any of its many aliases. (See Example 5-1.)

Example 5-1. Typical mailer.conf

```
sendmail      /var/qmail/bin/sendmail
send-mail     /var/qmail/bin/sendmail
newaliases    /var/qmail/bin/newaliases
```

Debian and Red Hat Linux have an "alternatives" scheme that uses symlinks. In a typical alternatives setup, */usr/sbin/sendmail* is a symlink to */etc/alternatives/mta,* which is in turn a symlink to the real sendmail program. You can just symlink */etc/alternatives/mta* to */var/qmail/bin/sendmail* or use the alternatives (Red Hat) or update-alternatives (Debian) command to make the links.

User Issues

There are two important differences visible to mail users when moving from sendmail to qmail: mailbox format and location, and *.forward* files. The standard qmail distribution includes some examples in */var/qmail/boot* to set up for various degrees of sendmail compatibility, discussed in Chapter 4.

Mailbox Format and Location

Sendmail invariably delivers mail into mbox format mailboxes, which are usually all located in */var/mail* or */var/spool/mail.* Qmail can deliver to either mbox or Maildir files, but normally puts each user's mailbox in the user's home directory. You have several options during a conversion.

The easiest option is to leave all the mailboxes in */var/mail* or a similar shared directory. The disadvantage is that */var/mail* isn't a very good place to put mail, because mail doesn't count toward individual disk quotas, and minor protection errors on mailboxes make it possible to snoop on mail. Because qmail doesn't have a built-in delivery agent that puts mail in */var/mail,* you must tell it to use an external one such as */usr/libexec/mail.local* (4.4 BSD and descendants) or */bin/mail* (older versions of BSD, System V, and Linux).

It is not a good idea to leave mail in */var/mail* other than for testing. A reasonable compromise is to have qmail deliver to mbox files in the home directories, and leave sendmail delivering to */var/mail*. Then when you're happy with qmail, copy all the old mailboxes to the new location using scripts described later in this chapter. You must also adjust the *.profile* and *.login* files so that they set the MAILBOX environment variable to point to the new location.

Although Maildir mailboxes have many operational advantages over mboxes, switching users over on systems with shell users is painful due to the dearth of Maildir mail clients. On systems where most or all of your users pick up mail with POP or IMAP, switching to Maildirs is easier, and I recommend it. Again, set up qmail with Maildirs, then when you stop sendmail, copy the contents of the old mailboxes into the new ones, converting mbox to Maildir at that time.

Qmail comes with a pair of scripts called *pinq* and *elq*, which copy the user's incoming mail from *~/Maildir* to *~/Mailbox* and then run pine or elm. While they work fine, if a user is going to use a mail client that expects an mbox, it makes more sense to deliver to the mbox in the first place. One semiplausible reason to use *pinq* or *elq* is if the filesystem to which the mail is delivered is on a different host than the one uses to read mail, with the files mounted using NFS. Because NFS has locking problems with mboxes, it makes sense to do the deliveries into Maildirs, which work reliably. Assuming the user runs only one copy of *pinq* or *elq* at a time, it can safely copy mail from the Maildir into an mbox on his local disk, and then run pine or elm.

Qmail and .forward Files

Sendmail shell users frequently have *.forward* files to handle their mail deliveries. The most common uses are to forward mail to another address and feed incoming mail to procmail for filtering and sorting, but the *.forward* scheme is quite general, albeit not very well specified.

Qmail offers two migration paths for *.forward*. The format of *.qmail* files is similar enough to *.forward* files that the most common *.forward* files can be turned into *.qmail* files with little or no tweaking. If you have a small number of shell users, turn them into *.qmail* files when you convert, to get rid of *.forward* files once and for all.

Alternatively, if you have a lot of *.forward* files, Dan has an add-on package called *dot-forward* that provides most of the sendmail *.forward* features. You can run qmail and make the default delivery instructions to be to run *dot-forward*. This means that anyone without a *.qmail* file will use *dot-forward* to interpret a *.forward* file, if any, while users who have created *.qmail* files will use those instead. This is the best approach for larger shell setups.

Keep in mind that *dot-forward* doesn't do everything that sendmail does, so some *.forward* files, notably those that use *:include:* to forward to a mailing list or group of people, won't work. The conversion to *.qmail* isn't hard, but someone has to do it before stopping sendmail.

System Issues

The *sendmail.cf* configuration file provides a fantastic amount of configurability to sendmail, some of which is quite useful. Most of sendmail's tricks have straightforward equivalents in qmail. It may be useful to print out *sendmail.cf* so you can check off each configuration option as you deal with it.

Deconstructing sendmail.cf

Much of the configuration information in a typical *sendmail.cf* needs no qmail equivalent. Since sendmail was written in an era when it wasn't clear what mail system would predominate, it can handle a wide variety of long-dead mail addressing formats, and much of *sendmail.cf* defines the syntax of email addresses, something that's built into qmail.

Nonetheless, *sendmail.cf* files usually do have some local customization that you need to translate. Because the configuration language is so arcane, most sites use a set of m4 macros to generate the file. In the following discussion, I mention primarily the m4 macros rather than the generated configuration codes.

Local Deliveries

Sendmail uses several macros starting with LOCAL_MAILER to define the local mail configuration. The qmail equivalent is the default delivery agent set at startup time. The sample boot scripts described in Chapter 4 cover most of the common cases.

If you want to deliver mail into mbox files in */var/spool*, use one of the binm boot scripts, whichever one calls the same mailer that sendmail is calling. If any of your users have *.forward* files, use the +df versions of the boot scripts.

If you want to deliver to mbox files in users' home directories, use the *home* or *home+df* boot script. If you want to deliver into Maildirs, start with the *home* or *home+df* script, but change *./Mailbox* to *./Maildir/*. Don't forget the trailing slash, which tells qmail that it's a Maildir. Qmail will not create Maildirs automatically, so you must create them yourself. If your user directories are all under */home*, running this script as root does the trick:

```
cd /home
for i in *
do
    maildirmake $i/Maildir
    chown -R $i $i/Maildir
done
```

If the sendmail configuration has FEATURE('local_procmail'), it's using procmail to deliver local mail. See "Procmail and Qmail" in Chapter 4 for details on setting up procmail.

Hostnames and Masquerading

Sendmail provides an elaborate masquerading system to rewrite addresses on mail. Historically, people used masquerading so that the syntax of mail addresses within an organization could be different from (generally simpler than) the addresses visible outside. While this made some sense when mail systems had different, incompatible, and mutually hostile addressing syntaxes, it's not a very good idea now that mail systems all use Internet-style addresses. Not surprisingly, qmail provides only minimal help for masquerading.

The one function of masquerading that is still useful is to hide hostnames within a network. If your domain were example.com with hosts named good.example.com and bad.example.com, you would probably like the return address on your mail to be fred@example.com rather than fred@good.example.com or fred@bad.example. com. Qmail makes this easy.

Several control files in */var/qmail/control* set the hostnames to use:

me
> The hostname of this host, such as good.example.com.

locals
> A list of local domains. Lists the local domain and the machine's hostname, for example:
>
> ```
> example.com
> good.example.com
> ```
>
> The domains in the sendmail *virtusertable* and *mailertable* files are virtual domains, not local domains, so don't list them here.

envnoathost
> If *qmail-send* encounters an unqualified address without a domain, add this host name. Make this the domain, such as example.com. Such addresses are only likely to occur in incoming SMTP mail.

defaulthost
> If *qmail-inject* encounters an unqualified address without a domain, add this hostname. Make this the domain, such as example.com. This handles addresses coming in via the sendmail compatibility program.

defaultdomain
> If *qmail-inject* encounters an address where the host part does not contain a dot, add this hostname. Make this the domain, such as example.com. This turns addresses like root@bad into root@bad.example.com, so on networks with multiple mail subdomains, local users can abbreviate the addresses.

These aren't all of the control files that affect addressing, but all of the others have reasonable defaults, so there's no need to create them.

Sendmail provides several ways to specify multiple names for the local host. If your sendmail setup has */etc/mail/local-host-names*, all the names in that file are names for the local host. Or you may have LOCAL_DOMAIN lines in the configuration file, each specifying another name for the local host. In qmail, all of these turn into lines in the *locals* file.

Local and Virtual Domains

Sendmail and qmail handle domains somewhat differently. Qmail has a simple division into local, virtual, and remote domains, whereas sendmail has many special cases. Fortunately, most of the special cases translate easily into virtual or remote domains.

Qmail's local domains treat mailbox names as mailboxes on the local computer.

Virtual domains can handle any domains that are neither treated as local mailboxes (local) or sent elsewhere via SMTP (remote). Virtual domains deliver to a set of mailboxes other than the standard set on the computer and route mail via something other than SMTP.

The usual sendmail approach to virtual domains is with a *virtusertable* file that contains instructions on how to route every address in every virtual domain. The easiest way to translate *virtusertables* is to use the add-on *fastforward* program, as described in Chapter 12.

Remote Domains, and Primary and Backup MXes

Qmail's remote domains deliver mail to other hosts via SMTP. Anything that's not local (listed in *locals*) or virtual (listed in *virtualdomains*) is remote.

Normally a host receives mail only for domains it handles itself, so the list in *rcpthosts* is the combination of local and virtual domains. Mail hosts can also be "backup" or "secondary" MXes, receiving mail for domains handled elsewhere, to provide a place to buffer the mail if the primary MX isn't available. To make qmail a backup MX, just add the domains to back up to *rcpthosts* or *morercpthosts*. If an incoming message isn't handled locally, qmail will automatically forward it to the primary MX when it can. Sendmail has some backup MX kludges, like the one that automatically provides backup service for any domain that has an MX pointing at the host. For security reasons, qmail doesn't do that; the list of domains has to be explicit. For systems that handle many domains, it's not hard to generate a suitable *morercpthosts* automatically from whatever database maintains the DNS, and it's more secure than letting any random domain point its MX at you and make you an unwilling relay.

Smarthosts

Many small systems deliver mail using a "smarthost," a larger or better-connected system that handles all outgoing mail, typically a gateway system on the local network or at one's ISP. Qmail has a very simple, if not obvious, way to specify a smarthost. Put the smarthost's name into *smtproutes* preceded by a colon, e.g.:

```
:mail.myisp.com
```

The syntax of each line in *smtproutes* is the name of the domain to route, colon, the name of the host to route it. A missing domain makes the entry the default to use for all domains that don't have explicit routes.

Uucp and Other Specialized Deliveries

Sendmail can specify that mail to particular domains be routed specially, for example, if the sendmail system is acting as a gateway to dialup uucp hosts. Qmail's virtual domain system is flexible enough that it can easily implement all sorts of gateway and specialized routing. See Chapter 12.

Spam Filtering

Sendmail can configure DNS blacklists and other spam filters in *sendmail.cf*. Qmail can do all of the same filtering, but it's set up completely differently because qmail's SMTP daemon, where the filtering happens, runs independently of the core mail delivery system. See Chapter 9.

Converting Your Aliases File

An important but tedious part of a transition from sendmail to qmail is to convert */etc/aliases*. There are two general strategies. The first is to create a *.qmail* file in *~alias* corresponding to each entry, which works fine for small alias files but becomes unwieldy after a few dozen entries. The other is to install the fastforward package (described at the end of Chapter 4) which handles a version of */etc/aliases* pretty close to sendmail's, and then just adjust the alias entries that *fastforward* doesn't handle well.

When sendmail runs a program for a delivery from the aliases file, it uses a variety of heuristics to decide which user runs the program. Qmail's model is much simpler: all programs run from *~alias*, including *fastforward* when it does */etc/aliases* deliveries, are run as the alias user. In most cases that's fine for deliveries that don't store messages or update files. For deliveries that do store messages or update files, you may need to rewrite the delivery rules to be sure that they're run as the appropriate, user as described next.

Address Forwarding

The syntax for addressing forwarding is:

```
address1: address2
address1: address2, address3, address4
```

Alias entries that just forward one address to another can be left in *aliases* as is. To rewrite them as a *.qmail* file instead, create *~alias/.qmail-address1* and put address2 in it. If an address is forwarded to multiple addresses, put each one on a separate line in the *.qmail* file.

Mailing Lists

The syntax for mailing lists is:

```
mylist: :include: /usr/fred/listfile
owner-mylist: fred
```

fastforward's aliases emulation supports sendmail-style lists directly. The only difference is that the included file has to be compiled into a *.bin* file using *newinclude*, as described in Chapter 4.

Although included lists are most easily handled by *fastforward*, it's also possible to convert them to *.qmail* files. Copy *listfile* to *~alias/.qmail-mylist*, stripping out any address comments that aren't permitted in *.qmail* files, and create *~alias/.qmail-owner-mylist* containing the address of the list owner. Qmail provides more facilities for list management, including easy ways for users to handle their own lists. See Chapter 14.

Program Deliveries

The syntax for program deliveries is:

```
progaddr: "|someprogram -flags"
```

Program deliveries are supported by *fastforward*, so long as it's acceptable to run the programs as the alias user. To run programs as any other user, rewrite the delivery instructions to forward to a subaddress of the desired user. If, for example, this program should run as user fred, change the aliases entry to:

```
progaddr: fred-progaddr
```

Then as user fred, create *~fred/.qmail-progaddr* with instructions to run the program:

```
|someprogram -flags
```

Program delivery lines in *.qmail* files start with a vertical bar and feed everything after the bar to the shell. See Chapter 10 for details of how qmail runs program deliveries.

Trusted Users

Sendmail has *trusted users* who can perform certain mail actions not permitted to the hoi polloi. Depending on your point of view, qmail either trusts all users or no users. Each user has full control over his own files and deliveries, but no user has any special ability to masquerade as others, run programs, or anything else. If a sendmail setup depends on trusted users (not many do), the setup must be redesigned to work with qmail.

## CHAPTER 6

Handling Locally Generated Mail

Mail comes from two conceptual places: inside your system and outside it. In this chapter, we look at mail that originates inside your system, mail generated locally on the host where qmail is running. We also take a first look at mail injected by MUAs on computers running on the same LAN, and mail injected by "roaming" local users elsewhere on the Net, which we address in detail in the next chapter.

qmail-queue

The only way to pass a message into qmail is *qmail-queue*. All of the other relay and injection programs, for both local and remote originated mail, call *qmail-queue* to queue a message and schedule it for delivery. This design has two advantages: it's easy to write new frontends to inject mail because they only need to call *qmail-queue* to pass along the mail, and by replacing *qmail-queue* with another program that offers the same interface, you can create interestingly different systems, such as mini-qmail. (See Chapter 16 for details.) It also offers security advantages, because *qmail-queue* is one of the few set-uid programs (to qmailq, not root) in the qmail package, so it can write files in the queue directories.

qmail-queue is intended to be run from other programs, not from the command line, so it has an interface that only another program could love. It takes no command-line arguments and reads its input from two file descriptors. The first input is read from file descriptor 0 and is the text of the message. *qmail-queue* treats the message as an uninterpreted block of bytes and doesn't change it at all, other than prefixing a Received: line at the front. The received line includes the PID, the message source, and a timestamp:

```
Received: (qmail pid invoked source); 4 Apr 2004 22:35:00 -0000
```

The source is `by alias` if the invoking user is the alias user; `from network` if the invoking user is qmaild, the daemon user that means the caller was the SMTP daemon; `for bounce` if the user is qmails, the qmail-send user; or `by uid NNN` otherwise.

Then *qmail-queue* reads the envelope information from file descriptor 1 in a concise binary format. (In most programs, that's the standard output, but this isn't most programs.)

```
Fsender@sender.com\0 Trcpt1@rcpt.org\0 ... Trcptn@rcpt.net\0 \0
```

First is the letter F, the sender's address, and a null byte. Then there is a list of recipient addresses, each preceded by the letter T and followed by a null byte. Finally there comes an extra null byte.

Once it has the message and the envelope, *qmail-queue* writes them in files in the queue directories and notifies *qmail-send* to process queued messages.

The only output from *qmail-queue* is the return code, which is zero if the message could be queued, and any of a long list of other values if not. (See the manpage for the list.) Because *qmail-queue* only queues a message, its return code says nothing about whether the message could be delivered, only that it could be queued for the rest of qmail to do something with it. If there are delivery problems, qmail reports them by sending bounce messages to the message's sender address.

Passing Input to qmail-queue

qmail-queue reads two input files from two file descriptors, and more often than not both input files are pipes from the calling program, so some care is needed to avoid deadlock. It's important to remember that *qmail-queue* reads the message from fd 0 first, then the envelope from fd 1. This isn't an implementation accident; it's part of the spec.

If you're writing programs that call *qmail-queue* and use pipes, be sure that you write the entire message first, then close the message pipe, and then write the envelope. If the structure of the program doesn't make that convenient, write the envelope information to a file in */tmp*. (You could write the message to a temporary file instead, but the envelope is usually a lot smaller than the message.)

If you're writing programs that use the same interface as *qmail-queue*, read the entire input message before reading the envelope. If you want to look at the envelope before doing anything with the message, you must stash the message in a file first. In practice, this isn't often a problem, because the message needs to be stored in a file anyway.

Other Queueing Programs

Qmail comes with one other compatible queueing program, *qmail-qmqpc*, the mini-qmail QMQP client that queues the mail on another host. Because the interface is so simple, it's quite simple to add a "shim" between the calling program and *qmail-queue* to do tasks like making a copy of all the mail (just add the address of the log mailbox to the list of recipients) or invoking spam filters. We'll see many of these elsewhere in the book.

Wrapping qmail-queue

If you want to replace *qmail-queue*, you have three alternatives. One is to move the real *qmail-queue* and rename or symlink the replacement to */var/qmail/bin/qmail-queue*. If you want to use the replacement every single time you normally use *qmail-queue*, this is the easiest approach. Mini-qmail (see Chapter 16) does this because it moves the entire mail queue to another system. More often, you only want to replace *qmail-queue* when a message is first introduced into the system, not every time it's forwarded, so a more flexible approach is called for. One possibility is to individually patch the code in *qmail-inject* and *qmail-smtpd* and *new-inject*, and whatever other programs you use to inject mail. This turns out to be extremely messy programming, because all of the programs in the qmail package use a single library routine to call *qmail-queue*, so you must create multiple versions of that routine.

A third approach, and the one I recommend, is the "qmailqueue" patch that takes the name of the program from the environment. Once it's applied, if the variable QMAILQUEUE is defined, it names the program to run instead of *qmail-queue*. There's a very short patch file at qmail.org (search for QMAILQUEUE on the home page) that's easy to apply to the qmail source. If you use the netqmail-1.05 package, it's already had the patch applied.

Several of Dan's add-on packages also call *qmail-queue*, using the same *qmail.c* library file, so you can use the same patch. These include dot-forward-0.71, fastforward-0.51, mess822-0.58, and serialmail-0.75. Either apply the patch to each of them, or copy the patched copy of *qmail.c* from the qmail or netqmail source directory into the source directories of the add-on packages. In each of the add-on packages, if you apply the patch file, the patch program will complain that the patch failed on *Makefile*, which you can ignore because in all of the add-ons, only *qmail.c* needs patching. Don't forget to recompile and reinstall all the packages you patched.

Cleaning Up Injected Mail

Unlike some other MTAs, qmail distinguishes between *injected* mail, new messages entered into the mail system, and *relayed* mail, which is delivered from somewhere else. The difference is that injected mail needs to have its headers cleaned up, while relayed mail doesn't. Configuring qmail to clean up injected mail isn't hard, but depending on your setup, there are several possible ways to handle it.

The *new-inject* package contains two programs: *new-inject*, which is a replacement for *qmail-inject*, and *ofmipd* (Old Fashioned Mail Injection Protocol Daemon), an SMTP daemon that includes the functions of *new-inject*. Although you can survive without *new-inject*, it's easy to install and I encourage you to use it.

Accepting and Cleaning Up Locally Injected Mail

The usual ways to inject local mail are to feed it to *qmail-inject* or *sendmail*. Both do the cleanup automatically. (The qmail version of *sendmail* is a small wrapper that runs *qmail-inject*.)

Because *new-inject* is almost completely upward compatible with *qmail-inject*, use it in place of *qmail-inject*:

```
# cd /var/qmail/bin
# mv qmail-inject qmail-inject.old
# ln new-inject qmail-inject
```

(I've saved the old *qmail-inject* as *qmail-inject.old* in case there turned out to be some application that needed exactly *qmail-inject*'s features, but after a year, I have yet to need it.)

Some programs inject local mail by opening an SMTP connection to the loopback address 127.0.0.1. If you've installed an SMTP listener following the instructions in Chapter 4, injecting mail via that route already works, but without any cleanup. There are two alternatives to clean up mail injected by SMTP: adjusting the setup of the regular SMTP server to detour locally injected mail through a cleanup program or setting up a separate SMTP daemon running *ofmipd* to receive locally originating mail. I discuss both options later in the chapter.

The standard way to give a freshly created message to qmail for delivery is to use *qmail-inject* or its replacement *new-inject*. Both programs accept a message from the standard input, clean up and complete the headers without modifying the message body, construct the envelope information from the message and command arguments, and pass the result to *qmail-queue* for delivery. A combination of flags on the command line and environment variables give you some control over the header rewriting and control where it gets the envelope addresses. In the following discussion capitalized names refer to environment variables passed to *qmail-inject* or *new-inject*.

The QMAILINJECT environment variable, if it exists, contains a string of letters from the set *cfimrs* that control the header rewriting, as described later. *new-inject* also accepts the uppercase letters FIMRS with the equivalent meanings and also accepts command-line –FIMRS flags.

For testing purposes, the –n flag causes the rewritten message to be copied to standard output rather than queued. To show the envelope addresses, *new-inject* prefixes Envelope-Sender: and Envelope-Recipients: headers, while *qmail-inject* puts the sender address in a Return-Path: line but doesn't do anything with the recipient addresses.

Setting the envelope addresses

Like *sendmail*, *qmail-inject* and *new-inject* can take the recipient addresses from the command line, from the message itself, or both. In the absence of any flags or with the −A flag, they deliver the message to the addresses on the command line if there are any, otherwise to the addresses in the To:, Cc:, Bcc:, and Apparently-To: (a sendmail-ism). *new-inject* uses Envelope-Recipients: line(s), if any exist, in preference to those headers. The −a flag says to use only command-line addresses, −h says to use only the header recipients, and −H says to use both. All addresses are rewritten as described in the later section "Address rewriting."

The envelope sender address is taken from the −f flag if present. Otherwise, unless the environment flag "s" is set, it uses Envelope-Sender: (*new-inject* only) or Return-Path:. If those headers aren't present, the user part of the sender is taken from QMAILSUSER, QMAILUSER, MAILUSER, USER, or LOGNAME. The host part is taken from QMAILSHOST, QMAILHOST, or MAILHOST, or if none of those are set, the *defaulthost* control file.

The environment flags "m" and "r" handle Variable Envelope Return Paths (VERP), a way to encode information about the message and its sender in the envelope return address to aid bounce processing. (VERP is discussed at length in Chapter 14.) If environment flag "m" is set, it appends a dash, the time in seconds, a dot, and the process ID as a per-message VERP. If environment flag "r" is set, it rewrites the sender address for the per-recipient VERP (described in Chapter 14). Either or both kinds of VERP can be present; for example, if the sender fred@example.com might be turned into fred-1059105280.24559-@example.com-@[ ]. Note that neither kind of VERP is done if the sender is set explicitly with −f; in that case it's up to you to put whatever you want into the sender string.

Header rewriting

Both *qmail-inject* and *new-inject* rewrite most message headers:

From:
> If environment flag "f" is set, any existing From: header is discarded; if not, an existing From: header is passed through. When creating a From: header, the user part is taken from QMAILUSER, MAILUSER, USER, or LOGNAME, and the host part is taken from QMAILHOST, MAILHOST, or the *defaulthost* control file. (Note that QMAILSUSER and QMAILSHOST don't affect the From: line, providing the occasionally useful ability to concoct different header and envelope return addresses.) The comment on the From: line is taken from QMAIL-NAME, MAILNAME, or NAME. If the environment flag "c" is set, *qmail-inject* uses the address (comment) style; otherwise it uses comment <address>. *new-inject* ignores the "c" flag and always uses comment <address>.

To: and Cc:
> Addresses are rewritten as described in the next section, and put into standard format with commas between the addresses and address comments in the preferred form. *new-inject* combines multiple To: lines or multiple Cc: into one. If there are no To: or Cc: addresses at all, it adds a syntactically valid Cc: group address of "recipient list not shown: ;".

Bcc: and Apparently-To:
> These lines are deleted.

Notice-Requested-Upon-Delivery-To:, and Mail-Reply-To: and Reply-To:
> The addresses are rewritten but otherwise don't affect delivery.

Date:
> If there's an existing date header with a date that it can decode, the date is standardized into the form 23 Jun 2004 12:02:00 -0500. If not, it adds a Date: header with the current time and date.

Message-ID:
> If there's an existing header, it's passed through, unless the environment variable "i" is set, in which case any existing Message-ID: header is deleted. In the absence of a passed-through header, it creates a new one. The domain part of the new Message-ID: comes from QMAILIDHOST if present, otherwise the *idhost* or *me* control files. The user part is always a combination of the date and PID in the form 20020623170200.2345.qmail.

Resent- headers
> *new-inject* moves these to the top of the message with the Received: headers but doesn't otherwise rewrite them. If *qmail-inject* sees any of them, it adds Resent-Date: and Resent-Message-ID:, and treats the Resent-To: as the header addresses to which the message is delivered. This is the most significant incompatibility between *qmail-inject* and *new-inject*, although it rarely causes trouble in practice because MUAs tend to put either a full set of Resent- headers on messages or none of them.

Mail-Followup-To:
> If this header is not already present, and the environment variable QMAILMFT-FILE is the name of a file that contains a list of mailing list posting addresses, one per line, and one of those addresses appears in the To: or Cc: line of the message, it adds a Mail-Followup-To: header containing all of the To: and Cc: addresses. This is a little-used feature intended for some varieties of mailing list software.

Content-Length:
> If this field is present, it's removed. Some MUAs attempt to use it to make it faster to scan mboxes, but it's not useful in mail in transit.

Address rewriting

Addresses in the message headers are rewritten into a standard form. (Envelope addresses aren't rewritten, other than with the VERP options discussed earlier. If the envelope recipients are taken from the headers, it uses the rewritten versions.)

The rewriting involves adding or completing the domain. Qmail's rewriting rules work best in an environment with multiple subdomains, such as a university where each department has its own subdomain (so fred@alchemy.bigu.edu and fred@phrenology.bigu.edu are different addresses, and on-campus users would likely abbreviate them as fred@alchemy and fred@phrenology).

If an address has no host part at all, it adds a default hostname from QMAILDE-FAULTHOST, or the contents of *defaulthost* or *me*.

If the host part (whether it came from the previous step or was already present) contains no dot, it adds a dot and QMAILDEFAULTDOMAIN, or the contents of *defaultdomain* or *me*.

If the host part ends with a plus sign, it changes the plus to a dot and adds QMAIL-PLUSDOMAIN, or the contents of *plusdomain* or *me*.

In the usual case of "flat" addressing where all the addresses are in the second or third-level domain, both *defaulthost* and *defaultdomain* should contain that domain. In the aforementioned campus example, *defaulthost* should contain the name of the local subdomain (such as alchemy.bigu.edu), and *defaultdomain* should contain the main domain (such as bigu.edu) so that short addresses like fred@alchemy and fred@phrenology work. Plus addresses are for the more esoteric situation where there are multicomponent subaddresses, so a user can type fred@lead.alchemy+ and have that turn into fred@lead.alchemy.bigu.edu.

new-inject has a more elaborate rewriting system controlled by patterns from *rewrite* (or if it exists, the file named by QMAILREWRITE.) See the rewriting(5) manpage for details. I don't recommend doing more elaborate rewriting, because that makes the addresses your users type into their MTAs different from the ones that the rest of the world uses, causing great confusion when they tell their friends to write to jerry@boam and it doesn't work because that address is locally rewritten into jerry@bo.am.bigcorp.com. However, rewriting is useful to compensate for users who insist on writing to stevec@aol when they mean stevec@aol.com.

Passing in Large Numbers of Addresses

The simplest way to send mail to a list of addresses is to put all the addresses in a file, and then either directly or, more likely, via a mailing list manager (such as ezmlm, majordomo, or mailman) type:

```
new-inject -a $(cat mylist) << EOF
To: mylist
Subject: Free beer

Look behind the coffee machine at 5 PM
EOF
```

This works as long as the list of addresses remains small enough to fit on a command line. The To: address in the message, which is normally the address of the list, is ignored for delivery purposes. But what happens when the list doesn't fit on a command line? A typical command-line limit is 20 K, which only fits a thousand 20-character addresses—not a very big list.

The usual way to get around the command-line limit is to queue the message directly, either by running *qmail-queue* or by connecting to the local port 25 SMTP daemon to send the mail. They both work, but they have the disadvantage of doing no header cleanup. Can we run *new-inject* and give it thousands of addresses? Yes.

The obvious approach is to put all the addresses on Bcc: lines, because they're normally copied into the envelope and deleted. But the problem is that addresses on the To: and Cc: lines are copied into the envelope as well. The To: address is generally the address of the list itself, so this is a fairly efficient route to a mail loop.* Instead, put the addresses into Envelope-Recipients: headers at the top of the message, either one huge line with addresses separated by commas (like all parts of qmail, it allocates line buffers to be as big as they need to be so there's no limit on line length) or in multiple header lines. Either way, all of the recipients will be extracted from those headers, and then the rest of the message will be cleaned up and sent on its way to all the recipients.

Accepting Local Mail from Other Hosts

Most networks have a small number of mail servers that handle the mail for many users who use MUAs on their individual PCs to read and send mail. Outgoing mail from these PCs is sent to the mail server using SMTP, at which point it is the mail server's job to clean up the headers and send the mail on its way.

Locally injected SMTP mail presents two problems. One is to tell which SMTP mail is injected mail from local users rather than the normal incoming mail. This is a crucial distinction, because local users can inject mail addressed anywhere, while incoming mail should be accepted only for the domains that this server handles. (Hosts that promiscuously accept and forward mail from third parties are known as "open relays" and tend to be quickly blacklisted, because the third parties are invariably spammers.) The other, simpler problem is to arrange to clean up the headers in the injected mail the way that *qmail-inject* or *new-inject* clean up locally injected mail.

Distinguishing Injected from Relayed Mail

All of these techniques involve configuring and patching the SMTP daemons. They're discussed in detail in the next chapter, but here is a short overview.

---

* A mail loop, for the fortunate few who have never encountered one, is a chain of forwarding addresses that forms a loop so that mail keeps recirculating forever, frequently growing at each stage as forwarders add headers or comments to the message. Qmail breaks mail loops by scanning the Delivered-To: headers at delivery time and bouncing any mail that has a Delivered-To: that's the same as the address it's delivering to now, but avoiding loops is far preferable to breaking them.

Hosts on the local network are easily recognized by their IP addresses. Each time *tcpserver* accepts a connection, it consults a rule database indexed by IP address and marks each connection as local or remote. In the common case that a network has a fixed, known set of IP addresses, and users on the network have PCs that use the qmail host to send and receive mail, this is the only setup needed.

Most networks have at least a few "roaming" users who sometimes or always connect from outside the local network. In order for the network to recognize their mail as local, the users have to provide a username and password. The most common way is SMTP AUTH, an extension to SMTP defined in 1999 that adds password authentication to SMTP. Qmail doesn't provide SMTP AUTH, but it's not hard to patch it into the SMTP daemon.

If you have old MUAs that don't handle SMTP AUTH, an older kludge called pop-before-smtp implicitly uses POP logins to authenticate SMTP. Each time a user logs in for POP (or IMAP, for systems that run an IMAP server), the system notes the IP address from which the user logged in. For an hour or so thereafter, SMTP connections from the IP address are treated as local. Users only need to check their mail before sending new mail, so MUAs need no special features to support it. Qmail doesn't support pop-before-smtp either, but add-on packages are available that fit in as "shims" that can be configured to run between the standard parts of the qmail POP and SMTP daemons. These are covered in the next chapter.

Most systems that support SMTP AUTH also support Transport Layer Security (TLS), the same cryptographic security scheme known as SSL on the Web. TLS permits authentication in both directions; the client can check the server's TLS certificate to be sure that the server is who it purports to be, and the client can also present a certificate to the server. In practice, most TLS systems use self-signed certificates that provide no authentication, but like SSL it adds extra security if the traffic passes through networks where it's subject to snooping. Patching qmail to use TLS is also straightforward, but the steps required to set up MUAs with appropriately signed certificates that can be used for authentication are a lot more difficult than setting up SMTP AUTH.

CHAPTER 7

Accepting Mail from Other Hosts

Unlike some other mail systems, qmail uses separate daemons for incoming and outgoing mail. Incoming mail is handled primarily by *qmail-smtpd*. As discussed at the end of the previous chapter, local mail injected from MUAs on other computers also arrives by SMTP, and it's important to distinguish the local from the incoming mail because they're handled differently.

Accepting Incoming SMTP Mail

Chapter 4 discussed the basic setup of the SMTP daemon in */service/qmail-smtpd*. The *supervise* daemon runs *tcpserver*, which listens for incoming connections, then runs *qmail-smtpd* to run the SMTP session and queue the received mail. The control file *rcpthosts* lists the domains for which it accepts mail. (If that file doesn't exist, it accepts mail for all domains and can be an open relay, which spammers see as an open invitation to abuse.)

The normal SMTP setup consults a *tcprules* file that lists the IP addresses from which to accept and deny connections. The rules file is */var/qmail/rules/smtprules.txt*, which is compiled into the binary */var/qmail/rules/smtprules.cdb* that *tcpserver* consults.

Accepting and Cleaning Up Local Mail Using the Regular SMTP Daemon

In the FAQ distributed with qmail 1.03, question 5.5 describes the classic technique for cleaning up remotely injected mail. The *smtprules.cdb* file that *tcpserver* consults contains lines that set the RELAYCLIENT environment variable for hosts allowed to inject and relay mail. If RELAYCLIENT is set, *qmail-smtpd* both skips the usual relay validation and appends the contents of RELAYCLIENT to all envelope destination addresses. If RELAYCLIENT has the value @fixme, mail addressed to fred@example.com is sent to fred@example.com@fixme. If you define fixme as a virtual domain, all mail from these hosts is handled as virtual domain mail.

More concretely, start by creating a fixme virtual domain in *virtualdomains*:

```
fixme:alias-fixup
```

Then create ~*alias/.qmail-fixup-default*:

```
| bouncesaying 'Permission denied' [ "@$HOST" != "@fixme" ]
| qmail-inject -f "$SENDER" -- "$DEFAULT"
```

The first line checks that the mail is really sent to the fixme virtual domain, so that sneaky bad guys can't relay mail by sending it to alias-fixup-victim@otherdomain@example.com (assuming example.com is your local domain.) The second line feeds the mail through *qmail-inject*, preserving the original sender and remailing it to $DEFAULT, which was the original destination address before @fixme was added. Finally, add the @fixme strings to the local network entries in *smtprules.txt* and rebuild *smtprules.cdb*:

```
127.:allow,RELAYCLIENT="@fixme"
172.16.42.:allow,RELAYCLIENT="@fixme"
172.16.15.1-127:allow,RELAYCLIENT="@fixme"
:allow
```

Use `svc -h /service/qmail-send` to make qmail notice the new virtual domain.

Although as we see in the next section, this is no longer the best way to handle mail injection, the basic model for treating mail depending on its source IP address remains useful. For example, I find that I receive certain spam from AOL over and over again with very predictable strings in the message. So I route all mail from AOL to a pseudodomain aoltrap in which commands in the *.qmail* file grep each message for the known spammy strings, forward the mail to an abuse reporting script if they find any of the strings, and otherwise forward the mail to $DEFAULT to deliver it normally. While I use a more general spam filter for other incoming mail, the stuff from AOL is different enough that it was worth setting up a special filter, particularly because it only took 10 minutes to set the filter up.

Using Separate Relay and Injection Daemons

Since the *new-inject* package includes *ofmipd*, which combines an SMTP daemon and the same mail cleanup that *new-inject* does, the best way to clean up incoming mail is to arrange for mail clients to inject mail through *ofmipd* rather than *qmail-smtpd*. *ofmipd* doesn't do relay checking, so you have to ensure that only authorized clients can use it.

If you assign more than one IP address to your qmail host, run *qmail-smtpd* on one address and *ofmipd* on another. It's also a good idea to run a copy of *ofmipd* on port 587, the SUBMIT port that is defined (and increasingly used) for mail submission (another name for injection) from MUAs on other hosts.* And you must run *ofmipd*

---

* If you have roaming users who connect from hotels and the like, SUBMIT is particularly important. Many networks block attempts to connect to port 25, but they permit connections to 587.

on 127.0.0.1 to accept mail from programs that inject mail by setting up a local SMTP session (such as pine and some mailing list packages). You must run separate copies of *tcpserver*, each bound to a separate IP address and port. First, change */var/qmail/supervise/qmail-smtpd/run* to run *tcpserver* only on a single IP address, which should be the address in the MX record pointing at the server, as in Example 7-1.

Example 7-1. The SMTP listening script for incoming mail

```
1. #!/bin/sh
2. limit datasize 2m
3. exec \
4.    tcpserver -u000 -g000 -v -p -R    \
5.     -x/var/qmail/rules/smtprules.cdb 10.1.2.3 25 \
6.    /var/qmail/bin/qmail-smtpd 2>&1
```

In the *log* directory, create a subdirectory *log/logfiles*, chown it to qmaill (the log user), and create *log/run*, as in Example 7-2.

Example 7-2. Log file script for SMTP and ofmip daemons

```
1. #!/bin/sh
2. exec setuidgid qmaill \
3.    multilog t s1000000 ./logfiles
```

In line 3, s1000000 says to make each log file a megabyte. Depending on how much log traffic the server generates, you may want to adjust this number up or down to adjust how far back the log data goes. The log setup for all of the servers described in this chapter is the same, so I won't repeat it.

Second, create directories */var/qmail/supervise/ofmipd* and */var/qmail/supervise/ofmipd/log* to run *ofmipd*. Set up the *log* directory the same as the one for *qmail-send* described in Chapter 4. Set the file modes the same as you did for SMTP service and create *ofmipd/run*, as in Example 7-3.

Example 7-3. The ofmipd script, for SMTP mail injected from other hosts

```
1. #!/bin/sh
2. limit datasize 2m
3. exec \
4. tcpserver -u000 -g000 -v -p -R         \
5.    -x/var/qmail/rules/ofmipdrules.cdb 10.1.2.4 25 \
6.    /usr/local/bin/ofmipd 2>&1
```

Third, create */var/qmail/rules/ofmipdrules.txt* to permit connections only from the local network and deny everyone else, and create */var/qmail/rules/ofmipdrules.cdb* from it:

```
172.16.42.:allow
172.16.15.1-127.:allow
:deny
```

Finally, symlink */var/qmail/supervise/ofmipd* to */service* and your injection daemon should start up. Telnet to your injection daemon's address, port 25, and use HELO, MAIL FROM, RCPT TO, and DATA commands to send yourself a test message.

Once that works, copy everything in */var/qmail/supervise/ofmipd* to */var/qmail/supervise/ofmipdlocal*, and */var/qmail/supervise/ofmipd/log* to */var/qmail/supervise/ofmipdlocal/log*. Then edit the run file to use 127.0.0.1, as shown in Example 7-4.

Example 7-4. The ofmipd script, for SMTP mail injected from this host

```
1. #!/bin/sh
2. limit datasize 2m
3. exec \
4.      tcpserver -u000 -g000 -v -p -R \
5.      127.0.0.1 25 \
6.      /var/qmail/bin/ofmipd 2>&1
```

You can omit the -x flag because only processes on the local computer can connect to 127.0.0.1. Now symlink */var/qmail/supervise/ofmipdlocal* to */service*, and test your local daemon by telnetting to 127.0.0.1 port 25, and send yourself another test message.

To create an *ofmipd* running on the SUBMIT port, create */var/qmail/supervise/ofmipdsubmit* and */var/qmail/supervise/ofmipdsubmit/log* with the same contents as */var/qmail/supervise/ofmipd* and */var/qmail/supervise/ofmipd/log*, except that the port number on line 5 is 587 rather than 25. It can (and should) share the same *ofmipdrules.cdb* file because the rules for who you accept mail from are the same, regardless of which port a client uses. Symlink */var/qmail/supervise/ofmipdsubmit* to */service*, telnet to your injection daemon's address, port 587, and send one more test message, and you're done setting up mail injection.

To someone familiar with sendmail, it may seem awfully complicated and perhaps slow to set up four separate daemons just to receive mail, but the four are all configured slightly differently, and because *tcpserver* is small and fast, it doesn't place an undue load on the system.

Deciding On the Fly Which Daemon to Use

Although I don't really recommend this approach, it's easy to arrange to run either *qmail-smtpd* or *ofmipd* on connections to the same IP address depending on the remote address from which a connection arrives. Do this by adding an environment variable to entries in *smtprules* that says which daemon to run, and testing that variable in the programs run from *tcpserver*. Let's put the name of the server to use in the SERVER variable, so *smtprules.txt* looks like this:

```
127.:allow,SERVER="ofmipd"
172.16.42.:allow,SERVER="ofmipd"
172.16.15.1-127:allow,SERVER="ofmipd"
:allow,SERVER="smtpd"
```

Now adjust the *run* file to use SERVER to decide what to run, as shown in Example 7-5.

Example 7-5. The SMTP listening script for incoming mail

```
1. #!/bin/sh
2. limit datasize 2m
3. exec \
4.     tcpserver -u000 -g000 -v -p -R     \
5.      -x/var/qmail/rules/smtprules.cdb 10.1.2.3 25 \
6.      sh -c 'case "$SERVER" in
7.       smtpd) exec /var/qmail/bin/smtpd ;;
8.       ofmipd) exec /usr/local/bin/ofmipd ;;
9.                          esac' 2>&1
```

When *tcpserver* receives an incoming connection, it runs the shell script[*] on lines 6-9, which in turn exec's whichever program SERVER tells it to. Be sure to use single and double quotes exactly as shown here, so that the value of SERVER is expanded by the shell run from *tcpserver*, rather than by the shell that interprets the *run* script.

Dealing with Roaming Users

The most difficult part of dealing with injected mail is to recognize mail from "roaming" users not located on the local network. You can recognize them directly by requiring a user/password when they send mail or indirectly by noting their IP when they log into the POP server, then treating mail from the same IP address as local. The former is SMTP authorization, the latter is pop-before-SMTP.

SMTP Authorization and TLS Security

To use SMTP authorization with qmail, you must patch *qmail-smtpd* to handle the AUTH command for remote users to log into the server. Although AUTH lets remote users prove who they are, it doesn't provide any security against third parties snooping on the mail as it leaves whatever network the roaming users are on, nor does it provide security against port redirection, where a network connects you to their own SMTP server rather than the one you asked for. (AOL does port redirection, not for malicious purposes, but because it lets their users send out modest amounts of mail as roamers without needing to reconfigure their MUAs, while blocking blasts of spam and viruses.)

---

[*] Because the script is in single quotes, it doesn't need \ at the end of each line.

Using an IP Tunnel

A different approach to the roaming user problem is to make the roaming user's computer logically part of the local network by assigning it an IP address on the local network, and arranging to "tunnel" the traffic over the Internet between the PC and the local network. Tunnels have the advantage that once they're set up, they allow access to any local-only service, such as intranet web servers.

The most popular tunnelling systems are the IETF's IP security (IPSEC) and Microsoft's point to point tunnelling protocol (PPTP). IPSEC is available on most recent Unix-like systems and on Windows 2000 and XP. It is quite tedious to set up but is very secure in use, with strong encryption on both the login and all the data that's passed through the tunnel. PPTP is built into all recent versions of Windows, and free Unix servers called poptop and pptpd are available. It's considerably easier to set up than IPSEC but is much less secure, passing data either unencrypted or at best using an encryption scheme that's known to be easy to break.

The widely used *ssh* secure remote login system provides a per-port version of tunnelling called "port forwarding." For example, users can specify that port 2025 on their remote machine is forwarded to port 25 on the mail host on the home network, then set up their mail application to use localhost:2025 for outgoing mail, with the SMTP server seeing the *ssh* host on the local network as the source of the mail. Even though it's possible to log into POP and IMAP servers directly from remote networks, it's also useful to forward remote ports to ports 110 or 143 on the mail server so that the login passwords and retrieved messages are transferred via ssh's encrypted connection rather than in the clear. *ssh* requires a shell login for authentication on the home network, and must be set up (one time) for each port that's to be forwarded. Regardless, *ssh* is often a good compromise, because it is easier to set up than IPSEC while still being reasonably secure.

The transport-level security (TLS) extension provides an encrypted channel for SMTP sessions similar to that used by SSL secure web servers. TLS is based on certificates that include the host owner's name and address along with the hostname and an email address. Each certificate is in two parts, the private key, which needs to be kept secret, and everything else including the public key, which is not secret. For incoming SMTP sessions, SMTP clients start a secure session, verify the server's certificate and check that the hostname in the certificate matches the name of the host that the client thinks it's talking to. The client can optionally present a certificate to the server for which the server can make the same checks. The server can also use the address in the client certificate to authenticate the user instead of a separate AUTH step, as described later in the sidebar "Authenticating Client Hosts with TLS."

There's a combined patch for *qmail-smtpd* that adds both SMTP AUTH and TLS, and a doubly combined patch that adds SMTP AUTH and TLS, as well as the badrcptto anti-spam patch described in Chapter 9 and some extra logging (the version that I use). The two combined patches both add the same SMTP AUTH and TLS code, so they're the ones I describe here. These are the largest patches described in this book, which makes it more likely that they contain bugs. I've looked at the code and it appears OK to me, but if you're concerned about security, you should read through the patch you use yourself.

For SMTP AUTH, the setup involves setting up a login/password checking program to validate the authorization values that remote hosts present and adjusting the *tcpserver* invocation of *qmail-smtpd*. If you're using the qmail POP server, use the same password validator. Users generally only need to set an option in their MUAs to use AUTH on outgoing mail using the same userid/password pair they use for POP or IMAP.

TLS requires the openssl library (included with many but not all recent Unix-like systems) and a TLS certificate for the SMTP server. If you happen to have an SSL web server with the same name as the mail server, use the same certificate it uses. Otherwise, make a new certificate. All certificates are signed; you can sign yours yourself, but most MUAs expect server certificates to be signed by a certificate authority (CA) that vouches for the authenticity of the certificate. The MUA has a set of validation certificates from well-known CAs built-in (Outlook and Outlook Express share their list with Internet Explorer), and if the signature isn't from one of the authorities in the list, the MUA at least warns the user that the certificate isn't properly signed, and in many cases refuses to transfer any mail. There's generally some way for the MUA's user to tell the MUA to accept the self-signed certificate from the server. If you have very sophisticated users, you can set up your own miniature CA to sign your certificates and try to get your users to install your CA certificate into their MUA's well-known lists. Alternatively, you can pay one of the well-known CAs to sign your certificate, which costs between $50 and $300 depending on the CA. At this point, most TLS users are sophisticated enough to get their MUA to accept one self-signed certificate for the smarthost they use regularly, but if you plan to offer TLS to a less technical user community, your easiest course is to pay a well-known CA for a signature.

If this all sounds like more trouble than it's worth, build your patched qmail with the TLS code turned off, and worry about it later if your users ask for it.

Installing and Building SMTP AUTH and (Optionally) TLS

Download either of the combined SMTP AUTH/TLS patches (see *www.qmail.org* for links to the latest versions), and apply the patch.

The TLS code depends on the open source openssl library. If you want to use TLS and your system doesn't have a recent version of the openssl library (0.9.6 or later), download the source from *http://www.openssl.org*, and build and install it. The configuration and installation procedure, documented in its *INSTALL* file, is straightforward.

If you don't want to use TLS, edit *conf-cc* to remove the option to compile in the TLS code. The patch changes the first line of the file to something like this:

```
cc -O2 -DTLS -I/usr/local/ssl/include
```

To turn off TLS, change it back to:

```
cc -02
```

(Because the compilation process uses only the first line of that file, add the simpler line in front of the patched one in case you want to try TLS later.)

Before you rebuild qmail, if you're using the standard checkpassword 0.90 or any other password checker that doesn't keep plain text passwords, you need to turn off one of the SMTP AUTH features. The patch supports three varieties of AUTH known as LOGIN, PLAIN, and CRAM-MD5. The CRAM-MD5 variety needs plain text passwords, so you must disable it if your password checker doesn't support them. (A modified checkpassword that supports CRAM-MD5 using a separate password file with plaintext passwords is available at *http://members.elysium.pl/brush/ cmd5checkpw*.) To turn off CRAM-MD5, edit *qmail-smtpd.c* and around line 40 is a definition of AUTHCRAM:

```
#define AUTHCRAM
```

Comment it out:

```
/* #define AUTHCRAM */
```

Now make to rebuild the patched qmail.

If you're using TLS, you must install a certificate for TLS to use. To create a self-signed certificate, become super-user and make cert. It will ask for identifying information for the certificate, including the host's two-letter country code (US for the United States), state name, company name, common name, and email address. Most of the info is merely for display if someone checks the certificate, but the common name should be the SMTP server's hostname, and the email address a contact address for the server's manager. It will put the public and private keys into *control/servercert.pem*, and also link it to *control/clientcert.pem* for use in outgoing mail. This is all the setup you need if clients who use TLS are willing to tell their MUAs to accept self-signed certificates. If you want a certificate signed by a CA, use make cert-req instead. It puts a "certificate request" into *req.pem*, which you can submit to the CA. When the CA sends back the signed version, add that to the end of *control/servercert.pem*.

Whether or not you're using TLS, now become super-user and make setup check to install the patched qmail. (If you have the new configuration files set up, it's OK to install this over the running version of qmail because the AUTH and TLS features do nothing until someone tries to use them.)

To configure AUTH, the *run* file for the SMTP server needs three new arguments to *qmail-smtpd*: the server's hostname, the password checker, and a dummy program that the password checker can run, usually */bin/true*. (See Example 7-6.)

Example 7-6. The SMTP listening script for incoming mail

```
 1. #!/bin/sh
 2. limit datasize 2m
 3. exec                                              \
 4.    tcpserver -u000 -g000 -v -p -R with SMTP AUTH \
 5.     -x/var/qmail/rules/smtprules.cdb 10.1.2.3 25 \
 6.    /var/qmail/bin/qmail-smtpd                     \
6a.    mail.example.com                               \
6b.    checkpassword                                  \
6c.    /bin/true 2>&1
```

The hostname in line 6a is used only for CRAM-MD5 authorization, but the argument has to be there regardless of whether CRAM is used. A common error is to leave out the hostname argument, making */bin/true* the password checker, which means that any user/password pair will be accepted, making the server an open relay.* After adding the new arguments, restart *tcpserver* with svc -t, and test out AUTH by sending mail from client MUAs with both valid and invalid logins, making sure that the invalid login is rejected. Because an invalid login doesn't end the SMTP session (it just doesn't authorize) you must address the test messages to an address that wouldn't be permitted without AUTH. If you're using TLS, test it from your favorite PC MUA. Just turn on the MUA option to use TLS on outgoing mail, send a message, observe that the MUA complains about the server's self-signed certificate, tell the MUA to accept it anyway, and check that the mail is delivered.

On outgoing mail, *qmail-remote* with TLS turned on automatically starts a TLS session whenever a server announces that it has TLS available. If *control/clientcert.pem* exists, its contents are used as the client certificate in outgoing sessions. Normally, make

---

* So don't do that.

cert links the *clientcert* file to the *servercert* file, but if you're sending TLS mail to a smarthost run by your ISP, the ISP may provide you a client certificate to use instead. If there are some SMTP servers to which mail should only be sent using TLS connections with signed certificates, create the directory *control/tlshosts*, and for each server, put the CA certificates of the allowable signers in *control/tlshosts/hostname.pem*. Usually all of the hosts share the same set of signers, so all of the *.pem* files are links to the same file. In practice, the only host that you're likely to verify this way is your ISP's smarthost.

POP-before-SMTP

An older and more indirect scheme for roaming user authentication is POP-before-SMTP, first used in 1997. It's a very simple idea and has been implemented many times. Whenever a user successfully logs in using POP or IMAP to pick up mail, it notes the IP address where the user logged in. For the next hour or so, that IP address is allowed to use the mail gateway. It has the practical advantage of working with any POP or IMAP MUA, merely by telling users to check their mail before sending. For MUAs that support SMTP AUTH, which is now most of them, AUTH is better than POP-before-SMTP because it doesn't require the extra mail check, and it identifies sent mail with a particular user, not just an IP address. But for the benefit of users who never upgrade their MUA, it's worth keeping POP-before-SMTP around.

I wrote a homebrew POP-before-SMTP system with a daemon that updates the *smtprules* files, but I now prefer Bruce Guenther's *relay-ctrl* package (*http:// untroubled.org/relay-ctrl/*), which has the advantage of not needing any patches to existing software and working reasonably well on clusters of multiple hosts running POP, IMAP, and SMTP servers.

POP-before-SMTP has three parts. The first part observes the POP and IMAP logins and notes the IP addresses. *relay-ctrl* uses the filesystem for its database, so if a user logs in from address 10.1.2.3, it creates a file */var/spool/relay-ctrl/allow/10.1.2.3*. The second part checks the IP address on each incoming SMTP connection, and if the IP has a corresponding file in */var/spool/relay-ctrl/allow*, it sets the environment to allow relay. The third cleans up stale entries by deleting files in */var/spool/relay-ctrl/allow* that are older than the window of time allowed for POP-before-SMTP. The *relay-ctrl* documentation suggests 15 minutes, but I've used times as long as a day without trouble. To keep the relay database reasonably secure, make */var/spool/relay-ctrl* owned by root with mode 0500 so that only root can chdir into it, but make */var/spool/relay-ctrl/allow* mode 777 so that the unprivileged program that notes logins can write there.

For clusters of multiple hosts, whenever a user is authenticated on one host, *relay-ctrl* sends notices to the other hosts about the IP that authenticated, using UDP packets.

To install *relay-ctrl*, download it from *http://untroubled.org/relay-ctrl/*. (This description is of Version 3.1.1.) Unpack it, adjust the *conf-cc*, *conf-ld* and *conf-man* if you need to reflect your local commands for compiling and linking, and the place to put the *man* files, then make. Become super-user and run *./installer* to install the various programs. The runtime configuration of the *relay-ctrl* package is almost entirely done through environment variables. I suggest creating a directory */etc/relay-ctrl* so you can use *envdir* from the daemontools package to set the environment. (Each file in the directory is the name of a variable, the contents of the file becomes the value of the variable.) Files and environment variables to create include:

RELAY_CTRL_DIR
> The directory where the relay data goes, usually */var/spool/relay-ctrl/allow*.

RELAY_CTRL_EXPIRY
> The time in seconds to permit relay after a user is validated. Defaults to 900 (15 minutes), but I suggest 3600 (an hour.)

RELAY_CTRL_RELAYCLIENT
> The value to use for the RELAYCLIENT variable when a user is allowed to relay. Defaults to the null string, but if you're using the "fixme" trick to clean up headers on injected mail, make it @fixme, the same as the value in RELAYCLIENT lines in the *smtprules* file.

RELAY_CTRL_LOG_IPS
> If defined, print log messages when an SMTP connection is authenticated for relay. The messages goes the same place as the log output from *tcpserver* and *qmail-smtpd*, typically the log files kept by *multilog*.

RELAY_CTRL_REMOTES
> A comma-separated list of IP addresses to which UDP messages containing notices of IP addresses should be sent when a host is authenticated. Not needed if you're not using multiple hosts.

RELAY_CTRL_PORT
> UDP port number to use for notifications. Defaults to 811, and there is no reason to change it unless something else on your network is using UDP port 811 packets.

RELAY_CTRL_TIMEOUT
> How many seconds to wait for each remote host to acknowledge a notification packet before retrying. Defaults to one second, and there is no reason to change it unless your mail hosts are very slow.

RELAY_CTRL_TRIES
> How many times to retry each notification if it doesn't get an acknowledgement. Defaults to 5, and there is no reason to change it unless your network is extremely congested.

Adding POP-before-SMTP to the POP Server

Chapter 13 describes the procedure for setting up the qmail POP server. Example 7-7 shows the modifications to handle POP-before SMTP, in the script */etc/popd/run*.

Example 7-7. The POP listening script with POP-before-SMTP

```
 1. #!/bin/sh
 2. limit datasize 2m
 3. exec                                      \
3a.   envdir /etc/relay-ctrl                  \
3b.   relay-ctrl-chdir                        \
 4.   tcpserver                               \
 5.     -HRv -l pop.example.com               \
 6.     -x /etc/popd/rules.cdb                \
 7.     0 110                                 \
 8.   /var/qmail/bin/qmail-popup pop.example.com \
 9.   checkpassword                           \
9a.   relay-ctrl-allow                        \
9b.   relay-ctrl-send                         \
10.   /var/qmail/bin/qmail-pop3d Maildir 2>&1
```

Line 3a sets the environment from the files in */etc/relay-ctrl*, and line 3b, which runs with root privileges, opens the *allow* directory so that later nonroot programs can modify it. Line 9a creates the *allow/nn.nn.nn.nn* file noting that the IP has authenticated, and line 9b sends UDP notifications to other local mail servers. (If you only have one server, leave out line 9b.) The rest of the script is unmodified from the version in Chapter 13.

Adding POP-Before-SMTP to the SMTP Server

The additions to the SMTP script in */var/qmail/supervise/qmail-smtpd/run* are similar to the ones for the POP server, as shown in Example 7-8.

Example 7-8. The SMTP listening script, with POP-before-SMTP

```
 1. #!/bin/sh
 2. limit datasize 2m
 3. exec                                          \
3a.   envdir /etc/relay-ctrl                      \
3b.     relay-ctrl-chdir                          \
 4.     tcpserver -u000 -g000 -v -p -R            \
4a.     relay-ctrl-check                          \
 5.       -x/var/qmail/rules/smtprules.cdb 10.1.2.3 25 \
 6.     /var/qmail/bin/qmail-smtpd 2>&1
```

Lines 3a and 3b set environment variables and open the *allow* directory, as before. Line 4a checks to see if *allow/nn.nn.nn.nn* exists and isn't too old (older than RELAY_CTRL_EXPIRY seconds), and if so sets RELAYCLIENT.

If you want to provide both POP-before-SMTP and SMTP AUTH, install the SMTP AUTH patches as described earlier in this chapter, and then add in the POP-before-SMTP programs to the *run* script, as shown in Example 7-9.

Example 7-9. The SMTP listening script with POP-before-SMTP and SMTP AUTH

```
 1. #!/bin/sh
 2. limit datasize 2m
 3. exec                                           \
3a.  envdir /etc/relay-ctrl                        \
3b.    relay-ctrl-chdir                            \
 4.    tcpserver -u000 -g000 -v -p -R              \
4a.    relay-ctrl-check                            \
 5.     -x/var/qmail/rules/smtprules.cdb 10.1.2.3 25 \
 6.    /var/qmail/bin/qmail-smtpd                  \
6a.    mail.example.com                            \
6b.    checkpassword                               \
6c.    /bin/true 2>&1
```

Using POP-before-SMTP with ofmipd

If you use *ofmipd* to accept injected mail, it's a little harder to use POP-before-SMTP. The reason is that *:deny* rules prevent `relay-ctrl-check` from running at all for IP addresses that aren't on the local network. There's a straightforward workaround using the anti-spam program *rblsmtpd*, discussed in Chapter 9.

Other POP-before-SMTP Daemons

Every once in a while, you should delete expired files from the *allow* directory to avoid clutter. There's no great urgency since `relay-ctrl-check` checks each time it uses a file that the file isn't expired, so running the cleanup program once a day is plenty. If your system has a *daily* or *daily.local* script that's run as root once a day, add a line to the end that says:

```
    envdir /etc/relay-ctrl relay-ctrl-age
```

If not, run that line directly from *cron* once a day.

Finally, if you have multiple mail servers, on each SMTP server you must run the UDP server that receives messages about IP addresses that have authenticated. The server does no validation at all of source addresses, so if possible you should adjust your router to discard all packets addressed to UDP port 811 (or whatever other port you use). Create directories */var/qmail/supervise/relay-ctrl/udp* and */var/qmail/supervise/relay-ctrl/udp/log*. The *run* file just starts the UDP listener as root, as in Example 7-10.

Example 7-10. The POP-before-SMTP UDP listener script

```
1. #!/bin/sh
2. exec                                    \
3.  envdir /etc/relay-ctrl                 \
4.    relay-ctrl-udp 2>&1
```

IMAP Before SMTP

If you use the Courier IMAP server or the Courier POP server, relay-ctrl is designed to work with them as well, using the Courier authorization library interface. See the *relay-ctrl README* file for more details.

## CHAPTER 8

Delivering and Routing Local Mail

Mail isn't very useful unless it's delivered successfully. This chapter looks at delivering mail addressed to local mailboxes, both for local delivery and for redelivery elsewhere.

Mail to Local Login Users

Local login users usually receive mail in mbox format in *~/Mailbox* and *~/.mail*.* Or they receive mail in Maildir format in *~/Maildir/*.

Local Delivery .qmail Files and Default Delivery Rules

In the simplest case, a user's *.qmail* file needs to contain only a single line to specify the user's mailbox, either the mbox format mailbox:

```
# deliver into $HOME/Mailbox
./Mailbox
```

or the Maildir:

```
# deliver into a file in $HOME/Maildir/
./Maildir/
```

I suggest that every shell user should have a *.qmail* file (add it to the set of skeleton files that your *adduser* procedure creates), but for users who don't, be sure to set a reasonable default as the argument to *qmail-start* in */service/qmail/run*, as described in Chapter 3.

---

* For historical compatibility, some still use */var/spool/mail/username*, but in this chapter I assume that you have at least moved your users' mailboxes into their home directories where they belong.

Maildirs and Mail Clients

Although Maildirs have all sorts of advantages over mboxes, they are not supported in many mail clients. For the popular elm and pine clients, qmail provides small scripts, *elq* and *pinq*, which move mail from the Maildir into an mbox, then run the client. These use the *maildir2mbox* utility, which requires three environment variables to be set. `MAIL` is the mbox file, usually `$HOME/Mailbox`. `MAILTMP` is the name of a temporary file used to hold a copy of the updated mbox, which must be on the same filesystem as $MAIL, usually `$HOME/Mailbox.tmp`. `MAILDIR` is the name of the Maildir, usually `$HOME/Maildir`.

While these two scripts work adequately, in the long run if you're using Maildirs, you should use a Maildir client. Unix and Linux command-line users can try mutt, a nice freeware client, Courier IMAP (see Chapter 13), and IMAP clients including pine and the KDE mail client.

Mail Sorting

Unless users receive very little mail, they generally want to sort it before they read it. While Windows mail users tend to pick up all their mail from a single POP mailbox and sort it into local mailboxes in their mail client, Unix users often arrange to sort the mail as it's delivered into mailboxes on the server, and use a client that can handle multiple mailboxes either directly or using IMAP.

There are two general strategies to mail sorting: use multiple incoming addresses or use a filtering program on incoming mail.

Mail Sorting with Subaddresses

The easiest way to sort mailing list mail is to subscribe to each list with a different subaddress. That is, if your address is mary@example.com, you might sign up for three lists as mary-gold@example.com, mary-nade@example.com, and mary-land@example.com.* If your system is set up with per-user subdomains as described in Chapter 12, the three addresses could be written as gold@mary.example.com, nade@mary.example.com, and land@mary.example.com. Then create three files *~mary/.qmail-gold*, *~mary/.qmail-nade*, *~mary/.qmail-land*, each with the delivery instructions for the list mail. If you are using a mail client that handles multiple mailboxes, either directly or through the Courier IMAP server (see Chapter 13), deliver each list to its own mailbox.

This scheme works very well when you only receive mail from a list and you can access the signup through a web site. I use a unique address every time I buy

---

* These are presumably lists about horticulture, cooking, and geography.

something from a web site that wants an email address. That's useful for both mail sorting and reminding me that a dubious looking piece of mail is in fact from a place to whom I gave the address. It doesn't work so well on discussion lists to which you send as well as receive mail, because it's not easy to put the subaddress on outgoing mail, either to set up the subscription or to send messages to the list. (I've occasionally been reduced to running *qmail-inject* and typing mail headers to it.) It's possible to write a wrapper around qmail's *sendmail* program or *qmail-inject* or, if you're using the QMAILQUEUE patch from Chapter 3, write a wrapper around *qmail-queue* that looks up the destination addresses for a user's outgoing mail in a file and adjusts the return address for mail going to lists. As far as I know, though, nobody's done so. The pragmatic approach is to subscribe both a subaddress and your regular address to a list, and set your regular address to NOMAIL or alias the two together if the list management software permits, so incoming mail from the list goes to the subaddress, while you send outgoing mail from your regular address.

Mail Sorting with Filter Programs

For mail that's sent to a user's regular address, procmail and maildrop provide flexible script-driven mail sorting. They both provide similar sets of features, with the largest difference being one of style. The procmail control language is extremely terse with single-letter commands and options, while maildrop's language is more reminiscent of the Unix shells or Perl. Maildrop includes some extra features to do simple text processing intended mostly for extracting and handling email addresses, and an optional interface to GDBM keyed files. A significant practical difference is that procmail reads an entire message into memory, which means it won't work on very large messages that don't fit. Maildrop falls back to temporary files so it can handle even the largest messages, slowly.

I use procmail, mostly because I've been using it since before maildrop was available. The size limit isn't a problem in practice, because I rarely get mail bigger than 10 MB (certainly not mail that I want), and the filtering I do doesn't need the extra features in maildrop.

Mail sorting with procmail

Procmail works well when run from *.qmail* files. It expects an mbox-style From line at the beginning of the message, so run it via *preline*:

```
| preline /usr/bin/procmail || exit 111
```

This tells procmail to read the standard control file *.procmailrc*, preceded by */etc/procmailrc* if it exists. The exit 111 is optional, but it's there to ensure that a message stays in the queue if procmail crashes, giving you a chance to fiddle around and figure out what went wrong and try again. On the other hand, if your procmail script sets the EXITCODE variable to return a particular value, you should leave off the exit so qmail sees your code.

The procmail documentation discusses special provisions for using procmail as a mail delivery agent, and the fine points of its set-uid code. None of this applies to qmail. When procmail starts, whether it's run explicitly from a *.qmail* file or implicitly as the default argument to *qmail-start*, it is like all delivery agents run under the recipient user's ID and home directory. You should *not* install procmail as setuid, because you don't need it and it would be a potential security hole.

If you have multiple mailboxes, either mboxes or Maildir subfolders, procmail can deliver to them directly:

```
# catch messages that appear to be duplicates based on msgid
# (this cryptic recipe cribbed from the procmail examples)
:0 Whc: msgid.lock
| formail -D 8192 msgid.cache

# file them in a subfolder
:0 a
Maildir/.duplicates/

# deliver mail about breakfast to an mbox
:0
* Subject:.*breakfast
Mail/breakfast

# deliver mail from the lunch list to a Maildir subfolder
# use the List-ID: tag to identify it
:0
* List-ID:.*lunchlist.example.com
Maildir/.lunchlist/

# bounce mail about dinner, we're on a diet
:0
* Subject:.*dinner
{
    EXITCODE=100
}

# deliver everything else to my regular Maildir
:0
Maildir/
```

Note that the Maildir deliveries end with a slash to identify them as Maildirs rather than mboxes, just like in *.qmail* files.

It's quite possible and often useful to combine tagged addresses with procmail. You'll generally want to create separate procmail files for the subaddresses, so put this in *.qmail-color* and tell it to use *procmail-color*:

```
| preline /usr/bin/procmail procmail-color
```

You can use all of qmail's environment variables in your procmail scripts, because procmail makes them available as variables in the script and in the environment of any commands it runs. All but one, that is, because procmail has its own (not very useful) definition of $DEFAULT, which overrides qmail's. Fortunately, this is easily circumvented by giving it a different name. Put this in *.qmail-color-default* to refer to the default part of the address as $SUBADDR:

```
| preline /usr/bin/procmail procmail-color SUBADDR="$DEFAULT"
```

Mail sorting with maildrop

In principle, anything you can do with procmail, you can do with maildrop, just differently. In practice, I've found maildrop's code to have severe portability bugs on non-Linux systems, so I can't recommend it for production use, at least not on BSD systems.

To use maildrop, run it from your *.qmail file*:

```
| maildrop
```

The script comes from */etc/mailfilter* if it exists, then *.mailfilter* in the user's home directory. With no arguments, it delivers mail to the default place determined when maildrop was built, usually *~/Maildir*. Here's the maildrop equivalent of the delivery script:

```
# catch messages that appear to be duplicates based on msgid
# (this code from the maildrop manual)
`reformail -D 8192 duplicate.cache`
if($RETURNCODE == 0)
  to Maildir/.duplicates

# deliver mail about breakfast to an mbox
if(/Subject:.*breakfast/)
  to Mail/breakfast

# deliver mail from the lunch list to a Maildir subfolder
# use the List-ID: tag to identify it
if(/List-ID:.*lunchlist.example.com/)
  to Maildir/.lunchlist/

# bounce mail about dinner, we're on a diet
if(/Subject:.*dinner/)
{
   EXITCODE=100
   exit
}

# deliver everything else to my regular Maildir
to Maildir
```

More Mail Sorting

Although procmail and maildrop are the most popular programs for mail sorting, it's not hard to roll your own. For example, using qmail's *condredirect* program, you can sort mail based on text strings:

```
| condredirect fred-breakfast grep -q 'Subject:.*breakfast'
| condredirect fred-lunch grep -q 'List-ID:.*lunchlist.example.com'
Maildir/
```

Because qmail doesn't include separate programs to store mail into mailboxes, conditional deliveries need to use separate subaddresses for each mailbox they use. If you have programs handy to do deliveries (mine's called *mds* for Maildir Store, available at *www.qmail.org*), you can write these as short shell commands:

```
| if grep -q 'Subject:.*breakfast'; then mds Maildir/.breakfast; exit 99; else exit
0; esac
... and so forth ...
```

(The grep command reads through the input message, so any program like *mds* has to be sure to rewind its input so it starts delivering the message from the beginning.) For most purposes, you're better off with procmail or maildrop, but if you find you want to do some sorting that you can't easily express in procmail-ese, you can always roll your own.

## CHAPTER 9

Filtering and Rejecting Spam and Viruses

Filtering spam and viruses out of incoming mail is an unfortunate necessity on today's Internet. It would be easy to write a book on spam filtering techniques, but this chapter is designed to present techniques and examples rather than a complete filtering strategy. (Even if it did have a complete strategy, by the time you read it, the character of spam would have changed enough that you'd have to change your filters anyway.)

Filtering Criteria

Spam and virus filters can use any of a wide range of message characteristics for filtering. They include:

- The IP address from which the message is received
- The information sent in commands in the SMTP session, including the argument to the HELO or EHLO command, the envelope sender in MAIL FROM, and the envelope recipients in RCPT TO
- The contents of message headers, including From:, To:, Subject:, and Received:
- The contents of the message body

It's also possible and often useful to make filtering decisions based on combinations of messages, such as the number of messages received per minute from a particular IP address, or "bulkiness" scores based on the number of messages seen with similar or identical contents.

Places to Filter

Filtering can be applied at several places in the receipt and delivery process. The earlier a filter is applied, the more quickly a message is dealt with. Filtering points include:

- At connection time, for IP address and rDNS-based filters
- During the SMTP session, before the message is received, for filters based on envelope information

- During the SMTP session, after the message is received, for filters based on message contents

- As the message is delivered, for user-customizable filters

Most systems use multiple filters applied at different points. The standard qmail SMTP daemon is very lightweight compared to most other MTAs, and does as little work as possible to collect the message and queue it, leaving all of the rest of the work for delivery time. Many of the spam filtering tools, such as Spamassassin, a complex filter that computes a "spamminess" score based on multiple criteria, can run at either SMTP time or delivery time.

If you run it at SMTP time, the disadvantage is that it ties up an incoming SMTP process a lot longer than normal, possibly causing mail to be rejected if *tcpserver* reaches its concurrency limit. Also, the SMTP daemon doesn't know where the mail will be delivered, which makes it hard to apply per-user parameters. The advantages of filtering at SMTP time are that mail can be rejected before it's queued, so the bounce goes back to the actual sending system rather than a probably forged return address; a message addressed to multiple recipients can be processed once rather than separately for each user; and in case of a barrage of spam, the *tcpserver* concurrency limits prevents mail from being accepted faster than it can be delivered.*

I used to think that only lightweight filters, such as IP address lookups in DNS blacklists and envelope address lookups in *badmailfrom*, should be run at SMTP time, but as the ratio of spam to real mail has grown, and I see blasts of spam come in that flood the queue and can take hours to filter at delivery time, now I think that it makes sense to run anything at SMTP time that isn't user-specific and doesn't need access to data that the SMTP daemon doesn't have.

Spam Filtering and Virus Filtering

Although spam and virus filtering have historically been different applications, their implementations are as much similar as different. The most important difference is that while nobody wants to get viruses (except perhaps the abuse desk so they can figure out where they're coming from), users have varying taste in spam filters, and many filters permit some user customization. The only way to detect a virus is to examine the body of a message and see if there's a virus inside, which means it has to be done either at SMTP time after the message is received or as the message is delivered. Virus-filtering vendors have come up with long, frequently updated lists to match all of the viruses that they're aware of. While there are plenty of commercial anti-virus products available that can be plugged into qmail (see qmail-scanner and Amavis), it's possible to catch just about every virus with a simple filter (see Russ Nelson's anti-virus patch).

---

* Hitting the concurrency limit and rejecting mail is good if the rejected mail is spam; it's not so good if the rejected mail isn't spam. But legitimate mail software will retry the delivery, so real mail will only be delayed, not lost.

Connection-Time Filtering Tools

The ucspi-tcp package contains a set of tools to accept, reject, or conditionally accept mail using rules that key on the IP address or rDNS of the remote site.[*] Some rules are locally defined and used only on a single host, while others are shared among multiple hosts. The standard way to handle shared rules is via DNS blacklists or blocklists (DNSBLs, either way). Local IP and rDNS rules are handled by *tcpserver*, using a rule file created by *tcprules*. This is the same rule file we set up in Chapter 8 to distinguish between local injection hosts and remote relay hosts. DNSBLs are handled by *rblsmtpd*, which runs between *tcpserver* and *qmail-smtpd*.

Using Local Filtering Rules

Local filtering rules go into the file that is used to build the CDB file used by *tcpserver*. If you set up your qmail system as suggested in Chapter 4, the CDB file is called */var/qmail/rules/smtprules.cdb*, and the source from which it's built is */var/qmail/rules/smtprules.txt*.

To refuse mail connections from hosts that you never want to accept any mail from, use a deny line:

```
10.1.2.3:deny
10.20.96-127.:deny
```

These rules reject connections from the single address 10.1.2.3 and the range 10.20.96.0 through 10.20.127.255. (Omitted components are considered to be wildcards and match any value.) You can also match on the rDNS name of a host. To reject connections from mail.imaspammer.com and any host whose rDNS ends with .dialup.badlyrunisp.net, use these lines:

```
=mail.imaspammer.com:deny
=.dialup.badlyrunisp.net:deny
```

Each time *tcpserver* gets an incoming connection. It looks first for a rule with a name in the form IDENT@IP and IDENT@=rDNS, if it's retrieved IDENT data for the connection, it looks for IP, then =rDNS, then wildcard IPs, then wildcard rDNS, then just an equals sign if there's any rDNS, and finally, an empty catch-all rule. For example, if the host IP is 10.1.2.3, its rDNS is mail.myvirt.com, and the IDENT info is fred, it looks for these rules in this order:

```
fred@10.1.2.3
fred@=mail.myvirt.com
10.1.2.3
```

---

[*] *tcpserver* can also use info from an IDENT (port 113) server on the remote host. IDENT has almost disappeared from the Net, so I won't say much about it beyond noting that if *tcpserver* receives IDENT data from the remote host, it's put in the TCPREMOTEINFO environment variable. See the *tcprules* documentation for more details.

```
=mail.myvirt.com
10.1.2.
10.1.
10.
.
=.myvirt.com
=.com
=
  (empty rule)
```

If there's no IDENT info (there usually isn't), it doesn't look for the first two rules. If there's no rDNS, it doesn't look for any of the rDNS rules with equals signs. Note the three different catchalls: a single dot that matches any IP address, a single equals sign that matches any host that has rDNS, and an empty name that matches anything. The dot rule and empty name both match everything, with the difference being that the dot rule takes precedence over rDNS wildcards. (Or to put it another way, if there's a dot rule, it never looks at rDNS wildcards because the dot rule matches first.) The actions in the rules can be :allow or :deny. An :allow action can be followed by any number of environment variable assignments, separated by commas.

A typical rules file has a few :allow rules with RELAYCLIENT for hosts on the local network that inject mail, a few IP-based :deny rules for hosts that send viruses or pure spam, often some rDNS :deny rules for IP ranges of retail dialup or broadband hosts that have sent nothing but viruses, and a catchall :allow rule. It's a bad idea to use rDNS-based :allow rules, because rDNS is technically easy to forge. If you're using POP-before-SMTP, described in Chapter 7, note that if an address has a :deny rule, *tcpserver* will summarily reject the connection, never giving the POP-before-SMTP program a chance. Fortunately, as we'll see in the next section, it's possible to use *rblsmtpd* to do the rejections in a way that makes POP-before-SMTP work:

```
# allow relay from this host
127.:allow,RELAYCLIENT=""

# allow relay from other hosts on this network
172.16.42.:allow,RELAYCLIENT=""
172.16.15-18.:allow,RELAYCLIENT=""

# reject all connections from spam source
10.10.88.99:deny

# reject connections from badly managed DSL pool
=.dsl.ineptisp.com:deny

# otherwise, allow connections but no relay
:allow
```

Using DNSBLs and DNSWLs

A rules file is a fine way to manage IP rejection rules for a single host. For a small network, it's practical to distribute copies of rules of CDB to all of the hosts using scp or rdist that need it. But to share a set of rules among hundreds or thousands of hosts, only a DNSBL will do. To use DNSBL, insert a call to *rblsmtpd* in between *tcpserver* and *qmail-smtpd*. Early versions of *rblsmtpd* could only check one DNSBL per invocation (dating from the era when Paul Vixie's RBL was the only DNSBL), but Version 0.88 checks any number, as shown in Example 9-1.

Example 9-1. Running the SMTP daemon

```
1.  #!/bin/sh
2.  limit datasize 2m
3.  exec \
4.     tcpserver -u000 -g000 -v -p -R      \
5.     -x/var/qmail/rules/smtprules.cdb 0 25 \
5a.        rblsmtpd -b \
5b.           -ahul.habeas.com \
5c.           -rsbl.spamhaus.org \
5d.           -rcbl.abuseat.org \
6.        /var/qmail/bin/qmail-smtpd 2>&1
```

rblsmtpd either runs the next program in line, generally *qmail-smtpd*, if the DNSBLs and DNSWLs don't tell it to block mail from the connecting IP, or else turns into a tiny SMTP "rejection server" that only accepts HELO, EHLO, MAIL FROM, and QUIT, returning an error message to anything else. With any luck, the SMTP client on the other end passes the error message back to the sender so that a human sender realizes there's a problem and mailing list software takes the address off its list. The message can be prefixed by either a 451 code, a temporary error that tells the sender to try again later, or 553, a permanent error that tells the sender that it can't send mail to that address. It drops the connection after 60 seconds if the client hasn't already done so. Normally it gives a temporary rejection unless it's run with the –b flag, as in the previous example. (These days most rejections are for mail that you'll never want delivered, so there's no point in retrying.)

To decide what to do, *rblsmtpd* first checks the environment variable RBLSMTPD that might have been set by *tcpserver* or the *run* script. If the variable is set to a null string, that's a whitelist entry so *rblsmtpd* runs the next program in the chain. If it's set to a string, RBLSMTPD runs the rejection server, using the string as the error message. If the string is prefixed with a hyphen, the rejection server gives permanent rather than temporary errors.

In the absence of RBLSMTPD, it then goes through the list of –r and –a flags, checking each DNSBL or anti-DNSWL in turn. The argument to each –r or –a flag is the name of the list to check. If a DNSBL has a TXT entry for the IP in TCPREMOTEIP, it starts the rejection server. If an anti-DNSWL has an A entry for the IP, it runs the next program. If it gets to the end of the list of DNSBLs and anti-DNSWLs with no matching entries, it runs the next program.

For the most part, you need to select only the DNSBLs you want to use, add them to your *run* file, and restart the SMTP daemon. Some of the DNSBLs I use in early 2004 include (all have web pages at the same address as the blocklist unless otherwise noted):

sbl.spamhaus.org
> The Spamhaus Block List, a manually maintained list of chronic spam sources

cbl.abuseat.org
> The Composite Block List, created mechanically from spam received at some high-volume spam traps

relays.visi.com
> A mechanically created list of open relays

opm.blitzed.org
> The Open Proxy Monitor, a mechanically maintained list of abused open proxy servers

dul.dnsbl.sorbs.net
> A manually maintained list of dynamically allocated IP addresses (mostly retail dialup ISP space) that shouldn't be sending mail directly

The one public DNSWL I currently use is the Habeas Users List. It requires a no-charge license agreement; see *http://hul.habeas.com/services/hul.htm*.

The list of effective DNSBLs and DNSWLs changes every month or two, and some of these may no longer be available or may have been replaced by the time you read this.

Sometimes you'll find that you want to override a few of the entries in one of the DNSBLs you use because they block mail from someone your users want to hear from. (If the listing is a mistake, most DNSBL maintainers take it out reasonably promptly, but your user will of course want it fixed right away.) *rblsmtpd* looks at the environment before it looks at any of the DNSBLs, so you can put override entries in your rules file. To whitelist an address, add an entry that sets RBLSMTPD to an empty string. To block an address with a rejection message, add an entry that makes the message the contents of RBLSMTPD:

```
# accept mail from this address, overriding any DNSBL entries
10.20.1.2:allow,RBLSMTPD=""

# send temporary rejections to this one
10.30.2.3:allow,RBLSMTPD="Please pay your bill to regain mail access"

# reject this entirely
10.40.5.6:allow"RBLSMTPD="-All mail blocked due to pornographic spam".
```

SMTP-Time Filtering Tools

Once *qmail-smtpd* has started, filters can use the message envelope and data to trigger more filter rules. Some of the filters require patching the filter code into *qmail-queue*, while others can use the QMAILQUEUE patch to run the filters on the incoming message before queueing it for delivery.

Filtering in the SMTP Daemon

The three most useful checks in the daemon itself are MAIL FROM rejection, RCPT TO rejection, and Windows EXE virus rejection.

The standard qmail control file *badmailfrom* lists addresses and domains to reject as MAIL FROM arguments. The addresses are listed literally, domains preceded by @, so an address annoying@example.com is rejected if either annoying@example.com or @example.com appears. The rejection actually happens at subsequent RCPT commands because it's clearer to some SMTP clients that the mail can't be delivered.

I wrote a "badrcptto" patch, available at qmail.org, that lets you list recipient addresses to reject by putting them in *badrcptto* or *morebadcptto*, which is compiled into *morebadrcptto.cdb* by the new program *qmail-newbrt*. It only lists addresses; the way to reject recipient domains is to not put them in *rcpthosts*. The rejections happen after the DATA command to deter dictionary validation attacks. (Typical dictionary attacks start by trying a garbage address or two, in order to see whether the recipient MTA rejects them, and if they're not rejected, the attacker goes away.) The main point of badrcptto is one of efficiency. My system has a lot of addresses that get nothing but spam, and it's much faster to reject mail to those addresses at SMTP time than at delivery time. Also, if the message has multiple RCPT TO recipient addresses, it's rejected and not delivered to any of them if any of the addresses appear in *badrcptto*, on the theory that one can presume that any message sent to a known-to-be-bad address is spam even if it's also sent to a valid address. Another minor point is that rejecting at SMTP time sends the rejection to the actual sending host, rather than to the innocent return address, in the usual case that the return address is a fake.

There's a "goodrcptto" version of my patch floating around that flips the sense of the test and accepts mail only to listed addresses. I don't suggest you use it, because it breaks mail sent to subaddresses and -default addresses, some of qmail's most useful features.

The third daemon check deals with viruses. I observed in 2002 that all current viruses are Windows *.exe* files, and it's rare for anyone to send mail with an individually attached *.exe* files that's not a virus. Russ Nelson wrote a simple and extremely effective anti-virus patch, available at *www.qmail.org*, that recognizes the fixed code pattern present at the beginning of each *.exe* file. I suggest you use it, and tell your users who just have to mail around *.exe* files to put them in ZIP files before sending.

There are some other filtering patches for the SMTP daemon, none of which I recommend. One fairly popular one does a DNS lookup on the domain of each MAIL FROM address and rejects any that don't resolve. Several years back, a lot of spam used nonexistent fake addresses, but once the DNS checks became popular, spammers started forging genuine domains to defeat the DNS check. Nowadays, the DNS check slows mail delivery, because it can require a round-trip DNS lookup to a far-away DNS server, but stops almost no spam.

Separate Filters Called from the SMTP Daemon

Once *qmail-smtpd* has collected the incoming message, it normally runs *qmail-queue* to queue the message for delivery. If you've installed the QMAILQUEUE patch recommended in Chapter 3, it will instead run whatever program is named by the QMAILQUEUE environment variable. In practice you almost always run a shell script that calls the various filtering programs. In the simplest case, run incoming mail through a filter and then queue it. For example, create */var/qmail/bin/smtp-spa* with the following contents, and chmod it 755 to make it executable, as shown in Example 9-2.

Example 9-2. Excessively simple Spamassassin SMTP-time filter

```
#!/bin/sh

/usr/local/bin/spamassassin | /var/qmail/bin/qmail-queue
```

This works because *qmail-queue* first reads the body of the message from file descriptor 0, which is connected to the pipe, and then reads the envelope from file descriptor 1, which the shell doesn't change because there's no output redirection. Then add a line to the SMTP run script (line 2a in Example 9-3) that sets the environment variable.

Example 9-3. Running the SMTP daemon with an SMTP-time post-filter

```
1.  #!/bin/sh
2.  limit datasize 40m
2a. export QMAILQUEUE=/var/qmail/bin/smtp-spa
3.  exec \
4.      tcpserver -u000 -g000 -v -p -R      \
5.      -x/var/qmail/rules/smtprules.cdb 0 25 \
5a.         rblsmtpd -b \
5b.         -ahul.habeas.com \
5c.         -rsbl.spamhaus.org \
5d.         -rcbl.abuseat.org \
6.      /var/qmail/bin/qmail-smtpd 2>&1
```

Note line 2, where the data limit is increased to be large enough for Spamassassin to run. This example works, assuming you have Spamassassin installed, but there are two reasons that you probably want to set up a slightly more complex filtering script. One reason is that if Spamassassin fails, the mail disappears without a trace and *qmail-queue* delivers an empty message instead. The other reason is that Spamassassin has quite a few user-adjustable parameters, but when it's run here it has no access to the users' home directories where the parameter files live. The first problem is easily solved by using *qmail-qfilter* (described next) in the shell script to run the filter programs, but the only way to solve the second is to run at least some of the filtering code at delivery time if you let your users customize their filters.

It's possible to install extremely complex and slow spam and virus filters to run at SMTP time, but in my experience, you quickly reach the point of diminishing returns. Most users don't customize Spamassassin very much, so I find it reasonably effective to run Spamassassin at SMTP time, configured to add headers with a spam score, then use procmail at delivery time to look at the score and decide what to do with it.

To do SMTP-time filtering, you need at least two parts. One is the program that runs the filters, such as *qmail-qfilter* or *qmail-scanner*; the rest are the actual filters. This can go to a third level if you do virus filtering with *amavis*, which unpacks a message into its individual parts and then passes each part to a third-party filter.

While *qmail-qfilter* is a fairly simple program that runs a message through a few filters you specify before handing it to *qmail-queue*, *qmail-scanner* combines built-in message scanning with separate virus and spam filters to provide one-stop mail filtering (which is fine if their stop is the one you want).

Filtering with qmail-qfilter

You can download *qmail-qfilter* from *http://untroubled.org/qmail-qfilter/*, as either an RPM or a *tar.gz* file. Pay attention to the note in the *README* file that points out that it defines TMPDIR in *qmail-qfilter.c*, the place to put temporary copies of messages as */tmp*, which you may want to change to */var/tmp* or */usr/tmp* if you have a small */tmp* on a ramdisk. Compile and install it like any other application; it's a separate program, not a patch. To use it, you must apply the QMAILQUEUE patch to qmail, as described in Chapter 3.

When *qmail-qfilter* runs, it takes as arguments the names of the filters to which it will pass the mail message. If there's more than one program, they're separated by --arguments. *qmail-qfilter* runs the filters one at a time, using temporary files to store the possibly modified message, and then if all of the filters succeeded (returned 0), passes the output of the last filter to *qmail-queue*. The QMAIL-QUEUE patch only passes the name of a command, so in practice *qmail-qfilter* is always run from a shell script. For example, Example 9-4 presents a script to run incoming mail through the popular Spamassassin spam filter using *qmail-qfilter*.

Example 9-4. Run incoming mail through a spam filter

```
#!/bin/sh

# spam filter incoming mail

exec /var/qmail/bin/qmail-qfilter \
    /usr/local/bin/spamassassin
```

The version I use first runs mail through DCC, which counts similar messages to estimate bulkiness (see *http://www.rhyolite.com/anti-spam/dcc/*), and then through Spamassassin, which already contains rules to use the info that DCC adds to the mail header. DCC doesn't have built-in support for qmail, but I wrote *qmaildcc* (available as always at *www.qmail.org*), a small Perl script intended to be run from *qmail-qfilter*, which passes incoming mail through DCC and adds a header noting the DCC bulkiness score (see Example 9-5). DCC can optionally also perform greylisting, temporary rejection of mail from unfamiliar sources, on the theory that real mailers will retry later but spamware won't.

Example 9-5. Run incoming mail through DCC and a spam filter

```
#!/bin/sh

# greylist, bulk count and spam filter incoming mail

exec /var/qmail/bin/qmail-qfilter \
    /usr/local/bin/qmaildcc -- \
    /usr/local/bin/spamassassin
```

DCC can optionally whitelist based on incoming IP address. Because *tcpserver* provides the IP address in the environment variable TCPREMOTEIP, *qmaildcc* can pass it along to DCC. Note the -- separating the DCC arguments from the call to Spamassassin. If you use a separate virus filter like Clamav, add it here, too.

This script doesn't try very hard to do per-user customization. *qmail-qfilter* passes the list of recipient addresses to the filter programs as the environment variable QMAILRCPTS, and *qmaildcc* has a little code that checks to see whether an address is in a domain in *locals*, in which case it passes the mailbox to DCC as the username, or a domain in *virtualdomains* in which it passes the first component of the corresponding address as the username. However, this only works for the simplest user setups. For better per-user customization, see delivery-time filtering, described next.

To hook this script into qmail, the QMAILQUEUE variable needs to be set. Assuming the script is called *dofilter*, the easiest approach is to set it in the *run* script, as we already did. In line 2, increase the datasize to be big enough to run whatever filter software you're running. Spamassassin is pretty big, but 40 MB should be enough. As always, whenever you change the *run* script, svc -t to reread the script and restart *tcpserver* (see Example 9-6).

Example 9-6. Running the SMTP daemon with an SMTP-time post-filter

```
 1. #!/bin/sh
 2. limit datasize 40m
2a. export QMAILQUEUE=/var/qmail/bin/dofilter
 3. exec \
 4.    tcpserver -u000 -g000 -v -p -R    \
 5.    -x/var/qmail/rules/smtprules.cdb 0 25 \
5a.        rblsmtpd -b \
5b.        -a'hul.habeas.com' \
5c.        -r'sbl.spamhaus.org' \
5d.        -r'cbl.abuseat.org' \
 6.      /var/qmail/bin/qmail-smtpd 2>&1
```

You can and probably should put some entries into the rules file to override QMAILQUEUE for some hosts, as shown in Example 9-7. For example, you probably don't want to spam filter injected outgoing mail, unless you have extremely unruly users, and there are probably some known friendly hosts that you can trust not to send unwanted mail, so there's no point in running slow spam filtering software on their mail.

Example 9-7. Sample smtprules line

```
# mail from a friend, no filtering needed
10.30.10.10:allow,QMAILQUEUE="/var/qmail/bin/qmail-queue"

# allow relay from this host, but clean up the mail (see below)
127.:allow,RELAYCLIENT="",QMAILQUEUE="/var/qmail/bin/qinject"

# allow relay from other hosts on this network
172.16.42.:allow,RELAYCLIENT="",QMAILQUEUE="/var/qmail/bin/qinject"
172.16.15-18.:allow,RELAYCLIENT="",QMAILQUEUE="/var/qmail/bin/qinject"
```

If your mail server handles injected mail, you can run the injected mail through *new-inject* to clean it up, like the *@fixme* trick described in Chapter 6, but without needing an extra trip through the delivery queue. Create a script called *qinject* (see Example 9-8).

Example 9-8. qinject: Using qmail-qfilter to clean up injected mail

```
#!/bin/sh

# unset potentially wrong env vars
unset MAILUSER; unset USER; unset LOGNAME; unset MAILNAME; unset NAME
unset MAILNAME

exec /var/qmail/bin/qmail-qfilter /var/qmail/bin/new-inject -n
```

This unsets the environment variables used to concoct a From: line, so that the mail won't seem to come from the qmail daemon user, then it runs the message through *new-inject*. *qmail-qfilter* sets QMAILUSER and QMAILHOST from the message's envelope sender, so *new-inject* can create a reasonable From: line if need be.

Create as many filtering scripts as you want and assign them to different hosts or sets of hosts via entries in the rules file. A plausible setup would be to do spam and virus filtering (if you don't use the EXE patch to *qmail-smtpd*) for incoming mail, just virus filtering for mail injected from local hosts that run Windows, and no filtering at all for mail injected locally or from other Unix systems.

In the previous examples, the filtering programs always accept the mail, but they don't have to. If a filter program returns a nonzero code, the code is passed back to *qmail-smtpd*, which returns an error message to the SMTP client. Useful return codes include 31 for a permanent "554 mail server permanently rejected message" error, 71 for a temporary "451 mail server temporarily rejected message" error, and 73 for a temporary "451 connection to mail server rejected" error. As a special case, return code 99 discards the message without returning an error.

Filtering with qmail-scanner

qmail-scanner is a large Perl script, also run via QMAILQUEUE, which runs mail through a gauntlet of tests and filters. Conceptually, *qmail-scanner* is simpler than using *qmail-filter*. You just download it from *http://qmail-scanner.sourceforge.net/*, run the configuration script as root which builds the Perl script to call the tools that are available, and plug it into QMAILQUEUE. In practice it's a little more complex.

Before you can use *qmail-scanner*, as well as the QMAILQUEUE patch, you must install maildrop (or at least the *reformime* program from maildrop), some Perl modules described in the *README* file, and all of the spam and virus filters you want it to call. You also need to create a separate user ID, usually called *qscand*, for it to run as. By default it "quarantines" incoming viruses in *~qspamd/Maildir*, so you must remember to look there from time to time and clean it out.

qmail-scanner does work, but it's extremely slow (the suggested timeout in case something hangs is 20 minutes) and is overkill for most qmail systems.

Delivery Time Filtering Rules

The most practical way to do delivery time filtering is to call filter programs from procmail or maildrop. (All these examples use procmail, but you can do the same things from maildrop.) Procmail is called in the context of the delivery user, so it's straightforward to use the user's personal preferences for filtering. These procmail rules, for example, call DCC and Spamassassin, both of which add X- message headers to the mail to report what they found. Tagged mail is filed in a separate mailbox, in this case a spam subfolder of Maildir where it's visible as a subfolder in Courier IMAP. The procmail rules can either go in */usr/local/etc/procmailrc*, the global file used by default, or go in an individual user's *procmailrc* for users who want to fiddle with their own rules (see Example 9-9).

Example 9-9. Filtering in procmail

```
# filter through dcc using the user's whitelist
:0 f
| dccproc -cCMN,40 -ERw .dcc/whiteclnt

:0
* X-DCC-IECC-Metrics: .*bulk
{
        LOG="Reject: tagged by DCC
"
        :0
        ./Maildir/.spam/
}

# filter through spamassassin for messages under 300K
:0 fw
* < 300000
| spamassassin

:0
* X-Spam-Status: Yes
{
        LOG="Reject: tagged by spamassassin
"
        :0
        ./Maildir/.spam/
}
```

Combination Filtering Schemes

You can mix and match the pieces described previously to construct hybrid filtering schemes. For example, on one of my servers I have some domains that deliver into a POP/IMAP "pop toaster," and other domains that deliver to a variety of shell accounts, mailing lists, and mail forwarders. For the pop toaster domains, I want to do the filtering at SMTP time, because all of the mailboxes are handled the same, while for the other domains I want to do it at delivery time.

To arrange this, I assigned two different IP addresses to the server, and set up the DNS so that the MX records for the pop toaster domains point to the first MX and the rest point to the second MX. Then I set up two separate SMTP server setups under */service*. The one for the pop toaster runs *tcpserver* with QMAILQUEUE set to point to the filtering script, while the other one leaves QMAILQUEUE alone, so mail is queued directly. Hence mail for the pop toaster domains goes to the first MX where it's handled by the first setup, filtered and then queued for delivery, and the *.qmail* files for toaster domains just deliver the mail. The rest of the domains go to the second *tcpserver* setup where mail is not filtered at SMTP time, but the .qmail files for the various recipients run procmail to do the filtering at delivery time.

In theory, a bad guy who knew the details of this setup could deliberately misroute mail for pop toaster accounts to the second MX, thereby avoiding the spam filtering, but that's unlikely because there's no obvious connection between the two sets of domains other than that the two IP addresses are numerically close. If it became a problem, I could set up two completely separate instances of qmail with separate configurations and separate *rcpthosts* files, as described in Chapter 17.

PART II
Advanced Qmail

The last nine chapters build on the foundation in the first part. They start with detailed definitions of qmail's local and remote mail delivery system, and then cover other topics, including virtual domains, mail pickup from remote PCs, running mailing lists, system tuning, and ways to use qmail to solve complex mail handling problems:

## CHAPTER 10

Local Mail Delivery

The way that qmail delivers local mail is fundamentally quite simple but is extremely configurable. This chapter looks in detail at the way that local mail is delivered, then looks at some common problems and applications.

How Qmail Delivers Local Mail

Every local message is delivered to the *local part* of its target address, the part of the address to the left of the at-sign. The local part may come directly from an incoming message, or it may be generated internally by qmail, particularly for mail to virtual domains (see Chapter 12), which construct the local part from a combination of the incoming address and information about the virtual domain.

If the local part of an address contains one or more hyphens, the part before the first hyphen is consider the *user* and the rest is the *extension*. If the local part doesn't contain a dash (hyphen), the local part is the user and there's no extension.

Identifying the User

The first step in a local delivery is to identify the user corresponding to the local part and retrieve several items about the user. The items are:

- Username, that is, the login name that is usually but not necessarily the same as the qmail user.
- The numeric user ID.
- The numeric group ID.
- The home directory.
- The dash character, if the local part had an extension. This is almost always an actual dash, although for maximum sendmail compatibility some people use a plus sign instead.
- The extension, usually the extension from the local part.

Qmail uses two techniques to retrieve the user information. First it checks the users database, which the qmail manager can and usually should create. (I discuss it in more detail Chapter 15.) If there is no users database or an address doesn't appear in the database, it runs *qmail-getpw* to get the information from the Unix password file. If both of those fail, it prepends alias- to the address and tries again, so that unknown addresses are treated as subaddresses of the alias user.

Locating the .qmail File

All local deliveries are controlled through a *.qmail* file. Once qmail has the user information corresponding to a local part, selecting the qmail file is straightforward. All *.qmail* files are located in the user's home directory.* If the local part has no extension, the *.qmail* file is called *.qmail*. If Fred's home directory is */home/fred*, mail for the address fred is handled by */home/fred/.qmail*. If there's an extension, it's *.qmail-extension*; for example, mail to fred-fishing would be handled by */home/fred/. qmail-fishing*. If the *.qmail* file for an address with an extension doesn't exist, qmail also looks for a *.qmail* file, replacing the extension with -default, as in */home/fred/. qmail-default*. If there are multiple levels of extension, qmail searches for defaults one level at a time, and mail for fred-fishing-lures is now handled by */home/fred/. qmail-fishing-lures*, or */home/fred/.qmail-fishing-default*, or */home/fred/.qmail-default*. Notice that a single extension is not defaulted to the plain *.qmail* file, so the final default for any address with an extension is *.qmail-default*, not *.qmail*. To prevent funny business, any dots in the address are replaced by colons in the filename, so the *.qmail* file for fred-fishing.stories is */home/fred/.qmail-fishing:stories*.

If a *.qmail* file is empty, qmail uses the default delivery instructions passed to *qmail-start* at startup time. If there is no plain *.qmail* file, qmail also uses the default delivery instructions. On the other hand, if *.qmail-default* doesn't exist, mail to addresses with an extension bounces.

The alias user is handled the same as any other user. This means that mail to unmatched addresses is handled by *~alias/.qmail-address* if it exists, otherwise *~alias/.qmail-default*. That means you can handle arbitrary addresses by creating *.qmail* files in *~alias*. You can also handle arbitrary addresses by running *fastforward* from *~alias/.qmail-default*, to look up addresses in a sendmail-style */etc/aliases* database. I cover that later in this chapter.

Processing the .qmail File

Once qmail has selected a *.qmail* file, it reads and processes the file one line at a time. The first character on the line determines the type of line:

- Lines that start with a sharp sign (#) are comments and are ignored.

---

* Well, almost. If the extension contains slashes, the *.qmail* file will be in a subdirectory of the home directory.

- Lines that start with a vertical bar (|) are commands. Qmail hands the command to the shell (*/bin/sh*, regardless of what your login shell might be) in a known approximation to the recipient's login environment. See "Program Deliveries" later for more detail on how qmail runs commands.

- Lines that start with a slash or a dot are mailboxes. The line is the filename of the mailbox. If the line ends with a slash, it's the name of a Maildir mailbox, otherwise it's the name of an mbox mailbox. See "Mailbox Deliveries" for more details.

- Lines that start with an ampersand (&) are forwards. The entire line after the ampersand is taken to be an envelope-format address to which the message is to be forwarded, with no comments, decorations, or extra whitespace other than whitespace at the end of the line, which is ignored. That is, if you want to forward your message to sarah@example.com, this line is correct:

  ```
  &sarah@example.com
  ```

  and these are all wrong:

  ```
  &sarah@example.com (Sarah Bande)
  &Sarah Nade <sarah@example.com>
  &sarah (Sarah Pheem) @example.com
  &sarah @ example.com
  ```

  If you want to forward to more than one address, put each address on a separate line. If you want to forward to addresses computed on the fly, use the *forward* program in a command line.

- Lines that start with a letter or digit are also taken to be forwarding addresses, as though they were preceded by an ampersand. Again, the entire line is taken to be an envelope-format address, with no comments or decorations.

- Completely blank lines are ignored, except at the beginning of a *.qmail* file where a blank line is an error.

A *.qmail* file can have any combination of these kinds of lines. The lines are interpreted one at a time. Command and mailbox lines are interpreted in sequence. (Maildir and mbox deliveries are handled by internal routines in *qmail-local* that return exit codes like commands do to indicate whether the delivery was successful.) If a command exits with a failure code (anything other than 0 or 99), the delivery failed and *qmail-local* stops immediately. If a command exits with code 99, the command is considered to have succeeded, but the rest of the *.qmail* file is ignored. If a command exits with code 100, the failure is permanent and the message bounces. If with code 111, the failure is temporary and qmail will retry the delivery (the entire . *qmail* file, not just the command that failed) later. For historical reasons, exit codes 64, 65, 70, 76, 77, 78, and 112 are also considered permanent failures, any other nonzero exit code is temporary failure, but for compatibility with future versions of qmail, programs should only return 0 for success, 99 for success and skip the rest of the file, 100 for permanent failure, or 111 for temporary failure.

If you want qmail to continue interpreting a *.qmail* file if a command fails, the qmail documentation suggests putting each command in a separate *.qmail-whatever* file and having the main *.qmail* file forward the mail to the subaddresses corresponding to each of those files. A much easier approach is to just force the exit code of each command line to zero:

```
| somecommand ; exit 0
```

The cabalistically inclined can abbreviate to:

```
| somecommand ;:
```

Forward lines are noted but not acted on until all of the lines in the *.qmail* have been interpreted. At the end of the file, if there were any forward lines and no command or mailbox line has failed, *qmail-local* calls *qmail-queue* to requeue the message to the forwarding addresses. If a command or mailbox delivery fails, *qmail-local* does no forwards, even if the forward lines preceded the failing delivery line in the *.qmail* file.

Defensive Features in qmail-local

Mail deliveries can be fouled up in a remarkable number of ways. *qmail-local* has several features intended to prevent mail foul-ups, or to limit the damage when a foul-up occurs:

- Every time *qmail-local* forwards a message or delivers it to a mailbox, it places a Delivered-To: line at the front of the message. (The Delivered-To: line is available to program deliveries as the DTLINE environment variable for programs that remail the message.) If a message already has a Delivered-To: line with the exact same address as the current delivery, *qmail-local* won't deliver the message and fails permanently. This prevents mail loops in which a circular chain of forwarding addresses keeps forwarding a message along forever.

- If the home directory in which the *.qmail* file resides is world-writable or the *.qmail* file itself is world-writable, *qmail-local* won't deliver the message and fails permanently, on the theory that the *.qmail* file might have been tampered with by someone other than the intended user.

- If the sticky bit is set on the home directory, *qmail-local* fails temporarily. Qmail uses that bit as a flag that the user is editing *.qmail* files. This allows a user to set the sticky bit, edit *.qmail* files, then turn off the sticky bit, to be sure that qmail won't attempt to interpret a partially edited or partially rewritten file before the edits are done.

- If the first line of a *.qmail* file is blank, *qmail-local* fails temporarily. It's not clear to me what problem this solves. Blank lines elsewhere in the file are ignored.

- If the execute bit is set on a *.qmail* file, the file should contain only forward lines, and mailbox or command lines will fail. This helps make mailing lists more secure, so even if a bad guy sneaks an address onto a list that looks like a mailbox or command, it won't do any damage. If a *.qmail* file contains a +list line, subsequent lines in the file must be forwards, which makes it possible to use mailing list files with a few commands at the front to validate the message or reset bounce counters. (The +list feature is undocumented.)

Mailbox Deliveries

Qmail has two built-in delivery programs: one for mbox mailbox files and one for Maildir directories. In either case, the delivery is attempted under the recipient's user ID and primary group ID, so the mailbox must be writable by the user.

If a line in a *.qmail* file starts with a dot or slash and doesn't end with a slash, it's taken to be the name of an mbox mailbox file. To do the delivery, *qmail-local* opens the file for appending, creating it if it doesn't exist. It then locks the file using the flock() or lockf() system call.* If it can't set the lock within 30 seconds, the delivery fails temporarily. Once the file is opened and locked, *qmail-local* writes a traditional separator line, then the Return-Path: and Delivered-To: lines to provide the message envelope information, then the message, and a newline at the end. Any message line that starts with From, possibly preceded by some number of > angle brackets is quoted by preceding the line with an angle bracket. (This makes it possible to recover the original message by deleting one bracket from any such line.) It then calls fsync() to flush the file to disk and closes the file. The delivery fails if *qmail-local* can't create or lock the file, or if any of the writes to the file or the fsync() fail.

If a line in a *.qmail* starts with a dot or slash and does end with a slash, it's taken to be the name of a Maildir directory. First, *qmail-local* forks, and the child process does the delivery. The child makes the Maildir its current directory, then creates a new file named *tmp/t.p.h* where *t* is the time in seconds since 1970 (the standard internal Unix time format), *p* is the process ID, and *h* is the hostname, so a typical name would be *tmp/1012345678.34567.mail.example.com*. It then writes the Return-Path: and Delivered-To: lines to the file, followed by the message. Unlike mailbox format files, the message is written literally and there is no need to quote lines. It then calls fsync() to flush the file to disk, closes the file, links the file from *tmp* to *new*, and unlinks the *tmp* file. The delivery fails if *qmail-local* can't change directory to the Maildir, create or lock the file, or if any of the writes to the file, the fsync, or the link fail. The delivery also fails temporarily if the delivery subprocess doesn't complete in 24 hours, an error I have never seen but might occur with deliveries to an unavailable NFS filesystem. Maildir deliveries do not need explicit locking because the operating system has internal locks that make system calls to create and rename files atomic.

---

* Some mail systems lock mailboxes in different ways, but qmail doesn't. If flock or lockf isn't adequate for locking your mailboxes, you should switch to Maildirs, which don't need locks to work correctly.

Program Deliveries

Qmail defines a complex but well-specified environment in which to run the programs specified in *.qmail* command lines. Each command is run under the user's user ID and primary group ID, in the user's home directory, via */bin/sh -c*. The command's standard input is the message file, while the standard output and standard error are a pipe back to *qmail-lspawn*, which logs anything the command writes to its output. If the program fails (exit 100), its output is mailed back to the sender as part of the error report. The message file is guaranteed to be an actual file, so that programs can read the message, seek back to the beginning, and read it again. (This isn't very useful for individual programs, but it's quite useful for programs like *condredirect* that fork off a child program that reads and analyzes the message, then when the child is done, reprocess the message itself.)

The program's environment variables are inherited from the *qmail-start* command that originally started qmail, with quite a few added variables to help manage the delivery:

USER
> The delivery username

HOME
> The user's home directory

LOCAL
> The local part of the recipient address

HOST
> The domain part of the recipient address

RECIPIENT
> The envelope recipient address, `$LOCAL@$HOST`

DTLINE
> The Delivered-To: line, `Delivered-To: $RECIPIENT\n`; any newlines within the recipient address are changed to underscores

SENDER
> The envelope sender address

NEWSENDER
> The envelope sender, modified for mailing list deliveries; see the later section "Special Forwarding Features for Mailing Lists"

RPLINE
> The Return-Path: line, `Return-Path: $SENDER\n`; any newlines within the sender address are changed to underscores

UFLINE
> The uucp From line, the separator line that would be written to an mbox file, `From $SENDER Thu Nov 29 21:33:09 1973\n`. If the sender is null, it uses MAILER-DAEMON, and any spaces, tabs, or newlines within the sender address are changed to dashes (not underscores)

EXT

The address extension, the part of $LOCAL that follows the first dash; if there's no dash, the null string

EXT2

The second address extension, the part of $LOCAL that follows the second dash; if there's no second dash, the null string

EXT3

The third address extension, the part of $LOCAL that follows the third dash; if there's no third dash, the null string

EXT4

The fourth address extension, the part of $LOCAL that follows the fourth dash; if there's no fourth dash, the null string.

DEFAULT

If the *.qmail* file is a default file, the part of the local part that matched the default (see "Subaddresses"); not set if this is not a default file

HOST2

The part of $HOST preceding the last dot

HOST3

The part of $HOST preceding the penultimate dot

HOST4

The part of $HOST preceding the antepenultimate dot

Other than the translations of whitespace to underscores or dashes, there's no attempt to defend against strange or hostile characters in environment variables, so scripts should be sure to double-quote variable references and remember that hostile senders can put any characters they want, including punctuation and spaces, into a message's envelope. Programs called from *.qmail* files should be equally cautious if they use the environment variables either directly or as program arguments. For example, if a Perl script uses a subaddress to select a file to use, be sure it does something reasonable when a sender sends you a message where the subaddress is |rm -f.

There is no provision for continuation lines in a *.qmail* file, so each command has to be on a single line. There's no limit to the length of that single line, so you can put arbitrarily complex shell commands in your *.qmail* file. In practice, if the shell script is more than about 100 characters, it's easier to put the script in a separate file and call the script file from the *.qmail* file.

Any program run from *.qmail* files should run to completion and exit. If it forks and continues in the background, the results are unpredictable, because all program and mailbox deliveries from a *.qmail* file share the same input file descriptor, and the program's file reads are intermixed with those of other commands run from the same *.qmail* file. (*qmail-local* resets the seek pointer to the beginning of the file before each delivery.)

Delivery programs should not take very long to complete. Qmail normally limits itself to 10 simultaneous local deliveries, so 10 long-running delivery programs lock out all other local deliveries.

Delivery Utilities

Qmail provides a small set of programs intended for use in deliveries.

forward

The most useful of the programs is *forward*, which remails the input message to all of the addresses given on the command line, as though the addresses were each on a forward line in the *.qmail* file. This is useful both because *forward* can be embedded in shell scripts to be run conditionally and the addresses can be calculated at runtime. For example, to forward a message to a different address depending on what the day of the week is, type:

```
| forward "day-$(date +%a)@example.com"
```

Or to route mail from one sender specially, type:

```
| case "$SENDER" in fred@domain.com) forward fredflame ;; *) forward inquiries ;;
esac
```

bouncesaying

Bounce a message back to the sender either unconditionally or if a program succeeds. Most often, *bouncesaying* is used to turn off addresses that are no longer active:

```
| bouncesaying "Sorry, this employee has left the company"
```

It's occasionally useful as a simple mail filter:

```
| bouncesaying "No tropical fruit, please" grep -q "guava|mango|papaya"
./Maildir/
```

This scans the message for forbidden words and bounces the message if the grep succeeds. Otherwise it delivers the message to the user's Maildir. Note that the -q flag keeps the grep command from producing unwanted output that would be mailed back with the bounce message.

condredirect

Conditionally remail a message to a different address. The arguments are the new address and a shell command to run. If the command succeeds and exits 0, the message is mailed to the new address, and *condredirect* exits 99, telling qmail to ignore any subsequent lines in the *.qmail* file. If the command exits 111, so does *condredirect*. If the command exits with any other code, *condredirect* exits 0:

```
| condredirect subscriptions grep -q -i "Subject:.*subscribe"
./Maildir/
```

Except in the most simple applications, it's usually easier to use procmail.

---

except

Reverse the exit code of a program:

```
| bouncesaying "Tropical fruit required here" except grep -q "guava|mango|papaya"
./Maildir/
```

The except command reverses the sense of the grep so the mail is bounced if the magic words don't appear in the message.*

Subaddresses

Qmail provides each user with an unlimited number of subaddresses, which are the user's address followed by a dash† and the address extension. Subaddresses are most useful with virtual domains, where qmail maps each address in the virtual domain to a domain-specific subaddress, but subaddresses are useful for regular users as well. Their primary use is for mail sorting. If you use a different subaddress for every mailing list to which you subscribe, you can use *.qmail* files to sort list mail into separate mailboxes or to reformat incoming mail. I also find it handy to use a unique subaddress every time I register on a web site so in case one of the site owners misuses the address, I know who to blame.

Remember that subaddressed mail must be handled by a *.qmail* file or it will bounce. Here's a handy one-liner to put in *.qmail-default*:

```
| sed "s/^Subject:/Subject: [$DEFAULT]/" | forward username
```

It puts the address extension in the Subject line of the message to make it easier to see in your mail program. (It will also have a Delivered-To: line showing the subaddress, but most mail programs don't display that.)

Special Forwarding Features
for Mailing Lists

Qmail has some relatively obscure features that make it easier to use *.qmail* files to manage mailing lists. They rewrite the envelope sender on forwarded messages that are remailed to forwarding addresses in *.qmail* files, so that bounces come back to the list owner, who can do something about them, rather than to the original sender, who can't. They can also rewrite the sender address in a special form that tells *qmail-send* to create per-recipient sender addresses, known as Variable Envelope Return Paths (VERPs). The rewritten sender address is used on any forwards, and is also placed in the NEWSENDER variable for command deliveries. Although these

---

* Yes, I could have used –v in the grep command. It's an example.

† It's possible to use a character other than a dash, but I ignore that option for now.

features are mostly used by automated list management packages such as ezmlm (see Chapter 14), they can also be useful for small manually maintained lists.

If the local part of the recipient address is user-ext and there is a file *.qmail-ext-owner*, *qmail-local* changes the sender address to user-ext-owner. If there is both *.qmail-ext-owner* and *.qmail-ext-owner-default*, *qmail-local* changes the sender address to *user-ext-owner-@host-@[]*. This latter address will be rewritten again by *qmail-send*.

Assume as an example that you're user fred@example.com, and you have a list fred-fishing. You list all of the recipients in *.qmail-fishing*, and set the execute bit on that file to tell qmail that it's a list so all of the entries are forwards. Now any mail sent to fred-fishing@example.com is forwarded to all of the people listed in the qmail file. But what if one of the recipient addresses bounces? The bounce goes back to the original sender. To fix that problem, create a file *.qmail-fishing-owner*, which stores responses in a mailbox or forwards them to someone who can read and act on them. (A simple &fred puts them in your regular mailbox.) Now mail to the list is resent with an envelope sender of fred-fishing-owner@example.com, which will be handled by *.qmail-fishing-owner*. For manually handled lists that's probably adequate, but to finish the example, let's also create *.qmail-fishing-owner-default* and put these lines in it:

```
| echo "$DEFAULT" | sed 's/=/@/' >> badaddrs
./fishingbounces
```

Now mail to the fishing list is queued with an envelope sender of fred-fishing-owner-@example.com-@[]. When *qmail-send* processes each recipient address, it further translates the sender address so that a message sent to, say, margaret@domain.com is sent to the recipient host with a sender address of fred-fishing-owner-margaret=domain.com@example.com. If that message bounces, the bounce is handled by *.qmail-fishing-owner-default*. The first line in that file takes $DEFAULT, which in this case is margaret=domain.com, changes the equals sign back to an at-sign, and appends the bouncing address to *badaddrs*. Then it saves the bounce in a mailbox, in case a person wants to look at it. In a more realistic case, the address from the bounce is used to remove the bad address from the list. A complete bounce handler is also needed to analyze mail to fred-fishing-owner-@example.com (that is, with a null $DEFAULT) since mail addresses for which qmail can't even attempt a delivery bounce differently. I cover that in more detail in "Bounce Handling."

The Users Database

We now return to the question of how qmail figures out what user handles each local delivery. Each local address is mapped to a set of user data including:

- Username
- Numeric user ID
- Numeric group ID
- Home directory

- Character to separate parts of a subaddress, usually a dash
- Extension, used to find an appropriate *.qmail* file

Qmail provides two schemes to find the user data. The preferred scheme is to use a static lookup table known as the users file. The table is a CDB file (Dan's Constant Data Base, designed for quick lookups) in */var/qmail/users/cdb*, which is created from */var/qmail/users/assign* by *qmail-newu*. For every local delivery, *qmail-lspawn* looks up the local part of the address in that file. If there's no match or the file doesn't exist (which it doesn't unless you create it), as a fallback it calls *qmail-getpw*, which invents user data on the fly from the system password database using the *getpwnam( )* system library routine. Either way, qmail obtains an appropriate users entry for an address, which *qmail-lspawn* uses to perform the delivery.

See Chapter 15 for more details on the users database.

Bounce Handling

Sometimes a message can't be delivered to the intended address. The process of dealing with an undeliverable message is known as bouncing the message, and a message sent back to report a delivery failure is known, somewhat ambiguously, as a bounce. Sometimes a bounce message can't be delivered, leading to a double bounce and, if a double bounce can't be delivered, occasionally to a triple bounce.

Bounces can originate in two ways. A message sent to a local address can bounce either because the address doesn't exist or because a program run from a qmail file exits with code 100 to tell qmail to bounce it. (There is considerable overlap between these two causes. Many qmail systems have a global default qmail file *~alias/.qmail-default* that runs *fastforward* to look up the address in a sendmail-style */etc/aliases* file. If the address isn't in the file, *fastforward* exits with code 100, which causes a bounce. From the point of view of the sender, the two kinds of local bounces look the same.) A message sent to a remote address may have an invalid domain with no DNS information, or the server(s) that handle that domain aren't available or won't complete an SMTP delivery, or the remote server may explicitly reject the recipient address or the entire delivery using a 4xx or 5xx error code.

In each case, qmail usually generates a bounce message and mails it back to the envelope sender of the original message. If the envelope sender is null, which is the case if the bouncing message is itself a bounce message, qmail handles it as a double bounce and treats it specially, as discussed next.

Single Bounces

If a message delivery attempt bounces, qmail sends a bounce message back to the sender. If a single message is sent to multiple addresses, all of the bounce reports are sent back in a single message.* Qmail produces bounce messages in qmail-send Bounce Message Format (QSBMF) that Dan Bernstein designed as a much simpler alternative to the rather baroque Delivery Status Notices (DSNs) defined in RFCs 1892 and 1894. (Qmail does use the three-part error numbers defined in RFC 1893, though.) QSBMF is defined in detail at *http://cr.yp.to/proto/qsbmf.txt*. Here's a typical QMSBF bounce message:

```
Return-Path: <>
Received: (qmail 17296 invoked for bounce); 19 Jul 2003 11:30:58 -0400
Date: 19 Jul 2003 11:30:58 -0400
From: MAILER-DAEMON@tom.iecc.com
To: ChrissyFoster52@yahoo.com
Subject: failure notice

Hi. This is the qmail-send program at tom.iecc.com.
I'm afraid I wasn't able to deliver your message to the following addresses.
This is a permanent error; I've given up. Sorry it didn't work out.

<regan@iecc.com>:
Sorry, no mailbox here by that name. (#5.1.1)

<scarlett@iecc.com>:
Sorry, no mailbox here by that name. (#5.1.1)

<scorpio@iecc.com>:
Sorry, no mailbox here by that name. (#5.1.1)

<shay@iecc.com>:
Sorry, no mailbox here by that name. (#5.1.1)

<shelton@iecc.com>:
Sorry, no mailbox here by that name. (#5.1.1)

--- Below this line is a copy of the message.

[ a complete copy of the bounced message appeared here ]
```

The message is a sequence of paragraphs separated by blank lines. The first paragraph starts with the string Hi. This is the to identify the message as a QMSBF report. (Yes, Dan has an odd sense of humor.) Subsequent paragraphs start with < to report failing addresses. Each failed address appears in angle brackets on the first line of the paragraph. A paragraph that starts with a hyphen is the break paragraph, which indi-

---

* A message can have multiple addresses if it is injected locally with multiple recipients, if a *.qmail* file remails it to multiple addresses, or if the message arrives via SMTP from a system that, unlike qmail, delivers to multiple recipients in a single SMTP transaction. If a message is sent from qmail system A to multiple invalid recipients on system B, system A sends a separate copy of the message to each recipient, so system B sees all the copies as separate messages. If system B rejects invalid addresses in the SMTP transaction, as sendmail systems usually do, the rejections are all be collected by system A into a single bounce message. But if system B accepts the messages and bounces them later, as qmail does, it sends back its own separate bounce messages for each address that bounces in whatever format B's mail system produces.

cates that the rest of the bounce message is a copy of the message that bounced. Each paragraph can and usually does include explanatory text for the benefit of people reading the bounce, so the computer doesn't need to try to interpret the rest of the text.

QMSBF messages are designed to be extremely easy for computer programs to parse, so that mailing list software can tell what list addresses are bouncing and do something about it. (See Chapter 14.)

You can control the return address in the From: line of single bounces if you want, although in practice the defaults are invariably fine. The local part defaults to MAILER-DAEMON but is overridden by the contents of *bouncefrom* in */var/qmail/control* if that file exists. The domain defaults to the local hostname from *me* but is overridden by *bouncehost* if that file exists.

Double Bounces

Single-bounce messages have a null envelope sender address, because the sender is a computer program that is unlikely to understand a response. If a message with a null sender bounces, that's a double bounce. In practice, most double bounces are due to incoming spam with forged return addresses.

Qmail normally sends double bounces to postmaster at the local host, but the local part and domain of the double-bounce target address can be overridden by the contents of *doublebounceto* and *doublebouncehost*. The From: line return address is set the same as in single bounces, but the envelope sender is set to the impossible address #@[ ].

The vast majority of double bounces are now due to spam with forged return addresses, so some system managers find that wading through them is more trouble than it's worth. To get rid of double bounces, create an address "nobody" that discards all mail sent to it by putting a line with a single # into *~alias/.qmail-nobody*. Then put nobody into *doublebounceto* to send the bounces there. If your system generates many double bounces, there's a small patch to *qmail-send* at www.qmail.org called doublebounce-trim that discards double bounces directly if *doublebounceto* exists but contains a blank line.

Triple Bounces

If a double-bounce message bounces, which should never happen because postmaster is supposed to be an address that's always valid, qmail logs the failure and discards the message. This means that if you want to send mail within your qmail system that doesn't provoke bounce messages if it's undeliverable, set the envelope sender to #@[ ].

CHAPTER 11

Remote Mail Delivery

Remote mail delivery is actually somewhat simpler than local mail delivery, because there's really only one way to deliver remote mail: locate a suitable host for the message and deliver the mail to that host.

Telling Local from Remote Mail

Any domain that is listed in *locals* or *virtualdomains* is local. Anything else is remote. Note in particular that whether a domain appears in *rcpthosts* or *morercpthosts* has no bearing on whether it's local or remote. (If a domain is in *rcpthosts* but isn't local, that makes this host a *backup* or *secondary MX* for the domain, which I discuss later in this chapter.)

qmail-remote

As we saw in Chapter 2, the main *qmail-send* daemon passes remote deliveries to *qmail-rspawn*, which runs *qmail-remote* to attempt each delivery. The arguments to *qmail-remote* are the remote hostname, the envelope sender, and the envelope recipients, with the message to send on its standard input. Within qmail, *qmail-remote* is always run with a single recipient, and the host is the domain part of the recipient address. Other applications can use *qmail-remote* as a simple mail sending application, with as many recipients per message as desired.

Once *qmail-remote* has attempted delivery, it writes recipient report(s) and a message report to its standard output. The format of the reports is documented in the *qmail-remote* manpage.

Locating the Remote Mail Host

qmail-remote can identify the remote host for a message in two ways. If the *smtproutes* control file has an entry for the recipient domain, that entry determines the remote host, and *qmail-remote* pretends it found a single MX record for that host with distance zero and makes a list of the IP addresses for that host. The list usually has one entry, unless the host has multiple IP addresses.

Failing that, the usual way is through DNS. First, it looks up the hostname and retrieves any MX records, randomizing the order of multiple MX records with the same distance, then finds the IP addresses for each of the MX hosts.

Once it has the list of IP addresses, DNS goes down the list, starting at the lowest distance, trying to contact each host. Once it finds a host that answers, that's the host used for the SMTP delivery. (This description is slightly oversimplified; the omitted details are covered shortly.)

The smtproutes File for Outbound Mail

It's sometimes useful to override MX data with explicit routes for particular domains. The *smtproutes* control file consists of a list of two- or three-field lines, with the fields separated by colons. The first field is the domain to route, the second is the name or IP address of the host to which to deliver mail for that host, and the optional third field is the port to contact on the delivery host, defaulting to port 25.

The three primary uses for *smtproutes* are to override MX data that's known to be wrong, or at least suboptimal, to route mail to private pseudo-domains, and to send outgoing mail to a smarthost. The first situation occurs if a domain has several equal-distance MX hosts, one of which accepts SMTP connections but doesn't actually accept mail on those connections. An *smtproutes* entry forces mail to a host that's working.

Within a local network, it can often be useful to have private pseudo-domains for special applications. For example, I set up a mail-to-news gateway on my news host in the pseudo-domain news so that mail addressed to comp.whatever@news is posted to the appropriate newsgroup. The news gateway isn't accessible to outside users and doesn't appear in the DNS, so I use entries in *smtproutes* on other hosts to route the news pseudo-domain to the gateway machine. (The gateway's *rcpthosts* doesn't list news, so gateway mail from outside is automatically rejected.)

If an entry in *smarthosts* has an empty domain field, that is, it starts with a colon, that entry is taken to be the default route for remote domains. This feature can be useful to send outgoing mail to a gateway host on a local network, or to an ISP's mail server for dialup or consumer broadband users.

When *qmail-remote* looks up domains in *smtproutes*, it looks for successive tails of the recipient domain; if the target domain is bad.example.com, an entry for example. com matches it, unless there's also a more specific entry for bad.example.com.

Secondary MX Servers for Inbound Mail

The DNS makes it possible to list multiple MX hosts for a domain. If the hosts don't have the same distance value, the ones with greater distances are known as *secondary* servers. The server with the smallest distance is the *primary* server. A large domain can have several primary servers, and the primaries all have the same MX distance.

The SMTP specification requires that senders check closer hosts first, so secondary servers receive mail only if the closer servers are all unavailable. Qmail automatically handles secondary mail service for incoming mail. If a domain lists the qmail server as an MX for a domain but the domain isn't in *locals* or *virtualdomains*, qmail assumes it's a secondary server for that domain. When *qmail-remote* looks for a host to deliver mail to, it always checks servers starting with the ones at the smallest distance, but if it's a secondary for the domain, it ignores any MX with an equal or greater distance than its own, so that it always forwards the mail to a closer server.

If there is no lower distance server for a nonlocal domain, mail to the domain fails with the message Sorry. Although I'm listed as a best-preference MX or A for that host, it isn't in my control/locals file, so I don't treat it as local. This always indicates a configuration error. If there is supposed to be a different primary server, the DNS configuration is wrong. If the qmail system is supposed to be the primary server, the domain should be listed in *locals* or *virtualdomains*.

For outbound mail, *qmail-remote*'s strategy, contacting the lowest-distance server for a domain, delivers to a primary server if one is available, otherwise to a secondary.

TCP Time-Outs

Sometimes an MX host is unavailable, either because the host itself isn't working or because there's a network failure somewhere between that host and yours. It can take a while for an attempted TCP connection to time out and tell a calling program that there's no answer at the other end, so an SMTP client should avoid trying to contact remote hosts that don't answer.

qmail-remote uses a simple scheme to track TCP failures. In the queue directory, the file *queue/lock/tcpto* contains a set of up to 64 entries of 16 bytes, each representing a failed remote host. (This makes the file size 1024 bytes, which generally fits in a single disk block that can be read or written in one operation.) Each entry in the file contains an IP address, the time the host was last tried, and the number of consecutive times it tried and failed to contact the host, capped at 10.

After *qmail-remote* makes its list of MX records to contact, before it tries to contact each MX, it looks up the host's IP address in *tcpto*. If the IP is present and has been tried at least twice, and it's been less than about an hour since the last try, it skips the host and goes on to the next. The exact wait time is randomized for each *qmail-remote* process, in the range of 60 to 90 minutes, to avoid having a whole bunch of simultaneous attempted connections when the time-out is up. Whenever *qmail-*

remote connects successfully to a host, its IP is removed from *tcpto*. If it tries and fails to contact a host, it updates the host's record, incrementing the retry count and resetting the last contact time (unless the last contact time is less than two minutes old). If the host isn't already in *tcpto*, and *tcpto* is full, it discards an old entry, using a heuristic that looks for an entry that was last tried a long time ago and has a low retry count.

The overall effect of this scheme is to track unavailable remote hosts and retry each host no more than about once an hour. Once a host starts responding again, connections are tried whenever needed. If *qmail-remote* finds that all of the MX hosts for a delivery are unavailable, either because it tried and failed to contact them or because they're listed in *tcpto* as recently tried, the delivery attempt fails, and *qmail-send* will reschedule the delivery later using its quadratic backoff rule.

Remote Mail Failures

Remote delivery attempts can fail in a myriad of ways. Failures fall into two general categories: temporary, which means that the delivery might work later and should be retried, or permanent, which means that the message can't be delivered at all. On a temporary failure, *qmail-send* retries the delivery later, while on a permanent failure, it immediately sends back a bounce message with whatever error report *qmail-remote* produced. Errors include:

Connected to host but greeting failed
> Temporary. The remote server accepted the connection but never sent the initial SMTP greeting.

Connected to host but my name was rejected
> Temporary. The remote host rejected the HELO command.

Connected to host but sender was rejected
> Temporary or permanent. The remote host rejected the MAIL FROM command. If the remote code was 4xx it's a temporary error, if 5xx a permanent error.

Host does not like recipient
> Temporary or permanent. The remote host rejected the RCPT TO command. If the remote code was 4xx it's a temporary error, if 5xx a permanent error.

Failed on DATA command
> Temporary or permanent. The remote host rejected the DATA command. If the remote code was 4xx it's a temporary error, if 5xx a permanent error.

Failed after I sent the message
> Temporary or permanent. The remote host accepted the DATA command and the text of the mail message, but returned an error code after the message was accepted. If the remote code was 4xx it's a temporary error, if 5xx a permanent error.

Qmail only delivers mail to one recipient at a time, but *qmail-remote* accepts multiple recipient arguments, and tries to deliver to multiple recipients. It returns separate status codes for each RCPT TO and sends the message if any of the recipients were accepted.

QMQP and QMTP

Dan has invented two host-to-host protocols for people who aren't thrilled with SMTP. Despite their similar names, QMQP and QMTP are not compatible with each other and are intended for very different purposes. Qmail comes with servers for both, called *qmail-qmqpd* and *qmail-qmtpd*. Both run from tcpserver and are set up the same way as *qmail-smtpd*.

The simpler one is Quick Mail Queueing Protocol (QMQP) described at *http://cr.yp.to/proto/qmqp.html*. QMQP is currently used only by mini-qmail, a stripped-down version of qmail that passes all mail directly to a smarthost for delivery. It has no queueing, no secondary hosts, and no internal security. To avoid creating open spam relays, the TCP rules for *tcpserver* must permit connections only from known friendly hosts and deny connections from everywhere else.

Mini-qmail is primarily useful to pass incoming mail across a firewall, and to run on clusters of computers that share a single smart host (running regular qmail) for mail queueing and delivery. It's also occasionally useful for mailing list load sharing with ezmlm running on one host, passing messages for delivery to a smarthost. See Chapter 17 for details of setting up mini-qmail.

QMQP does *not* require or encourage single recipient deliveries; if a message has many recipients, the message and all of the recipient addresses can be transferred quickly via QMQP. This means that for mailing list load sharing, there's no need to split or cache the subscriber database on the smarthost. For each message distributed to a list, ezmlm can send the message and all of the recipient addresses quickly via QMQP, even if there are many recipients.

Quick Mail Transfer Protocol (QMTP) is intended as a replacement for SMTP. It's much simpler than SMTP, and just transfers a messages along with an envelope sender and a set of envelope recipients. To receive QMTP mail, set up *qmail-qmtpd* the same way you set up *qmail-smtpd*. To control mail relay, it uses the same *rcpthosts* and *morercpthosts* files and RELAYCLIENT *tcpserver* variable as *qmail-smtpd*.

The only QMTP client currently available is in the *serialmail* package, *maildirqmtp*, which is invoked exactly the same way as *maildirsmtp*. Although QMTP indisputably transfers mail faster than SMTP, almost nobody uses it. Partly this is because the QMTP client isn't integrated into qmail (and isn't available at all in other MTAs), but mostly this is because there's no standard way for a server to announce that it has a QMTP server available, analogous to a DNS MX record for SMTP. Dan proposed in 1997 to redefine the distance value in MX records to encode both the server distance and the service (smtp, qmtp, etc.), and Russ Nelson offers a patch to make *qmail-remote* use both qmtp and smtp, but QMTP remains an oddity not in general use.

Serialmail

Qmail was designed for an environment with fairly fast network connections, where the roundtrip delay on a connection dominates the data transfer time, so it's faster to have multiple single-recipient deliveries in progress that can share the connection. In environments where this is not true, the *serialmail* add-on package delivers one message at a time. It's also useful to deliver mail to hosts via intermittent dialup connections.

To use *serialmail*, first configure qmail to deliver mail to a Maildir, then run programs from the *serialmail* package to take mail out of the Maildir and send it across the Net. You can run it on a schedule to push out mail to a slow host or on demand to send mail when a dialup host connects.

The *serialmail* package is installed the same way as other DJB software. It depends on the *tcpclient* program that is in the UCSPI package. (That's the same package that contains *tcpserver*, so you should already have it installed.) The most useful programs in the package include:

maildirserial
> The driver program that selects messages from a Maildir, calls another program to try to deliver them, and deals with the results

serialsmtp
> The actual SMTP client called indirectly from *maildirserial*

maildirsmtp
> A shell wrapper that calls *maildirserial* to deliver the files in a directory via SMTP

setlock
> Runs a program with a file locked to ensure that multiple copies of the program aren't running simultaneously

To deliver mail to a domain with *serialmail*, first define the domain as a virtual domain and deliver all its mail into a Maildir. If you want to handle the domain bad.example.com, add a line to *virtualdomains* like this:

```
bad.example.com:alias-badex
```

Then create *~alias/.qmail-badex-default*, containing ./*bemaildir/*, to deliver all of the mail for that domain into *bemaildir*.

Then, when it's time to deliver the mail, run a command like this:

```
setlock bemaildir.lock \
 maildirsmtp bemaildir alias-badex- 10.2.3.4 my.example.com 2>&1 |
   splogger serial
```

The `setlock` command uses *bemaildir.lock* as a semaphore to keep a new delivery session from starting if a previous one hasn't finished yet. It runs *maildirsmtp* to do the deliveries. To find messages to deliver, it looks in bemaildir for files with Delivered-To:

lines starting with alias-badex-, which is the string that the virtual domain alias pre-fixes to mail delivered there. (It ignores files with other Delivered-To: lines, so you can store mail for several different domains in the same Maildir, running *maildirsmtp* with different address prefixes.) It connects to IP address 10.2.3.4 to deliver the mail, and in the SMTP session uses my.example.com as the argument to the HELO command, which should be the name of this machine. The messages are sent by SMTP, with the envelope recipient addresses being the ones in the Delivered-To: lines with the alias-badex- removed, so the mail is redelivered to the original addresses.

All of the details are handled by *maildirserial*: finding the files, passing their names to *smtpserial*, checking the return codes and deleting the files if the delivery was suc-cessful, sending back a bounce if the delivery failed and the file has been there too long, and leaving the file for another try otherwise.

Using Serialmail

If you're delivering to a slow host at a fixed address, the easiest way to push out the mail is to run *maildirsmtp* from *cron* on a suitable schedule. Run it once an hour, or if the remote host is busier at some times of day than others, run hourly during the slow part of the day.

If you're delivering to a host that connects intermittently via dialup, start *maildirsmtp* from the script that runs when the remote host connects. Typically the script will have a variable like $REMOTE with the current IP address of the remote, which you can use in the call to *maildirsmtp*. If the host stays connected for a long time, you may want to push out mail periodically while it's connected. There's no elegant way to do that, but see Chapter 18 for an example of a serviceable approach.

If your host is one that dials into a hub, you can also use *maildirsmtp*. In *virtualdomains* set a catch-all route to put all outgoing mail into a Maildir:

```
:alias-catchall
```

with *~alias/.qmail-catchall* delivering into the maildir. Then run *maildirsmtp* from the dialout startup script to send your mail to the hub. Again, if you stay connected for a long time, you may want to run it periodically while you're connected.

In qmail-speak, a *virtual domain* is one handled locally but with a different set of mailboxes from the home domain. Qmail's virtual domain handling is one of its strongest features, thanks to a simple and clean design.

How Virtual Domains Work

Qmail turns addresses in a virtual domain into subaddresses of a local user, then handles the subaddressed message like any other local message. The translation from virtual to local addresses is in the control file *virtualdomains*. Assume, for example, that it contained the line:

```
myvirt.com:virtuser
```

Then mail addressed to *marvin@myvirt.com* is translated to *virtuser-marvin*, and then delivered normally. If there's a user *virtuser*, it checks for *~virtuser/.qmail-marvin* or *~virtuser/.qmail-default*. If there's no such user (which is often the case), the address is turned into *alias-virtuser-marvin* and delivered under the control of *~alias/.qmail-virtuser-marvin* or *~alias/.qmail-virtuser-default* or *~alias/.qmail-default*.

When qmail translates the mailbox part of a virtual domain address, it does *not* change the domain. That is, in the previous example, *marvin@myvirt.com* is translated to *virtuser-marvin@myvirt.com*. This seems like a mistake, because this is not Marvin's address, until you realize that the translated address is used only within qmail. The virtual domain remains with the address throughout the delivery process, so delivery programs can check $HOST or $RECIPIENT to tell whether a message was addressed to a virtual domain or to the (nearly) equivalent local address. Later in this chapter, *fastforward* makes good use of this ability.

Some Common Virtual Domain Setups

Although qmail's virtual domain mechanism is extremely flexible, most of its applications fall into a few common models.

In each case, you must pick a local user or subaddress to assign the virtual domain to. It can be a real user in */etc/passwd*, or if you use qmail's users mechanism (see Chapter 15), a qmail-only user. If you handle several virtual domains in the same way, all the domains can share a user, with delivery programs distinguishing among them by checking $HOST or $RECIPIENT. If you're only forwarding mail, you can handle virtual domains under *~alias*; otherwise, it's a good idea to set up separate user IDs per virtual domain or per kind of virtual domain so that the programs you run can only smash that user's files when they break. Also, if you want to delegate the management of a virtual domain to someone else, make a separate Unix user account for the domains so the manager can log in as that user and change the domain's mail setup.

If you want people outside your network to be able to send mail to the virtual domain, you must list the domain in *rcpthosts*. If you're using a virtual domain as a service gateway for your own users to a fax server or the like, don't put it in *rcpthosts*.

Finally, each time you change the contents of *virtualdomains* or *locals*, you must tell qmail to reread them by sending a hang-up signal. Assuming you're running qmail under daemontools, use:

```
# svc -h /service/qmail
```

Mapping a Few Addresses with .qmail Files

In the simplest case, you can just create a *.qmail* file per address. Assume you have the domain *myvirt.com*, with addresses *william*, *wilbur*, and *wilfred*, which you want to forward to local addresses *biff*, *buddy*, and *butch*, respectively. This example doesn't do any special processing on the mail, so just set it up as a subuser of alias. Add this to *virtualdomains*:

```
myvirt.com:alias-myvirt
```

(Don't forget to signal qmail to reread the configuration.) Now you need to create only three *.qmail* files in *~alias* and you're done:

```
.qmail-myvirt-william    &biff
.qmail-myvirt-wilbur     &buddy
.qmail-myvirt-wilfred    &butch
```

That's it. Mail to the three addresses is now forwarded to the three mailboxes.

In a realistic example, you'll probably want to define a few more standard addresses such as postmaster and abuse. Either you can create individual control files like *.qmail-myvirt-abuse*, or you can make a catchall file to collect mail to all other addresses in the domain, *.qmail-myvirt-default*. A catchall file catches mail to misspelled versions of the three explicit addresses as well as to other administrative addresses such as webmaster, hostmaster, and support. Unfortunately, the majority of mail to other addresses is likely to be spam. If you have a spam filter, aim the default file at a filtering program and deliver whatever survives the process, or do nothing about the process and bounce the mail. If you have no *.qmail-myvirt-default* in *~abuse*, but there is a global catchall *.qmail-default*, the global catchall will handle all of the misaddressed myvirt mail, which you do not want. To bounce any misaddressed mail, put something like this in *.qmail-myvirt-default*:

```
| bouncesaying "Not a valid address at myvirt.com."
```

Mapping Many Addresses with fastforward

If you have more than a handful of addresses to forward, rather than creating dozens or hundreds of *.qmail* files, it's easier to put the forwarding instructions in one file and use *fastforward* to forward the mail. The table for *fastforward* is created by either *newaliases* (from */etc/aliases*) or *setforward* (from any file you want). For virtual domains, *setforward* is more convenient.

If you have several virtual domains, either put the forwarding rules for each domain into a separate file or put the rules for several domains into a single file. Unless the rules for all the domains are identical or nearly so, it's easier to have a file per domain.

First, set up the *virtualdomains* line(s) for the domain in question. Each *fastforward* file needs a different user or subuser. Again, the forwarding can be via subaddresses of *~alias* or else delegated to a different user. Here are some lines for three domains handled in a single file and a fourth domain handled separately, all in *~alias*:

```
example.com:alias-example
example.org:alias-example
example.net:alias-example
myvirt.com:alias-myvirt
```

Then create the *.qmail* files. In *.qmail-example-default*, put:

```
| fastforward -d example.cdb
```

And in *.qmail-myvirt-default*, put:

```
| fastforward -d myvirt.cdb
```

The –d flag tells *fastforward* to use $DEFAULT@$HOST as the address to forward rather than the normal $RECIPIENT. The difference is that with –d the user prefix is stripped off, so that even though mail to, say, *fred@example.com* is delivered to *alias-example-fred@example.com*, the address that *fastforward* uses is stripped back to *fred@example.com*.

Put the forwarding instructions in files called *example* and *myvirt*, and set up *Makefile* to make the CDBs:

```
# makefile for two fastforward files
example.cdb: example
        /var/qmail/bin/setforward $@ $@.tmp < example

myvirt.cdb: myvirt
        /var/qmail/bin/setforward $@ $@.tmp < myvirt
```

Finally, make the files of forwarding instructions. As described in Chapter 4, the instructions are either addresses to forward or programs to run. In the single-domain file, each address is just a mailbox:

```
fred: phred
```

In the multidomain file, each address is just a mailbox if it applies to all of the domains, or it can include the domain if the address is handled differently in the various domains:

```
# fred@example.com, fred@example.org, and fred@example.net all same
fred: phred@realdomain.com
# robert handled differently
robert@example.com: bob
robert@example.org: robbie
robert@example.net: | bouncesaying "No such mailbox. Go away."
```

One thing that *fastforward* cannot do is deliver directly to a Maildir or mailbox. If a few of the addresses in a domain go to mailboxes, you can create *.qmail* files for those addresses, but handle everything else with *fastforward*. If, say, you want to put all the *abuse* mail in a mailbox, create *.qmail-myvirt-abuse* or *.qmail-example-abuse* containing:

```
./abuse.mbx
```

You can't distinguish among domains without running a command that tests the value of $HOST, so you can't distinguish domains and deliver to a mailbox in one step. If you want to deliver the three example abuse addresses to separate mailboxes, forward each of them to a different local address, then make *.qmail* files for each of those local addresses.

Per-User Subdomains

Although qmail makes it possible to give users an unlimited number of subaddresses using hyphens, some people dislike hyphenated addresses, either because they confuse their correspondents or because it's too easy to "untag" the address by removing the part after the hyphen. Using virtual domains, you can give each user a separate subdomain, so that, for example, if user ella has a subscription to the "mental" list and wanted to use a tagged address, she could use *mental@ella.myvirt.com*, which qmail could internally handle as the subaddress *ella-mental*.

This trick turns out to be extremely easy to set up. First, put wildcard subdomain entries into *virtualdomains* (note the leading dot):

```
.myvirt.com:alias-sub
```

and into *rcpthosts*:

```
.myvirt.com
```

Then create *.qmail-sub-default* containing:

```
| forward "$HOST3-$DEFAULT@myvirt.com"
```

You may want to treat a few administrative addresses specially, so that the system manager still gets all of the mail to postmaster and abuse. That's easily arranged (all on one line, although it's split here):

```
| case "$DEFAULT" in postmaster|abuse) forward $DEFAULT ;;
    *) forward "$HOST3-$DEFAULT@myvirt.com" ;; esac
```

Now mail to any subdomain of *myvirt.com* is handled as a virtual domain, and the *.qmail* file takes the subdomain ($HOST3, because it's the third component of the hostname from the right) sticks it in front of the existing mailbox name, and then forwards to that address.

This trick works well so long as all subdomains of a given domain are to be treated as mailbox addresses. If some subdomains are used for other purposes, such as hostnames or web server names, I find the results confusing, particularly if some of the hostnames appear in *locals*. Either use a virtual domain for mail that isn't used for anything else or, if the number of users is small, list the individual user subdomains in *virtualdomains* or *rcpthosts*, so mail to subdomains you don't use won't be accepted:

```
# in virtualdomains
alan.myvirt.com:alias-sub
barb.myvirt.com:alias-sub
chad.myvirt.com:alias-sub
debi.myvirt.com:alias-sub
ella.myvirt.com:alias-sub
fred.myvirt.com:alias-sub

# in rcpthosts
alan.myvirt.com
```

```
barb.myvirt.com
chad.myvirt.com
debi.myvirt.com
ella.myvirt.com
fred.myvirt.com
```

Service Gateways

Virtual domains provide an elegant mechanism for gateways from SMTP email to other services. They're useful both for sending mail by other means such as uucp, and for nonmail services such as mail-to-usenet and mail-to-fax. The mailbox part of the address tells the gateway how to pass the message to the other service. For uucp, it is the username on the remote system, for a usenet gateway, the newsgroup, for a fax server, the phone number to fax to. It's also possible to encode other information in the address; in my local mail-to-news gateway, I encode hints about moderated groups and bounce handling of unforwardable messages, as described in the next section.

The general strategy for a service gateway is to create a virtual domain, then deliver all the mail for that domain to a program that performs the gateway function. Depending on how long the gateway program takes to run and how quickly you want messages passed along, you can either set up the gateway program to run each time a message arrives or collect all the messages in a Maildir and run the gateway program every once in a while to process all the messages in a batch.

Gateway design

When setting up gateways, take a few minutes to be sure that your setup will work well for your users. Most importantly, be sure that the gateway setup makes sense from the point of view of users, and not just for the convenience of the gateway administrator. One of the worst mistakes of sendmail's design is that the syntax of addresses depends on the scheme used to transport the mail to a remote system, a detail that users rarely care about. When setting up service gateways, be sure not to recreate the same mistake. If you're setting up a gateway to forward mail by uucp, don't create a local virtual domain called uucp with addresses like *fred@faraway.uucp* or *faraway!fred@uucp*, thereby forcing remote users to use awful hacks like *fred%faraway.uucp@example.com* or *faraway!fred%uucp@example.com*. Instead, use a naming system that reflects the details that matter to the user. If faraway is a system that sends and receives mail, integrate its addresses into the rest of the mail addressing system, something like *fred@faraway.example.com*. This means, among other things, that if the remote system switches to a different mail system, user addresses don't have to change.

It's not hard to arrange your virtual domain setup so that the choice of the remote service is entirely handled by the *virtualdomains* file. Assume you have three uucp peers called faraway, distant, and pluto. Then you could set them up like this, and have the gateway program check $HOST or, more likely, $HOST3 to pick out just the hostname:

```
faraway.example.com:alias-uucp
distant.example.com:alias-uucp
pluto.example.com:alias-uucp
```

As discussed in the next section, you can easily handle all three with a single gateway.

Gateway addressing

A little planning when setting up your gateway can make it both easier for people to use and easier for you to implement. If the gateway is to another email system, the only sensible approach is to give the other system a domain name so mail to its users looks like mail to any other domain on the Net.

If the gateway is to another service, try to arrange for addresses to be easy to remember. For example, a fax gateway would take addresses like *13115552368@fax*, but you might as well also accept *1-311-555-2368@fax* and *311-555-2368@fax* and, if all the users are in the same area code, *555-2368@fax*. For a mail-to-news gateway, use addresses like *alt.flame@news*.

Sometimes it makes sense to embed some options into the gateway address. For example, in my mail-to-news gateway, I sometimes want the gateway to add an Approved: header to the posted article, and sometimes I want to avoid sending bounce messages about failed posts (newsgroups that log filtered spam, for example, which mostly has fake return addresses*). The easiest way to encode flags into the address is with a prefix like *approve-alt.flame@news* and *nobounce-local.spamtrap@news*. You can also encode the flags into the domain, like *alt.flame@approve.news*, but I've found prefixes to be easier to use.

Per-message service gateways

Running the gateway program for each message is usually the easiest approach to implement. Create a *.qmail-default* file that runs the program, and either pass the value of $DEFAULT as a program argument or have the program pick it up from the environment.

To continue the uucp example, a simple gateway for a single system could be set up in *virtualdomains* like this:

```
faraway.example.com:alias-faraway
```

In *~alias/.qmail-faraway-default*, it would be:

```
| uux -p "faraway!rmail" "$DEFAULT"
```

---

* If you create a local moderated newsgroup corresponding to a mailing list, set the moderator's address for that newsgroup to the list's submission address, and route incoming mail from the list to the mail-to-news gateway address with the approval option, you get a pretty good two-way gateway.

To generalize this for multiple uucp hosts, route all the uucp domains to alias-uucp, and create *~alias/.qmail-uucp-default* containing:

```
| uux -p "$HOST3!rmail" "$DEFAULT"
```

Now the hostname, which precedes *.example.com* in the domain name, is picked out and handed to uucp. If you have a variety of mail gateways, you need to adjust only the lines in *virtualdomains* to control which domains are sent through which gateways.

For a gateway to a different kind of service, such as net news or fax, you must write your own gateway program in C or Perl to read through the message headers to pick up any lines the gateway needs, such as Subject or Date (not To, that comes from $DEFAULT), and pass the body to the program for the other service.

In the special but fairly common case that the gateway looks up an address in a database of some sort and remails the message, your gateway program can run qmail's *forward* program to do the remailing; there's no need to write your own if you don't want to.

If your gateway encodes options into the address (such as *approve-* in the previous section), you can easily handle them with an extra *.qmail* file, such as *.qmail-approve-default*, that calls the gateway program with whatever extra arguments it needs to implement the option.

Batched service gateways

Sometimes it's easier to run the gateway program periodically, either from *cron* or when some other event happens, such as when a remote system connects via PPP. In that case, you can have all of the mail for a virtual domain or group of virtual domains delivered into a Maildir, then have the gateway program take the messages out of the Maildir and do whatever it does with them, looking at the Delivered-To: line at the front of each message to tell what the message's recipient address is.

The serialmail package, discussed in Chapter 9, provides a general purpose framework for building batched gateways. The *maildirserial* program looks through a Maildir for files with a Delivered-To: line that matches a specified pattern (this lets several similar gateways share a Maildir), passes the names of matching files to a gateway program, reads delivery reports from the gateway, and optionally sends bounce reports for undeliverable messages.

When you run *maildirserial*, you give it the name of the Maildir, the address prefix, and the name of the gateway program to run. When it runs the gateway program, it sends to the gateway the names of files to process, and the gateway sends back delivery reports. The gateway program should process all the files that *maildirserial* gives it, but if it doesn't, *maildirserial* reruns the gateway until it either produces a delivery report for each file or makes no further progress.

The gateway program runs with the Maildir as its current directory, and pipes to and from *maildirserial*. The names of files to process arrive on the standard input, separated by nulls. It sends delivery reports to standard output. Each report consists of the filename and a null, as received from stdin, followed by a one-letter status code, an optional line of descriptive text for the logs or bounce message, and a newline. The status code is K if the message was delivered successfully, Z if the delivery failed temporarily and should be tried later, and D if the delivery failed permanently and the message should be bounced. If either the delivery succeeded or it failed permanently and a bounce message was sent, *mailderserial* will delete the file; otherwise the file stays so the delivery can be tried again.

As a concrete example, here's the framework of a Perl gateway program. It takes one command-line argument, the target address prefix. It reads null-separated filenames, opens the files, picks up the envelope sender and recipient addresses from the Return-Path: and Delivered-To: lines, does something with the file, and sends back a delivery report:

```perl
$prefix = shift or die "need prefix";

while(!eof STDIN) {
    {   local $/ = "\0"; # read null separated file names
        $fn = <STDIN>;
        chop $fn;
    }

    open(MSG, $fn) or die "cannot open 'fn\n";

    if(<MSG> =~ m{Return-Path: <(.*)>}) {
        $sender = $1;
    } else {
        close MSG;
        print "$fn\0Dno sender address\n";
        next;
    }
    if(<MSG> =~ m{Delivered-To: $prefix(.*)}) {
        $recip = $1;
    } else {
        close MSG;
        print "$fn\0Dno recipient address\n";
        next;
    }

    ### do something with the message here ###

    close MSG;
    print "$fn\0Kmessage delivered\n";
}
```

If this script were called ~/bin/gate, the local address is *alias-myvirt*, and the Maildir is called *myvirtmail*, then invoke it as:

```
setlock myvirtmail.lock \
  maildirserial -b -t604800 myvirtmail alias-myvirt- \
    ~/bin/gate alias-myvirt- 2>&1 | \
splogger serial
```

The call to *setlock* prevents two copies of *maildirserial* from running at once, and piping through *splogger* sends the results to syslog. Note that *alias-myvirt-* occurs twice, once for *maildirserial* and once for *gate*, and that it ends with a hyphen to prune off everything before the virtual domain mailbox. The –b flag tells *maildirserial* to bounce mail in case of a permanent failure, and the –t flag tells it to treat a temporary failure as permanent after a week. Other than for debugging, you should always include them, perhaps adjusting the time limit for temporary failures. Run *maildirserial* from *cron* if you want to push stuff through the gateway on a fixed schedule, or if the gateway depends on a network or dialup connection that's not always available, start it from the script that starts the connection, as described in Chapter 9.

When debugging your gateway program, rather than firing up *maildirserial*, mail a few test messages to your gateway that will land in your Maildir files, then use a text editor to create a file containing the names of those files, each followed by a null character (typed as Ctrl-V Ctrl-@ in *vi*, or Ctrl-Q Ctrl-@ in *emacs*). Then run your gateway with input redirected from that file. You can rerun it as often as you need to, because your gateway program doesn't delete its input files.

If your gateway program uses a TCP/IP connection to a remote system, place *tcpclient* between *maildirserial* and your gateway program to open the connection, like this:

```
setlock maildir.lock \
  maildirserial -b -t 1209600 maildir prefix \
  tcpclient -RH10 host port \
    gatewayprogram prefix
```

The gateway program reads and writes from and to the network on file descriptors 6 and 7, still using 0 (stdin) and 1 (stdout) for filenames and delivery reports. See Appendix A for a mail-to-news gateway using *maildirserial* and *tcpclient*. To debug programs running under *maildirserial* and *tcpclient*, I usually redirect the network connection to my tty so I can manually play the part of the remote server and step through the sequence of commands. To do that, use some shell redirections for the input file mentioned previously and the terminal:

```
gatewayprogram <listofinputfiles 6</dev/tty 7>/dev/tty
```

Internet services including SMTP and NNTP require a return character before the line feed at the end of each line, while input from */dev/tty* just has a newline. To work around that, I write my scripts so they strip out the \r and work either way. Alternatively, if the server needs to send more input than you can easily type, put a sequence of input messages in a file, edit in the \r at the end of each line, and run the gateway program redirecting file descriptor 6 from that file.

The example code shown here handles the messages sequentially, one at a time in order, but *maildirserial* doesn't require that you do so. Your gateway can process the files it passes in any order, individually or all at once, so long as it sends back an appropriate status report for each file that it's processed. The status reports do not need to be sent in the same order that the filenames were received, and the program can receive as many filenames as it wants before sending back any reports. (*maildirserial* runs as two independent processes: one reading the Maildir and sending the filenames, and the other receiving the reports, deleting processed files, and sending bounces.)

If your gateway won't ever bounce back messages sent to invalid addresses or have a temporary gateway failure, you don't need to use *maildirserial*. Just run your program as needed (from *cron* or otherwise). It should read the Maildir's *new* subdirectory and process all the files it finds there, deleting each one as it's done. You should still use *setlock* or the equivalent so that you don't get multiple copies of the gateway running at once.

If you encode options into your gateway address or domain, your gateway program must decode the address from the Delivered-To: line to pick out the options. I write most of my gateway programs in Perl, so the decoding takes only a few lines of code.

Mapping Individual Addresses

A rarely used virtual domain option maps individual addresses in a virtual domain. It's primarily useful to short-circuit mail to local users who also have addresses in other places. Let's say you're at the two-person East Podunk office of your company, connected by a slow dialup line, with user addresses *fred@epodunk.example.com* and *ethel@epodunk.example.com*, but the company uses a standardized addressing scheme so to the outside world the addresses are *fred@example.com* and *ethel@example.com*. If Fred sent a message to *ethel@example.com*, it has to go out over the dialup link and be forwarded back, probably a lot later. To avoid that, you can special-case the two addresses to be local:

```
fred@example.com:alias
ethel@example.com:alias
```

This routes these two addresses locally to *alias-fred* and *alias-ethel*, which you can handle with *.qmail* files, while leaving the rest of the *example.com* domain to be routed normally.

It's not very useful to override individual entries in local virtual domains, because you receive almost exactly the same effect by using *.qmail* files; that is, if the mail for *fred* is to be handled differently from everyone else's and everyone else's mail is handled by *~myvirt/.qmail-default*, you can put Fred's special rules in *~myvirt/.qmail-fred*.

POP Toasters

A POP toaster is a virtual domain in which all (or nearly all) of the mailboxes are routed to mailboxes that users can retrieve via POP and other remote access services. POP toasters are covered in detail in Chapter 13.

Some Virtual Domain Details

Finally, here are a few virtual domain odds and ends.

qmail-foo Versus qmail-alias-foo

After qmail rewrites a virtual domain address into a local address, the local address is then handled just like any other address. In particular, if there's no match for the rewritten address, it's handled by ~alias. This means that if there's no local user *myvirt*, these two lines are equivalent:

```
myvirt.com:myvirt
myvirt.com:alias-myvirt
```

Use the latter version, to make it explicit that you're not expecting the user to exist. That way if someone later creates a user *myvirt*, mail to that virtual domain won't mysteriously start failing.*

Local-Only Domains

If you provide a service gateway, such as mail-to-fax or mail-to-news, you'll probably want to let users on the local network use it, but not outsiders. To ensure that, create a subdomain for the gateway, (e.g., fax.example.com), but don't put the domain in the DNS. (If you have split-horizon DNS, with internal hosts seeing different data than external hosts, it's OK to put the gateway domain in the DNS visible to local hosts.) Also be sure not to put the gateway domain in *rcpthosts*, so that the only people who can send mail to the gateway domain are local users and authorized SMTP users who can send to nonlocal domains. Finally, in the gateway delivery program, check that the mail was sent to the virtual domain, not to the equivalent local address. If you do individual deliveries, that's easily handled in the *.qmail* file:

```
| case "$HOST" in fax|fax.example.com) exit 0 ;; *) bouncesaying "Not authorized." ;;
esac
| gatewayprogram "$DEFAULT"
```

If you do batched delivery via a Maildir, this trick also works, because qmail treats a Maildir delivery as a program delivery using an internal program:

```
| case "$HOST" in fax|fax.example.com)exit0;;*) bouncesaying "Not authorized.";;esac
./faxmaildir/
```

---

* Guess how I learned about this trick.

In either case, the delivery program can check the domain itself, by checking $HOST in individual deliveries or by checking the domain in the Delivered-To: line in batched gateways, but it's usually easier to check in the *.qmail* file so the gateway doesn't have to be coded to know what domain it's handling.

An alternate approach is to make all addresses virtual. That is, create a virtual domain for all the local mailboxes, and put something like *localdomain* in *locals* but not *rcpthosts* for miscellaneous, locally generated mail. If you have many local users, this approach is painful because you have to map all the users' mail from the virtual domain into their mailboxes, but it's not a bad idea on systems that are supposed to be POP toasters or gateways without local shell users.

## CHAPTER 13

POP and IMAP Servers and POP Toasters

If you want to access your mailbox across a network using mail user agents (MUAs) such as Eudora, Microsoft Exchange, Pegasus, mutt and fetchmail, you must run the qmail POP server. The qmail POP server allows these clients to read and delete mail from their mailbox, but doesn't include a method for sending email; use *qmail-smtpd* or *ofmipd* for that.

Consistent with qmail's component design, the qmail POP server is actually three separate programs that cooperate to create the POP service. (Traditional POP servers such as *qpopper* are typically implemented as a single large program.)

The qmail POP server only handles Maildirs, not mbox mailboxes or anything else. If you are installing qmail on an existing mail system, you must convert any existing mailboxes to Maildir if you want to use the qmail POP service. (If you want to keep using mboxes, you can use the popular *qpopper* POP server, which is not covered here.)

POP Mail Versus Local Mail Clients

If you want to be able to read your mail both with a local mail client running on your mail host and with POP, you have a few options, described in "Reading Your Mail" in Chapter 4. If you're using Maildirs, your best bet is to use either the freeware mutt MUA or Courier IMAP, described later in this chapter, and an IMAP client such as pine. Or you can deliver to mboxes, using *qpopper* for POP and any of the many MUAs that handle mboxes.

Each Program Does One Thing

The qmail POP server consists of a set of three cooperating programs (or four if you include the copy of *tcpserver* that runs the rest of the server):

qmail-popup
> Read the username and password from the network connection

checkpassword
> Validate the username and password

qmail-pop3d
> Handle requests to read and delete mail from the user's Maildir

The Flow of Control

In detail, a POP session proceeds as follows:

- *tcpserver* listens for network connections on the POP3 port 110 and spawns *qmail-popup*.

- *qmail-popup* inherits the environment variables and the socket created by *tcpserver*. (*qmail-popup* actually has no idea that it is connected to a socket; it merely reads from stdin and writes to stdout—knowing this comes in handy when we want to test the POP Server.) *qmail-popup* performs one very simple function. It understands just enough of the POP protocol to read the username and password sent across the network. Once this data is read, *qmail-popup* spawns *checkpassword*, passing it the username and password. *qmail-popup* has now completed its part in this session.

- *checkpassword* checks the username and password against the password file. (It uses *getpwnam( )* which usually reads */etc/passwd*, but this detail varies considerably from one version of Unix to the next.) If the password is correct, *checkpassword* extracts information about that user from the password file, does enough of a login process to permit *qmail-pop3d* to do its work, and now spawns *qmail-pop3d*.

- *qmail-pop3d* handles the rest of the POP3 session with the client. When *qmail-pop3d* exits, the POP session is completed.

Functional Partitioning

Using four programs to establish each POP session might seem like a lot of needless work. But each program is small and consequently easy to understand, easy to test, and creates very little load on a Unix system.

Clean functional partitioning is not just a theoretical ideal. It has two very practical benefits: flexibility and testability.

Flexibility

The clean functional boundary between the different parts makes it very easy to replace any part with a program that meets your specific needs.

checkpassword is the most obvious and popular candidate for replacement, especially by large installations that tend to use a network directory service such as LDAP or a proprietary database such as Oracle for their repository of username and password information. (See the sidebar "Qmail and LDAP" later in this chapter.) Given that the core of *checkpassword* is less than 150 lines of C code, writing a replacement program is not hard. Anything you might want to do on a per-user basis is possible by replacing one small program, *checkpassword.*

Testability

The qmail POP server is very stable and very reliable. When installed correctly it does work and it does work well. Almost invariably, a new installation doesn't work because the installation instructions haven't been followed precisely.

The qmail POP server consists of four components rather than just one, so each component can be tested individually to identify problems. For example, test *checkpassword* separately from the network, test *qmail-pop3d* separately from *checkpassword*, and so on.

Starting the Pop Server

Setting up the POP server is similar to setting up the qmail SMTP server.

Prerequisite Packages

The POP server depends on the daemontools and ucspi-tcp packages. If you've set up qmail as described in Chapter 3, these tools are already installed and available. You also need a checkpassword package. If you want to use the same passwords that you use for shell logins, the standard checkpassword package at *http://cr.yp.to/ checkpwd.html* will do the trick. The checkpassword section of www.qmail.org has a long list of other versions to handle virtual domains, retrieve passwords from databases, support multiple mailboxes per user, and other options. The discussion here presumes that you're using the standard version, but the component design of the POP server means that you can substitute your own version without changing the rest of the setup.

Directories

Two directories need to be created: one that contains the scripts and data files used to run the POP server, and the directory that will contain the log files. (You can put these directories anywhere you want, but the following names are chosen to match the names used in the widely used "Life With Qmail" setup.)

As root, create the script and data file directories, and the log directory (see Example 13-1).

Example 13-1. Creating the POP server directories

```
# mkdir /var/qmail/supervise/qmail/pop3d
# mkdir /var/qmail/supervise/qmail/pop3d/log
# chmod u=rwx,go= /var/qmail/supervise/qmail/pop3d

# mkdir /var/qmail/supervise/qmail/pop3d/log
# mkdir /var/qmail/supervise/qmail/pop3d/log/main
# chown qmaill /var/qmail/supervise/qmail/pop3d/log/main
# chmod u=rwx,go= /var/qmail/supervise/qmail/pop3d/log
```

The Listening Script

Example 13-2 has been purposely written to be as flexible as possible and will work for most situations. It goes into */var/qmail/supervise/qmail-pop3d/run*.

Example 13-2. The listening script

```
1. #!/bin/sh
2. limit datasize 2m
3. exec                                           \
4.   tcpserver                                    \
5.   -HRv -l pop.example.com                      \
6.   -x /var/qmail/supervise/qmail-pop3d/rules.cdb \
7.   0 110                                        \
8.   /var/qmail/bin/qmail-popup pop.example.com \
9.   checkpassword                                \
10.  /var/qmail/bin/qmail-pop3d Maildir 2>&1
```

Once created, the script needs to be made executable with:

```
# chmod +x /var/qmail/supervise/qmail/pop3d/run
```

The beginning of this script should be familiar from the SMTP daemon setup, from the exec on line 3 to the rules file on line 6, and the IP address and port number on line 7. (If you want to run the new POP server in parallel with an old copy of *qpopper* for a while, pick a specific IP address not used by *qpopper* instead, or temporarily run the server on a port other than 110.) Line 8 runs *qmail-popup* with a single command-line option of pop.example.com, the domain name used in the POP protocol to get the username and password. Line 9 is the command that *qmail-popup* runs once it has the username and password. In this case it is checkpassword. There are no command-line options for checkpassword. Line 10 is the command that *checkpassword* runs once it has verified the username and password. In this case it is qmail-pop3d. qmail-pop3d uses the supplied command-line option as the path of the Maildir to access. *checkpassword* switches to the user's home directory, so this will be the user's own Maildir.

There are variations possible with this script. Here are a few of the most likely ones:

- The limit set on line 2 may need to be increased if the mailboxes have a very large number of messages (more than 10,000) because the POP server uses a small amount of memory to keep track of each message.

- Removing the "HR" options from line 5 provides more information for logging at the expense of increasing the time it takes to establish a connection. See the *tcpserver* manpage for details.

- If you allow POP connections from anywhere on the Internet, then you can remove line 6. Note that the username and password are sent over the POP connection in the clear, which makes these connections vulnerable to snooping. So be careful when making the decision to allow POP connections from networks outside of your control.

The Logging Script

The second script needed as part of the POP server is the script that runs *multilog* to log the connection details (see Example 13-3). Put this script into */var/qmail/ supervise/qmail-pop3d/log/run*.

Example 13-3. POP log/run

```
1. #!/bin/sh
2.   exec setuidgid qmaill \
3.   multilog t s4000000 ./main
```

Once created, the script needs to be made executable with:

```
# chmod +x /var/qmail/supervise/qmail-pop3d/run
```

This script is the same as the ones used for *qmail-send* and *qmail-smtpd*.

tcpserver Rules

The last step before putting this all together is to populate the *rules.cdb* file with the networks that are allowed to access the POP server. The discussion of setting up SMTP servers in Chapter 7 explains, how to create rules files and run *tcprules*, so just populate the file with a rule that allows access from everywhere, as shown in Example 13-4.

Example 13-4. Populating rules.cdb

```
# cd /var/qmail/supervise/qmail-pop3d
# echo :allow >rules.txt
# tcprules rules.cdb rules.tmp <rules.txt
```

Putting It All Together

It is finally time to start the POP server.* With *svscan* running, link the newly created service directory into */service*:

```
# ln -s /var/qmail/supervise/qmail-pop3d /service
```

---

* If you have another POP server running, you must stop that first of course, or else run the POP server on a different IP address.

Within five seconds, *svscan* will notice the new entry in */server* and start the POP server.

Testing Your POP Server

The easiest way to test the POP server is to connect to it with your favorite MUA. Can you retrieve mail? If so, congratulations.

If the POP server doesn't work, check the log file */service/qmail-pop3d/log/main/ current* if that file exists. If it doesn't exist, *multilog* isn't running, probably due to a protection error or typo in the *log/run* file, so do a ps and look for clues in the readproctitle line. If the log file exists, it may contain a diagnostic message that identifies the problem. If this doesn't work, check each installation step to diagnose the problem. There are two major categories of problems. Either you can connect to the POP server and then "something" goes wrong or you cannot connect to the POP server at all.

You Cannot Connect to the POP Server

If you cannot connect to the POP server at all but the other parts of qmail are running, it is likely that there's a typo or protection error in the *run* file.

As root run:

```
# svstat /service/qmail-pop3d /service/qmail-pop3d/log
```

You should see something like this:

```
/service/qmail-pop3d: up (pid 37197) 5021 seconds
/service/qmail-pop3d/log: up (pid 37198) 5022 seconds
```

showing "up" as the status for both. If not, check the permissions and contents of the failing *run* file.

You Can Connect, but Then Something Fails

This is actually a good sign as it means that the *supervise* processes are running and the run scripts are at least partially correct. There are two primary reasons for a connection starting and then failing; a good way to find out the precise nature of the problem is to use *telnet* to manually step through the POP session to see exactly what happens.

First connect to the POP server with *telnet* like this:

```
telnet localhost 110
```

(If the POP server is running on a particular IP address or different port, *telnet* to the appropriate place.) After a few seconds you should see a banner from the POP server, something like this:

```
Connected to example.com.
Escape character is '^]'.
+OK <54559.982199402@example.com>
```

If you don't get the "+OK" line, then check the run script for typos. Most likely the *qmail-popup* line is wrong in some way. If that looks right check that the *tcprules* (*/service/popd/rules.cdb*) has been created with the correct entries.

If you receive the +OK line, *tcpserver* has successfully started *qmail-popup*. The next step is to try and log in by entering the login and password like this:

```
USER yourlogin
PASS yourpassword
```

(Substitute a valid login and password for "yourlogin" and "yourpassword.")

If the output is like this:

```
-ERR authorization failed
Connection closed by foreign host.
```

and you are sure you entered the login and password correctly, then the problem is likely to be that *checkpassword* is unable to check the login and password.

For debugging purposes, run it directly from the shell:

```
# perl -e 'printf "someuser\000topsecret\000123456\000"'>foo
# ./checkpassword sh 3<foo
$ id
uid=174(someuser) gid=84(somegroup) groups=84(somegroup)
$ pwd
/home/someuser
$
```

The input to *checkpassword* is on file descriptor 3, consisting of a username, password, and timestamp, or other added info, each terminated by a null byte. (The standard version of *checkpassword* ignores the contents of the timestamp, but the field has to be present.) In this example, the Perl line puts the input into a file. Be sure to put double quotes inside single quotes. Then, as superuser, so it can change to another user ID, run *checkpassword* opening the file on descriptor 3, and tell it to run the shell as the next program. Then use id and pwd to verify that the user, group, and home directory are correct. This test isn't very useful for the standard version of *checkpassword* but can be a major timesaver when you're debugging a custom version for a POP toaster, as I explain later in this chapter.

POP Servers and POP-before-SMTP

The POP-before-SMTP relay control scheme, discussed in Chapter 7, requires a few extra items in the listening script in order to track the IP addresses from which users have logged in for POP mail. The modified version of the listening script with the extra steps is described in Chapter 7.

Qmail and LDAP

Lightweight Directory Access Protocol (LDAP) is the most common system used to handle address book-style data shared over a network. It's far more complex than what qmail needs to drive a POP toaster, but for organizations that already use LDAP to keep the company directory, *qmail-ldap* at *http://www.nrg4u.com/* (described in "Life with qmail-ldap" at *http://www.lifewithqmail.org/ldap/*) does a good job of integrating qmail with LDAP. The LDAP directory keeps all of the information for user accounts such as its email addresses, the username, what host it's on in a clustered system, and a variety of qmail-like delivery options such as deliver to a Maildir, forward to another address, or run a program.

Installing and integrating *qmail-ldap* is considerably more work than any of the other patches mentioned in this book, both because the LDAP directory has to be adjusted to include the fields that *qmail-ldap* needs, and because the patch itself is very extensive and has a lot of options that the system manager needs to understand and configure. The patch does work, and it's reported to be in use in mail systems that support millions of users, so for a really big system, it's definitely worth a look.

Building POP Toasters

A *POP toaster* is a system that provides POP mail service for a potentially large set of mailboxes. Rather than create each mailbox as a Unix user account, a POP toaster generally runs as a single user, puts all of the mailboxes in virtual domains, keeps its own database of usernames, and arranges for mail deliveries and POP/IMAP sessions to use that database for validation.

The widely used vpopmail package (previously called vchkpw) is available from *http://www.inter7.com/vpopmail.html*. It provides all of the POP toaster functions, along with some nice additions, such as POP-before-SMTP relay validation for roaming users, database interfaces so the user information can be kept in a MySQL, Pgsql, or Oracle database, and a design that makes it straightforward to create clustered mail servers for added performance or reliability. At the time of this writing, the current version of vpopmail is 5.3.16.

Installing Vpopmail

Vpopmail uses the conventional autoconf configuration scheme. Download it from *http://www.inter7.com/vpopmail.html*, and unpack it into a directory. Don't try to build it yet; you must create the vpopmail user ID first. It depends on ucspi-tcp (the package that contains *tcpserver*) so be sure you've installed that already, as described in Chapter 3.

All of vpopmail's mailboxes and control files belong to the same Unix user. The usual user and group IDs are *vpopmail* and *vcheckpw*. If you can, create them with numeric user and group IDs of 89. (Some versions of FreeBSD may already have them defined as 89.) If your vpopmail setup expands to multiple machines, you want to have the same numeric IDs on all of them, and 89 is as good a number as any. Be sure that the disk partition on which you create the vpopmail home directory has sufficient space for all of the mail directories you plan to create. In some cases, you can move directories around later and use symlinks to splice the subtrees together, but you might as well allocate enough space in the first place and avoid the trouble.

If you plan to have many thousands of mailboxes, you should put them on a separate partition. Since Maildirs put each message in a separate file, the average file size on a mail partition is smaller than on general purpose partitions, so you must build the partition with extra inodes. You can estimate that average messages are about 5K, so divide the size of the partition by 5K and allocate that many inodes.

In the following examples, I use /var/vpopmail as the home directory for the mailboxes. It doesn't matter for vpopmail's configuration whether it's a partition mount point or not.

Before you configure vpopmail, you have to make a few decisions:

- Do you want to handle mailboxes not in virtual domains? If your system has shell users that get their mail in Maildirs in their home directories, yes. Otherwise, if your system is just a POP toaster or the shell users don't pick up their mail remotely, no.

- Do you want to allow roaming users to send mail through your SMTP server? Usually yes.

- Do you want to enforce mailbox quotas at delivery time? Probably, unless you don't have many mailboxes or use a different way to clean out mailboxes.

- Do you want to allow mailbox extensions? If you do, mail to fred-foo will be delivered to fred if fred-foo doesn't exist. If not, hyphens aren't treated specially. Extensions and subaddresses are a useful feature to let users track places to which they've given their addresses, so unless you have a strong reason to allow users to select mailbox names with hyphens, you should allow extensions.

To configure vpopmail, become the super-user (it needs to look at password files to figure out your mail setup), and in the *vpopmail* directory, run *configure*:

```
# ./configure --enable-passwd \
    --enable-roaming-users=y \
    --enable-defaultquota=50000000 \
    --enable-qmail-ext=y
```

Leave out the options you're not using. The number after *defaultquota* is the default mailbox quota to use, in bytes. Quotas can also be written in the form 1000000S,400C to set limits on both the mailbox total size in bytes and maximum message count. After configure runs, leave super-user and type make (or gmake if your system's normal make program isn't GNU make) to build all the programs. Then become user again and make (or gmake) install.

Setting Up Vpopmail

To get your mail going, create the virtual domain(s) the mailboxes will use, create user mailboxes in those domains, and start up the POP server to let people pick up their mail.

Creating virtual domains

Use *vadddomain* to create a domain. As the super-user:

```
# cd ~vpopmail
# bin/vadddomain myvirt.com topsecret
```

The arguments are the name of the virtual domain, and the password to assign to the postmaster mailbox in that domain. A few options are available for unusual situations:

-e *address*
> Normally, mail to a nonexistent mailbox in a virtual domain bounces. The -e flag specifies an address that delivers mail to nonexistent addresses.

-q *quota*
> The mailbox quota for the postmaster mailbox.

-d *directory*
> Create the domain's files in this directory, rather than *~vpopmail/domain*.

(See the manpages in *~vpopmail/doc*.)

When you create a vpopmail virtual domain, it creates a directory for the domain under *~vpopmail/domains*, and (somewhat disconcertingly) automatically updates the files in */var/qmail/control* and */var/qmail/users*. It adds a line to */var/qmail/users/assign* creating a qmail user with the same name as the domain, adds a line to */var/qmail/control/virtualdomains* routing mail to the domain to the user it just created, and adds a line to *rcpthosts* or *morercpthosts* to accept mail for the domain. It doesn't do is to create DNS MX records to tell the world to send mail for the domain to your mail host. You have to do that yourself by editing zone files or your DNS server's equivalent.

If you create a lot of domains at once, use the -0 flag for all but the last *vadddomain* to speed up creation. In practice, it's unlikely that you'll create enough domains to worry about it.

Creating mailboxes

You create individual mailboxes with *vadduser*, running as either vpopmail or root. The arguments are the address of the mailbox to create and optionally the password. If you supply no password, it prompts you to type one. You can optionally supply a password on the command line, or let it generate a random one:

```
$ vadduser able@myvirt.com dontguess
$ vadduser -r baker@myvirt.com
Random password: LMd%tusw
```

Arguments include:

-r

Generates a random password.

-n

Uses no password.

-c 'user info'

Sets the "gecos" field in the user file, which usually contains the user's real name.

-q quota

Set the user's quota, if different from the domain's default.

-s

Doesn't regenerate the password database. Use in all but the last of a series of *vadduser* commands for speed.

If you have a file with usernames and password pairs, it's easy enough to use a script to add them all:

```
( read lastuser lastpass
while read user pass
do
        vadduser -s $user $pass
done
# do the last one without -s to force database rebuild
vadduser  $lastuser $lastpass
) < userfile
```

Once the database is rebuilt by a command without -s, the mailbox exists and is ready to use. You can change passwords or other mailbox parameters with *vmoduser* and delete mailboxes with *vdeluser*. Run each with no arguments to see what the options are. (There's an online manual, but it is way out of date.)

Starting the POP service

Starting the vpopmail POP server is a minor variation on starting the regular qmail POP server, mostly involving replacing the standard password checker with the vpopmail version. If all of your POP-able accounts are managed by vpopmail, you can make another small change to run the whole POP server as the vpopmail user, which is somewhat more secure. Assuming you've already set up the POP listening script as described earlier in this chapter, the changes for vpopmail are minimal (see Example 13-5).

Example 13-5. The listening script

```
 1. #!/bin/sh
 2. limit datasize 2m
 3. exec                                             \
 4.    /usr/local/bin/tcpserver                      \
 5.      -HRv -l pop.example.com                     \
 6.      -x /var/vpopmail/rules.cdb                  \
 7.      0 110                                       \
 8.    /var/qmail/bin/qmail-popup pop.example.com    \
 9.    /var/vpopmail/bin/vchkpw                      \
10.    /var/qmail/bin/qmail-pop3d Maildir 2>&1
```

On line 6, move the *rules.cdb* file into the vpopmail home directory, and on line 9, use the vpopmail password checker rather than the standard one. If you've enabled roaming users, *~vpopmail/etc/tcp.smtp* contains the fixed *tcpserver* relay rules, so put the info there to permit local users to relay; for example:

```
# allow from localhost
127.:allow,RELAYCLIENT=""
# allow from local network
10.1.2.:allow,RELAYCLIENT=""
```

Then modify your SMTP listening script, which is in */var/qmail/supervise/qmail-smtp/run*, so that it uses the vpopmail rules, as in Example 13-6.

Example 13-6. Change the SMTP server rules

```
5.     -x/home/vpopmail/etc/tcp.smtp.cdb 0 25         \
```

Then start or restart your SMTP server, and you're all set.

The */etc/passwd* users can log in with their usernames and system passwords, while vpopmail users log in with their full email address, such as *myname@myvirt.com* and their vpopmail passwords. For the benefit of people using mail clients that don't like to put at-signs in their configuration data, vpopmail also accepts a percent or slash, for example, *myname%myvirt.com* or *myname/myvirt.com*. If you are only picking up vpopmail mailboxes, run the POP server as the vpopmail user, as shown in Example 13-7.

Example 13-7. Change the POP server rules

```
4.     /usr/local/bin/tcpserver -u89 -g89            \
```

Substitute in the actual user and group IDs, if they're not both 89. This makes it somewhat more secure in the face of unexpected bugs.

Roaming users

Vpopmail includes support for POP-before-SMTP that is very easy to set up. Assuming you've set up *tcp.smtp* as described in the previous section, *vchkpw* automatically adds each address that logs in for POP to *~vpopmail/etc/open-smtp* and rebuilds *tcp.smtp.cdb* to include those addresses, and if you've modified your SMTP tcpserver commands as described previously, it lets POP-before-SMTP users relay mail.

The only other thing you have to do is to run the *clearopensmtp* daemon that removes out of date entries from the *open-smtp* list. Run it from *cron* once an hour, with an entry like this in */etc/crontab*:

```
0 * * * *        root /var/vpopmail/bin/clearopensmtp
```

If your POP server only picks up vpopmail mailboxes and runs as the vpopmail user, run *clearopensmtp* as vpopmail. Otherwise you have to run it as root, because *vchkpw* writes the *open-smtp* file as root.

Some Handy Vpopmail Tricks

Although vpopmail's normal setup delivers mail only to individual mailboxes, you can configure it to do just about anything that qmail can do.

Handling unknown users

When mail arrives for a mailbox that doesn't exist, it can bounce the message, discard it, or deliver it to a default mailbox either in the domain or elsewhere. When you create a domain with *vadddomain*, the -e flag sets the default, but it's easy to change later. In the domain's directory, usually *~vpopmail/domains/domainname*, the *.qmail-default* line controlling deliveries to the domain looks like this:

```
| /var/vpopmail/bin/vdelivermail '' defaultinstruction
```

The second argument (the first, the two quotes, is just a placeholder) is the instruction to control the default behavior. If the instruction is the string `bounce-no-mailbox`, mail to undefined addresses bounces. If the instruction is the string `delete`, mail to undefined mailboxes is discarded. If the instruction is anything else, it's taken to be the email address to forward the mail to. If you want to deliver unknown mail to a default mailbox within the domain, you must write out the full address, e.g., *catchall@myvirt.com*. An unqualified address is treated as a local qmail address, which is rarely what you want. To change the default behavior, just edit *.qmail-default* as needed.

Forwarding a user's mail and other per-user special handling

For each mailbox, vpopmail creates a directory with the same name as the mailbox and, in that directory, a Maildir. Usually the mailbox directory is in the domain's directory; in very large domains the directory is split up using intermediate directories named with small numbers. When *vdelivermail*, the vpopmail delivery program, delivers a message, it normally deposits it into the Maildir. But if the mailbox directory contains a *.qmail* file, *vdelivermail* processes that *.qmail* file using a subset of the qmail rules. Lines ending in */Maildir/* are taken to be Maildir names to which the message is delivered. Lines starting with a vertical bar are commands run by the shell. Anything else is treated as an email address, perhaps preceded by an ampersand. As a special case, if the mailbox's own address appears in the *.qmail* file, it's ignored to prevent mail loops. (Use *./Maildir/* to deliver the message.) Neither comment lines nor mbox deliveries are supported, but the features that are supported are quite adequate to handle forwarding to other addresses, vacation programs, and other common mailbox features.

Enforcing mail quotas

Vpopmail allows you to set a per-mailbox disk quota. If mail arrives for a mailbox that's over quota, it's bounced rather than delivered. You can customize the bounce message, and you can also arrange to deliver a warning message to a recipient when a mailbox is about to be over quota.

When you build vpopmail, the `--enable-defaultquota` sets the quota for each mailbox. When you create a domain, the `-q` flag to *vadddomain* can override the quota for the postmaster mailbox, and when you create a mailbox, the `-q` flag to *vadduser* can override the quota for that user. You can change the quota for an individual user or a whole domain with *vsetuserquota*:

```
$ vsetuserquota @myvirt.com 25M # 25 megs all user
$ vsetuserquota fred@myvirt.com 20M # 20 megs for fred
```

In each case, the quota can be a plain number that is the total size of messages in the mailbox; `10MS,999C`, to set limits on the total size and count of messages; or the string `NOQUOTA` to turn off quota checking. In the message size limit, the letters K and M have the usual meaning.[*]

When a message arrives for a user who is over quota, it is bounced back to the sender. If a file named *.over-quota.msg* exists in the domain's directory or in *~vpopmail/domains*, the contents of that file is used in the bounce message in place of `user is over quota`, permitting per-domain customized bounce text. In addition, if a file named *.quotawarn.msg* exists in either of those two places, its contents is delivered to the user. That file should be a complete mail message with headers, saying

---

[*] The binary meaning, 1024, and 1024*1024.

something like "your mailbox is over quota and you won't get any more mail until you delete some of it." The delivery program remembers when it's delivered the over-quota message and won't deliver it to a user more than once a day.

Mail bulletins

A useful service originated by the *qpopper* POP server is bulletins, messages sent to all users in a domain. Vpopmail provides *vpopbull* to deliver bulletins to all mailboxes in a domain or all mailboxes in all domains, by copying or linking the bulletin message into everyone's Maildir. To use it, create the bulletin in a file, formatted as an email message called something like *bulletin1*. (If you plan to copy rather than make links to the file, omit the To: line, because it'll be added to each copy automatically.)

```
From: support@myvirt.com (Support)
To: Myvirt Users :;
Subject: Mail server interruption

Due to a server upgrade, you won't be able to pick up your mail
between 3:00 and 5:00 PM on Saturday.  But if you come by the
office, there'll be free beer.

The Management
```

Then distribute it. As vpopmail, run:

```
$ vpopbull -s -f bulletin1 myvirt.com
```

You can list one or more domains to distribute the bulletin to users in those domains, or no domain at all to distribute the bulletin to all vpopmail users. A few useful options include:

-f *file*
: The message file to distribute

-n
: Don't distribute a bulletin; either -f or -n is required

-e *file*
: Exclude list, a file containing addresses that are not to get the bulletin

-c
: Copy the message file into each Maildir

-h
: Hard link message file into each Maildir

-s
: Soft link the message file into each Maildir

-V
: Verbose; list all the mailboxes affected

If you know that the total number of mailboxes is less than the per-file hard link limit on your system (usually 32767), -h will run the fastest. If you have more mailboxes than that, use -s. Only copy the file if you need to put each user's address on the To: line—for example, to defeat overenthusiastic spam filters.

A Cheap Trick to List All Your Vpopmail Mailboxes

If you run *vpopbull* with -n and -V, to do nothing verbosely, it'll list all the mailboxes in the domains you specify, or in the absence of any specific domains, all of the domains that vpopmail manages.

Storing user data in a database

Normally, vpopmail stores the user info for each domain in a file called *vpasswd* in the domain's directory, compiled into *vpasswd.cdb* for fast access. For large mail setups, the user info can instead go into a SQL database. While this is slower than direct access to a CDB file, it's considerably more flexible, and makes it easier to distribute mail and POP service across multiple hosts. There are database interfaces for Pgsql, Oracle, Sybase, but by far, the most popular database used with vpopmail is MySQL, so that's the one covered here.

Before building a MySQL version of vpopmail, you must define a MySQL database for vpopmail to use, along with a MySQL user that has full access to that database and a password for that user. Edit *vmysql.h* and put in the server name, username, and password into the definitions near the beginning of the file. There are two sets of definitions, one for the server from which to read data and the other for the server to which to send updates. Unless you turn on MySQL replication, the READ versions are ignored, but you might as well make them the same:

```
/* Edit to match your set up */
#define MYSQL_UPDATE_SERVER "localhost"
#define MYSQL_UPDATE_USER   "vpopmail"
#define MYSQL_UPDATE_PASSWD "verysecret"

#define MYSQL_READ_SERVER   "localhost"
#define MYSQL_READ_USER     "vpopmail"
#define MYSQL_READ_PASSWD   "verysecret"
/* End of setup section*/
```

Vpopmail manages the database tables itself, but you must make one decision about how it should do so, the so-called "many-domains" option. Normally, when many-domains is on, it puts all the user information for all domains into a single table called vpopmail, with the key being the combination of the pw_name field, the mailbox name, and pw_domain, the domain name. If many-domains is off, vpopmail can make a table of the mailboxes in each domain, with the table having the same name as the domain,[*] and the table key is just the mailbox name. If you have a small number of domains each with a large number of mailboxes, turning off many-domains can save space because the domain names don't need to be stored in the database tables. Unless you have many thousands of mailboxes, accept the default that is to turn many-domains on.

Now become super-user and rerun the configuration script, adding `--enable-mysql=y` to the arguments. If the MySQL include files and shared library aren't in the default places, you must provide arguments to tell vpopmail where to look for them. Here's the configuration command for our system:

```
# ./configure --enable-qmail-ext=y --enable-roaming-users=y \
    --enable-defaultquota=50 --enable-passwd \
    --enable-mysql=y \
    --enable-incdir=/usr/local/mysql/include/mysql \
    --enable-libdir=/usr/local/mysql/lib/mysql
```

To turn off many-domains, add `--enable-many-domains=n`. Then rebuild and reinstall vpopmail as previously described.

If you already have created virtual domains with mailboxes, the *vconvert* program can convert the CDB database into MySQL. Run it, giving it the list of domains to convert:

```
$ vconvert -c -m myvirt.com ...
```

The –c and –m flags say to convert from CDB to MySQL. The various vpopmail programs work the same as always.

Data replication and other MySQL tricks

The MySQL support in vpopmail is considerably more extensive than I have room to describe here. Using MySQL's database replication features, you can build multi-host systems with the SMTP server on one set of hosts and the POP servers on another set of hosts. See Chapter 17 for more details.

The MySQL module also supports mailbox aliases, a pseudo-mailbox that is delivered to one or more real mailboxes. This is handy when a user changes his email address but wants to keep getting mail to the old address.

You can use MySQL for logging, with an entry added for every POP login attempt, successful or not.

And finally, with modest programming effort, you can add your own fields to the database tables (edit *vmysql.h*). Vpopmail won't use them, but your own programs can use them for other user maintenance purposes.

---

[*] Actually, the table name replaces dots and hyphens with underscores for SQL compatibility, so *myvirt.com* becomes *myvirt_com*.

Picking Up Mail with IMAP and Web Mail

Although POP is by far the most common way for users to collect their mail, many mail servers also offer IMAP and web mail. IMAP is conceptually similar to POP except that the client program has a full set of tools to manipulate the mailbox on the server. The advantage of IMAP over POP is that the mailbox remains on the server, so the user can use different mail programs from different locations, seeing consistent mailbox contents at all times. While qmail provides no IMAP server of its own, the IMAP server from the Courier mail package uses Maildirs as its mailbox format and works well with qmail. I describe its setup below.

Web mail provides access to a mailbox using a web browser as the mail client. Many web mail packages are available on the Net that use POP or IMAP to access the user mailboxes. They're not specific to qmail, so I don't describe them here. The Courier package includes a web mail component called SqWebMail that uses Maildirs as its mailbox format. I describe its installation later in this chapter.

Maildirs don't have to be locked while a client reads or updates them, so the POP and IMAP servers and SqWebMail can access the same mailbox simultaneously without trouble. Systems based on mboxes can't do that. I routinely have my mailbox open in pine on a BSD system, Pegasus and Opera 7 on a Windows laptop, and SqWebMail on a web browser, all at the same time without any trouble. You can download the sources for Courier IMAP and SqWebMail by following the links from *http://www.courier-mta.org/download.php*. As of the time this book was written, the current version of Courier IMAP is 1.7.0 and of SqWebMail is 3.5.0.

Courier IMAP and SqWebMail share the same user validation scheme, an "auth" framework that calls out to a variety of authorization modules to handle everything from passwd files to vpopmail to MySQL (different from the vpopmail flavor) to LDAP. Once you have it set up for one, it's easy to transfer to the other. Courier IMAP includes a POP server that provides no more function than the qmail one but uses the Courier authentication scheme, letting your POP and IMAP login rules be consistent.

Courier's Extended Maildir++

All of the pieces of the Courier package support an upwardly compatible extended version of Maildirs known as Maildir++. The extensions allow subfolders within a Maildir and provide a convention for folders that can be shared among multiple users (a feature used by the IMAP server).

A subfolder is merely a Maildir that exists within another Maildir. For example, a subfolder called *spam* would be *Maildir/.spam* and *spam.mmf* would be *Maildir/.spam.mmf*. Even though folders can be logically nested, all subfolder directories are directly located in the main Maildir. Each subfolder has the usual *tmp*, *cur*, and *new* directories, as well as a zero-length file named *maildirfolder* that tells programs that it's a subfolder and to look in the parent directory for quota files and the like. From qmail's point of view, a subfolder is just a Maildir, and qmail can deliver messages to them the same as to any other Maildir. This comes in handy for delivery-time mail sorting. If, say, you want mail tagged by your spam filter to go into a separate subfolder, your *.qmail* or *.procmailrc* can deliver the spam to *Maildir/.spam/*, and the rest of the mail to *Maildir/*.

A shared Maildir is one that's world-readable. By convention, the file *shared-maildirs* in a regular Maildir contains a list of shared Maildirs, each on a line in the form:

```
nickname tab path-to-shared-Maildir
```

Courier IMAP and SqWebMail create symlinks as needed to make the messages in folders in the shared Maildirs look like they're in folders in the user's own Maildir.

The Courier programs create a lot of other files in the Maildirs, such as the signature and address book for SqWebMail. Qmail ignores everything but the three defined directories, so the extra files cause no compatibility trouble.

Installing Courier IMAP

Once you've downloaded the Courier IMAP source, unpack it into a directory (see the sidebar "Unpacking bz2 Files"). The configuration for Courier IMAP is intended to be almost entirely automatic, detecting whether you have packages such as OpenSSL, MySQL, and vpopmail installed and, if so, compiling optional subpackages for them. When the automated scheme works, it's great. When it doesn't quite work, it's a pain in the neck.

Read the *INSTALL* file carefully before building and installing the package, because the installation instructions may have changed from the ones here. First configure it by running *configure*. The configuration process runs recursively in a long set of subdirectories, so it can take several minutes. Then build it with *make*. (The instructions say to use GNU *gmake* on BSD systems, but I've found that the configuration files are built for the BSD *make*.) Assuming that works, become super-user and type `make install` to install the files, and then type `make install-configure` to configure the installed files. This installs the package into */usr/lib/courier-imap*.

Courier's Authorization Daemon

The usual configuration for the Courier package uses an authorization daemon to handle login authorization. The idea is to keep a pool of daemons running and to call them to do the authorization rather than running a separate program each time. For relatively slow authorizers that need to connect to remote databases, this can speed the login process, but the authorization daemon is notoriously hard to get working correctly. If your system looks up authorization in */etc/passwd* or another local file or database, the daemons offer little speed advantage. You can turn off the daemon by configuring Courier-IMAP and SqWebMail with `--without-authdaemon` to run each authorization program as needed. If speed isn't a problem or you have trouble getting the daemon to work, reconfigure to turn it off and get IMAP and SqWebMail working without it.

Once it's installed, you have some more setup to do before you start up the servers. There are separate servers for POP and IMAP. If you have OpenSSL installed, there are two more servers for POP-SSL and IMAP-SSL. To add to the confusion, some clients connect to the regular server on the regular POP or IMAP port, and then use a "starttls" command to switch to secure mode, while other clients connect to different ports (993 for IMAP, 995 for POP) and start the secure mode negotiation immediately. Courier IMAP supports both modes, but you have to start them separately.

If you're using SSL, this is a good time to generate your SSL certificates. The certs that Courier generates are self-signed, which makes most MUAs pop up warning messages, but they're adequate for debugging. To get rid of the warnings, you must get your certificates signed by one of the signing services that signs web server certs, at about $100 per signature. The files *etc/imapd.cnf* and *etc/pop3d.cnf* contain the info needed to create the certificates. You must change the CN line from the default localhost to the name of your mail server or some MUAs, including Eudora, won't talk to you at all. While you're at it, you might as well update the C (Country), ST (State), L (Locality), O (Organization), and emailAddress lines so that when users check the certificate, which they will when their MUAs complain about it, the values look reasonable:

```
[ req_dn ]
C=US
ST=NY
L=Trumansburg
O=The Example Organization
OU=Automatically-generated IMAP SSL key
CN=mail.example.com
emailAddress=postmaster@example.com
```

Once you've fixed up the certificate data, run share/mkimapdcert and share/mkpop3dcert to create the SSL certificates.

Now check the server configuration files *etc/imapd, etc/imapd-ssl, etc/pop3d*, and *etc/pop3d-ssl* (each is a shell script that sets variables imported into the startup scripts), and make any needed adjustments. The most likely variables to use are ADDRESS and SSLADDRESS if you want your servers to run on a specific IP address, and use MAXDAEMONS to limit the number of simultaneous sessions. Also check *authdaemonrc*, which controls the authorization daemon that validates logins, in particular the authmodulelist line, which lists all of the authorization modules it'll use. You'll often want to remove some of them. See *man/man7/authlib.7*, which describes all the modules. Now you're ready to start up the daemons:

```
# cd /usr/lib/courier-imap/libexec
# ./imapd.rc start      # start imap on 143
# ./pop3d.rc start      # start pop3 on 110
# ./imapd-ssl.rc start      # start ssl imap on 993
# ./pop3d-ssl.rc start      # start ssl pop3 on 995
```

Check that you can log into your new server. To test the POP server, *telnet* into it as described earlier in this chapter in the discussion of the qmail POP server. IMAP is an extremely complex protocol, but fortunately the commands to log in and check a mailbox are pretty simple. In this example, you literally type c1, c2, and c3, which are transaction identifiers used to match up responses with requests:

```
$ telnet yourserver imap
Trying 10.31.42.80...
Connected to yourserver.
Escape character is '^]'.
* OK Courier-IMAP ready. Copyright 1998-2003 Double Precision, Inc.  See COPYING for
distribution information.
c1 login yourname yourpassword
c1 OK LOGIN Ok.
c2 select INBOX
* FLAGS (\Draft \Answered \Flagged \Deleted \Seen \Recent)
* OK [PERMANENTFLAGS (\Draft \Answered \Flagged \Deleted \Seen)] Limited
* 31 EXISTS
* 0 RECENT
```

```
* OK [UIDVALIDITY 1043726086] Ok
c2 OK [READ-WRITE] Ok
c3 logout
* BYE Courier-IMAP server shutting down
c3 OK LOGOUT completed
```

To check that SSL is working, log into the various servers from MUAs and check that it works. If your MUA supports SSL, it will complain about the self-signed certificates before it lets you log in. Assuming you're happy with the results, add the previous startup lines to one of the */etc/rc* files on BSD systems. On System V and Linux systems, see the *courier-imap.sysvinit* script created in the build directory but not installed. Again, read the lengthy *INSTALL* for the most up to date installation instructions.

Courier IMAP and Pop-Before-SMTP

Although Courier IMAP supports about 15,000 different features, a general purpose POP-before-SMTP is not one of them unless you're using vpopmail. If you are, build Courier IMAP without authdaemon, and add -DHAVE_OPEN_SMTP_RELAY to the DEFS line in the *authlib Makefile* to have it include the relay code. The vpopmail FAQ at *http://www.inter7.com/vpopmail/FAQ.txt* has more details at question 34.

For other authorization schemes, this oversight is easily remedied. Each of the *.rc* files, when it starts a server, runs *couriertcpd*, a TCP daemon similar to *tcpserver*. Like *tcpserver*, it takes as its arguments a cascade of programs to run whenever an incoming connection arrives. Also like *tcpserver*, salient facts about the connection are placed in the environment, including TCPREMOTEIP for the remote host. In *imapd.rc*, for example, this rather complex command starts the server:

```
/usr/bin/env - /bin/bash -c " set -a ;
        prefix=/usr/lib/courier-imap ;
        exec_prefix=/usr/lib/courier-imap ;
        bindir=${exec_prefix}/bin ;
        libexecdir=/usr/lib/courier-imap/libexec ;
        . ${prefix}/etc/pop3d ; \
        . ${prefix}/etc/pop3d-ssl ; \
        TLS_PROTOCOL=$TLS_STARTTLS_PROTOCOL ; \
        export TLS_PROTOCOL ;
        /usr/lib/courier-imap/libexec/couriertcpd -address=$ADDRESS \
                -stderrlogger=/usr/lib/courier-imap/libexec/courierlogger \
                -stderrloggername=imapd \
                -maxprocs=$MAXDAEMONS -maxperip=$MAXPERIP \
                -pid=$PIDFILE $TCPDOPTS \
                $PORT ${exec_prefix}/sbin/imaplogin $LIBAUTHMODULES \
                        ${exec_prefix}/bin/imapd Maildir"
```

This sets variables, reads two configuration scripts from *etc*, and runs *couriertcpd*. When a connection arrives, it runs *imaplogin*, which after validating the login, runs *imapd*. If you're using relay-ctrl, the instructions for integrating it with Courier IMAP are in the *ANNOUNCEMENT* file. First you make a symlink in */usr/lib/courier-imap/libexec/authlib* to */usr/sbin/relay-ctrl-allow*. Then add relay-ctrl-allow to the end of the list of *AUTHMODULES* in the file */usr/lib/courier-imap/etc/imapd*, which tells IMAP to run that program every time someone logs in. Finally, insert this line in front of the `couriertcpd` line in the startup script:

```
envdir /etc/relay-ctrl relay-ctrl-chdir \
```

and restart Courier IMAP. You must modify all four *.rc* scripts to do POP-before-SMTP, but you can add the same line to each of them to use the same openrelay script.

Binc IMAP

Although Courier IMAP is the most widely used Maildir IMAP server, a worthy alternative is Andreas Hanssen's Binc IMAP (Binc Is Not Courier), available at *http://www.bincimap.org/* or *http://www.bincimap.andreas.hanssen.name/*. It is designed to be smaller and faster than Courier IMAP, and more compatible with qmail's design and use the same tools as the qmail POP server. It can run under *tcpserver* and uses *checkpassword* for its authentication. It can use Maildir++ subfolders, the same as Courier does, and notes on the web site tell how to use it with relay-ctrl and vmailmgr.

Binc isn't as mature as Courier, but if you're setting up an IMAP server, it's definitely worth a look because it's a lot easier to set up.

Installing SqWebMail

Once you have Courier-IMAP installed, SqWebMail is a snap to install. Unpack the bzipped file, configure, and install. SqWebMail runs from your web server, so the main program is installed in a *cgi-bin* directory and run on demand from the web server. If you're planning to run it from a virtual domain, create the web server directories for the domain's home page and cgi-bin if you haven't already done so. The installation process creates a directory of icon files that must be the *webmail* subdirectory of the domain and a directory tree of auxiliary files that shouldn't be visible via the web server at all, usually in */usr/local/share/sqwebmail*. If you're not using Courier-IMAP, and you're using the authorization daemon, you must add a line to your system startup scripts to start the daemon. If you are using Courier-IMAP, use the same daemon it uses. The configuration script has an enormous set of options, but the ones you most likely need are the ones to set the location of the cgi-bin and image directories. If you've installed Courier-IMAP with authdaemon, you also must tell SqWebMail to use the same authdaemon directory:

```
./configure \
        --enable-cgibindir=/var/www/cgi-sqweb \
        --enable-imagedir=/var/www/sqwebmail/webmail \
        --with-authdaemonvar=/usr/lib/courier-imap/var/authdaemon \
        --disable-autorenamesent
```

The last option to the configure command turns off a feature that automatically creates monthly subfolders of sent mail, which I don't find useful. Once the lengthy configuration process completes, build and install the program following the INSTALL instructions:

```
$ make configure-check
$ make
$ make check
$ su    # installation must be superuser
# make install       # or make install-strip to strip symbols
# make install-configure
```

Start authdaemon if needed, following the hints displayed by the install program, and then try *sqwebmail* with a URL like *http://mail.myvirt.com/cgi-bin/sqwebmail*.

The installation program lists many further possible customizations. One you should install is */usr/local/share/sqwebmail/sendit.sh*, the script that actually sends outgoing mail from SqWebMail. The version I use is this, to send mail using *qmail-inject*:

```
# $1 is the return address, $2 is the logged in sqwebmail user
{
    echo "Received: from [$REMOTE_ADDR] ($2); via SqWebMail 3.5.0"
    cat
} | /var/qmail/bin/qmail-inject -f "$1"
```

CHAPTER 14
Mailing Lists

The original impetus for writing qmail was to send out list mail faster than existing MTAs, so it's not surprising that qmail has excellent built-in support for mailing lists. The first part of this chapter looks at its list handling support, which is quite adequate for small and medium-sized lists. Then it covers ezmlm, the automated mailing list package designed to work with qmail, and other qmail-compatible list management software.

Sending Mail to Lists

The easiest and most common way to handle a small list is to put the list in a *.qmail* file. To reiterate an example from Chapter 10, assume a user's name is fred, and the list is about fishing. Then the list goes into *~fred/.qmail-fishing*, one address per line like any other *.qmail* file (see Example 14-1).

Example 14-1. Fred's fishing list

```
fred@example.com
jim@example.org
mary@myvirt.com
&/fn=hunt/ln=dash/@bigcorp.com
```

Note that the third address, an X.509 address that contains slashes, is preceded by an ampersand to keep it from being interpreted as a filename. Also, Fred's address is in the list so he gets copies of messages sent to it. To send mail to this list, one needs only to send a message to *fred-fishing*, and it's redistributed to all of the list members.

Maintaining List Files

Qmail provides a small but useful set of functions to maintain list files. To edit a file safely, set the otherwise unused "sticky" bit in the user's home directory, edit the file, then unset the sticky bit:

```
$ cd
$ chmod +t .
$ emacs .qmail-fishing
$ chmod -r .
```

Should any mail arrive for addresses handled by a *.qmail* file in the directory while the sticky bit is set, *qmail-local* notices the sticky bit and exits with code 111 so the delivery is retried later.

This list file example highlights a possible security hole when an address looks like a filename.[*] There are three ways to solve the problem. The simplest, but most error prone, is to put an ampersand in front of each name, or at least in front of each name that might look like a filename or command. The second is to set the owner execute bit on the file, which tells *qmail-local* that the file should only contain forwarding addresses, so any file or program deliveries fail. The third (undocumented) is to put a line containing +list in the file, which tells *qmail-local* that subsequent lines have to be forward addresses. This permits a few setup lines at the beginning before the addresses. For example, to require that each message's subject line has a keyword, see Example 14-2.

Example 14-2. Fred's fishing list with subject checking

```
| egrep -qi "^Subject:.*(largemouth|smallmouth|squid)" || bouncesaying "Not fishy enough."
+list
fred@example.com
jim@example.org
mary@myvirt.com
&/fn=hunt/ln=dash/@bigcorp.com
```

In the examples so far, the list has an address that is a subaddress of a user address. List files can equally well live in *~alias* in which case they have regular addresses; the list file *~alias/.qmail-fishing* has the address *fishing*.

Bounce Handling and VERP

One of the most tedious and difficult parts of mailing list management is bounce handling, identifying and removing addresses that are no longer valid. The most difficult aspect of bounce management turns out to be identifying the address that's bouncing, and a secondary problem is getting the bounces sent to an address that can do something useful with them.

When a message bounces, the host doing the bounce, which may be the one where the message was injected or another one to which the message was relayed by SMTP, sends back a failure report to the message envelope sender address. On qmail systems, all the bounces from the injecting system are sent back in one message in

---

[*] This isn't a new problem; in some ancient versions of Unix you could send mail to /etc/passwd and it'd add your message to the end of the password file.

QSBMF (qmail-send Bounce Message Format, described at *http://cr.yp.to/proto/ qsbmf.txt*). Bounces from remote systems arrive one per bouncing address, because qmail sends remote mail to one address at a time. Remote bounces arrive in whatever format the remote system chooses to use. Qmail systems use QSBMF; some MTAs use DSNs (delivery status notices), a complex format originally described in RFCs 3461-3464; and a lot of systems use ad-hoc formats not standardized or documented anywhere. Also, the envelope address on outgoing list mail needs to be the address of the mailing list manager (human or software), not the address of the original sender—only the list manager can update the list.

Manual bounce handling

The way to set up a qmail list for manual bounce handling is simply to create an owner mailbox. That is, if the list's qmail file is *.qmail-fishing*, create *.qmail-fishing-owner* and set it up to deliver mail someplace that the owner will see it, usually either forwarding to the owner's regular address or putting the mail in an mbox or Maildir.

When *qmail-local* processes *.qmail-fishing*, it checks to see if *.qmail-fishing-owner* exists, and if so, changes the envelope sender to *fred-fishing-owner@example.com*, or more generally to *LOCAL-owner@ HOST* where LOCAL and HOST are the local and host part of the original address. When bounces arrive, it's up to the list owner to read them and update the list appropriately by removing addresses that consistently bounce.

Automated bounce handling

For a list of any size or with a significant amount of traffic, manual bounce handling is an impossible amount of work. Fortunately, software does as good a job of bounce handling as people can, particularly when it uses qmail's VERP to identify the bouncing addresses.

Variable Envelope Return Path (VERP) encodes the recipient's address in the envelope sender of each message sent out, so if a message bounces, the address that bounced can be recovered from the address the bounce message is sent to. The recipient's address is placed at the end of the mailbox part with the @ sign changed to an = sign. For example, VERP would arrange that mail from Fred's fishing list to recipient *mary@myvirt.com* has return address *fred-fishing-owner-mary=myvirt.com@example.com*. If her mail bounces, the bad address is recovered from the bounce address by picking out the text at the end of the local part and changing the = back to an @ sign.

To use automated bounce handling, along with a *-owner* file, create a *-owner-default* file, which delivers to the bounce handling program. If *qmail-local* sees both of those files,[*] it rewrites the sender to *LOCAL-owner-@HOST-@[]*. This peculiar sender address turns on VERP, by telling *qmail-send* to rewrite the address again on each

---

[*] Both files have to be present, even though nothing will be delivered to the plain *-owner* address. This is debatably a buglet, although the owner address should exist anyway for humans to write to.

remote delivery to *RUSER@RHOST* so the envelope sender is *LOCAL-owner-RUSER=RHOST@HOST*. The overall effect of this is that all bounce mail is delivered to the *-owner-default* address, with local bounces delivered to *LOCAL -owner-* (note that trailing hyphen).

The bounce script can now easily determine the bouncing addresses, by parsing the QSBMF message in local bounces and picking the return address out of the address in remote addresses. The code to do so isn't very complex. It's wordy in C because of all of the string processing, so Example 14-3 shows it in Perl.

Example 14-3. Sample Perl code to handle bounces

```
$addr = $ENV{DEFAULT} # set by qmail-local
if ($addr) {
    $addr =~ s/=/\@/;         # VERP bounce, pick up address
    while(<>) {
        # ignore bounces that aren't really bounces
        exit 99 if /THIS IS A WARNING MESSAGE ONLY/;
        exit 99 if /^Subject: WARNING: message delayed at/;
        exit 99 if /^Subject: Returned mail: Deferred/;
    }
    dobounce($addr);
} else {
    # locally generated bounce, must be QSBMF
    $/=""; # slurp up a paragraph at a time
    $_=<>; # get rid of the email header.
    $_=<>; # get the QSBMF
    /^Hi. This is the/ || die "This is not a qmail bounce message";
    while(<>) { # handle each address section
        last if /^-/;
        /^<(.*)>/ || die "No recipient address";
        dobounce($1);
    }
}
```

Once the bounce code has the address, it should remove addresses from the list that bounce too often, for an appropriate definition of "too often" that has to depend on the nature of the traffic to the list.

This scheme won't handle 100% of all bounce mail, because some MTAs act in hostile ways, sending bounces other than to the envelope sender, but this gets about 90% of the effect of more comprehensive bounce handlers with about 5% of the work.

Bounce handling for mail without .qmail file forwarding

Mailing list software that doesn't keep the list in a *.qmail* file can also take advantage of qmail's automated bounce handling by setting the return address appropriately. No matter how mail is injected into qmail, whether it's via *qmail-inject*, by SMTP, or by calling *qmail-queue* directly, any envelope return address that ends with *-@[]* receives automatic VERP handling. (It's also possible for list software to generate 100 messages with 100 return addresses for 100 recipients, but that's pointless unless the messages differ in more than the envelope address.) At the moment the only mailing list software that takes advantage of qmail's automated VERP are ezmlm* and *majordomo2*,† but it wouldn't be hard to add it to other list management software.

Using Ezmlm with qmail

The most popular list manager used with qmail is ezmlm-idx, an extended version of Dan Bernstein's ezmlm. The original ezmlm has a very solid core of mailing list functions: subscription and unsubscription, message distribution and bounce management, and simple message archiving and retrieval. Unlike most list managers, ezmlm lets individual users run automatically managed private lists using subaddresses of their user addresses, as well as the more conventional arrangement where the system manager sets up a list with an address of its own. Ezmlm-idx adds more complex features such as digests, moderated lists, remote list management, and distributed lists with sublists. Nearly all ezmlm users use ezmlm-idx, because the basic ezmlm lacks now-essential abilities such as letting only list members post to a list. The following discussion all applies to ezmlm-index.

Installing Ezmlm-idx

Ezmlm-idx is a little bit tricky to install, because you have to combine the original ezmlm with the additions and patches for ezmlm-idx yourself. The easiest place to find the ezmlm and ezmlm-idx tarballs is *http://www.ezmlm.org*, where you can click the Download link near the top of the page to find a nearby archive with *ezmlm-0.53.tar.gz* and *ezmlm-idx-0.40.tar.gz* (or a newer version if available). While you're there, if you plan to run large lists (tens of thousands of addresses), you might also want to patch qmail, as discussed in Chapter 16, to increase the number of parallel deliveries above 255.

To install ezmlm-idx once you've installed the two archives:

1. Unzip and untar *ezmlm-0.53.tar.gz* into a directory in any convenient place, creating a subdirectory *ezmlm-0.53* containing the ezmlm files.

2. Unzip and untar *ezmlm-idx-0.40.tar.gz* in the same directory, creating an adjacent subdirectory *ezmlm-idx-0.40*.

3. Move all of the ezmlm-idx files, which include both new files and patching instructions for existing files, into the *ezmlm* directory:

   ```
   $ mv ezmlm-idx-0.40/* ezmlm-0.53
   ```

* Because it was written to work with qmail
† Because I wrote the qmail VERP code myself.

4. Go into the *ezmlm* directory and apply the patches. The *patch* program should report that all of the patches succeeded. (If not, either you have an obsolete patch program and need to install the current GNU version, or the files in the *ezmlm-0.53* directory were already modified, so delete the directory and recreate it from the *.gz* file.)

```
$ cd ezmlm-0.53
$ patch <idx.patch
Hmm... Looks like a unified diff to me...
The text leading up to this was:
--------------------------
|--- ezmlm-warn.1      1998/02/17 00:32:45      1.1
|+++ ezmlm-warn.1      1998/12/21 04:35:16      1.5
--------------------------
Patching file ezmlm-warn.1 using Plan A...
Hunk #1 succeeded at 3.
Hunk #2 succeeded at 21.
   ... more patch reports ...
--------------------------
|--- ezmlm-weed.1      1999/08/01 16:45:46      1.1
|+++ ezmlm-weed.1      1999/12/19 16:53:18      1.3
--------------------------
Patching file ezmlm-weed.1 using Plan A...
Hunk #1 succeeded at 7.
Hunk #2 succeeded at 35.
Hunk #3 succeeded at 113.
done
```

5. Look at the *conf-** files, and adjust them if needed for your local C compiler and qmail installation. One file not present in other packages is *conf-cron*, the location of the *crontab* program used to schedule commands for periodic execution. You may also want to change *conf-bin* from the default */usr/local/bin/ezmlm* to a directory that's in the standard search path, such as */usr/local/bin*, to make it easier to type the commands to your shell. For now you can ignore *conf-sqlcc* and *conf-sqlld*, which are used to build a version of ezmlm-idx that stores its data in SQL databases. Now type make to build ezmlm and make man to format the manpages.

If you want to test ezmlm-index before installing it, *INSTALL.idx* has test instructions. Briefly, create a user account called eztest (or if you already have a test account set up for other purposes, edit the ezmlm-test script to set EZTEST to the account name), then su to the test account, and in the ezmlm-index build directory, run *./ezmlm-test*:

```
$ ./ezmlm-test

testing ezmlm-idx:      ezmlm-idx-0.40
Using FQDN host name:
your host name
ezmlm-make (1/2):       OK
Using RDBMS support:    No.
testing for qmail:      >=1.02
ezmlm-reject:           OK
```

```
ezmlm-[un|is]sub[n]:   OK
ezmlm-send (1/2):       OK
ezmlm-tstdig:           OK
ezmlm-weed:             OK
ezmlm-make (2/2):       OK
ezmlm-clean (1/2):      removed mod queue entry 3 that wasn't due
```

Assuming it worked, become the super-user and make setup to install all the pieces you just built.

Ezmlm List Names

Every ezmlm list has a list name, which is an email address. The list's address is the submission address to which list mail is sent, with subaddresses used for subscription management, fetching archived articles, and bounce management. If an individual user has set up the list, the list address is a subaddress of the user's address, and all of the list's *.qmail* files and list-specific files are in a subdirectory of the user's home directory. Or the list can have an address of its own in the local domain, in which case its files are in *~alias* because addresses that are neither user addresses nor subaddresses are treated as subaddresses of *alias*. Or the list can have an address in a virtual domain, using qmail's normal virtual domain features.

It's probably easiest overall to put public lists into a virtual domain, so the lists belong to the virtual domain's owner rather than to *~alias*.

Creating an Ezmlm List

The ezmlm-make command creates and manages ezmlm mailing lists. It's not hard to use, but it's fussy about its arguments, particularly file and directory names that have to be specified as absolute paths. The information for each ezmlm list is stored in a directory full of files and subdirectories. (The ezmlm(5) manpage describes the directory's contents, nearly all of which is maintained automatically.) The directory name need not have any relation to the list name, although it's hard to think of a good reason to name the directory anything else. The directory is usually in the owning user's home directory or a subdirectory, although it can be anywhere so long as the user has write access.

Create a list with a user's subaddress; if the list were called *joe-fishing@example.com*:

```
$ # log in as joe
$ ezmlm-make -u ~/fishing ~/.qmail-fishing joe-fishing example.com
```

The arguments are flags, the full pathname of the directory (abbreviated here with ~ that the shell expands), the full pathname of the list's *.qmail* file, the mailbox for the list, and the domain. The –u flag only permits subscribers to post to the list, and is highly recommended. Other options include –m to moderate the list and –d to create a digest version. See the ezmlm-make manpage for the entire huge list of options.

Along with the directory, ezmlm-make creates *.qmail-fishing*, *.qmail-fishing-default*, *.qmail-fishing-owner*, and *.qmail-fishing-return-default*, all linked to newly created files in the *~/fishing* directory. If the list is moderated or has a digest version, there will be two more *.qmail* files for each of those options.

To create a list with a name in the local domain, become *alias* and run ezmlm-make:

```
$ # su to alias
$ ezmlm-make -u ~alias/fishing ~alias/.qmail-fishing fishing example.com
```

Whoever administers this list has to su to alias to run administrative commands, which can be a security problem.

Ezmlm Lists in Virtual Domains

Not surprisingly, ezmlm meshes easily with qmail's virtual domains. If individual users want to run lists, each user who runs lists can have a virtual domain. Or a system that hosts a lot of lists can set up a master list management account controlling many lists in multiple domains. (Or both, of course.) To extend this example, assume that user joe wants to run a set of lists about fish. Create a virtual subdomain, add appropriate MX records in the DNS, and route the subdomain's mail with an entry in */var/qmail/control/virtualdomains*:

```
ichthy.myvirt.com:joe
```

Now Joe can make as many lists as he wants:

```
$ # log in as joe
$ ezmlm-make -u ~/flounder ~/.qmail-flounder flounder ichthy.myvirt.com
$ ezmlm-make -u ~/tilapia ~/.qmail-tilapia tilapia ichthy.myvirt.com
```

This makes two lists, *flounder@ichthy.myvirt.com* and *tilapia@ichthy.myvirt.com*, both managed by Joe.

A larger system with multiple lists in multiple domains isn't much harder to set up. Create a user lists to be the list manager, and then map each virtual domain to a subaddress of the lists user:

```
fish.myvirt.com:lists-fish
fowl.myvirt.com:lists-fowl
fare.myvirt.com:lists-fare
```

To make it a little easier to keep track of all of the lists, each domain has a directory to hold its list directories:

```
$ # log in or su to lists
$ mkdir fish fowl fare
$ ezmlm-make -u ~/fish/scrod ~/.qmail-fish-scrod scrod fish.myvirt.com
$ ezmlm-make -u ~/fowl/duck ~/.qmail-fowl-duck duck fowl.myvirt.com
$ ezmlm-make -u ~/fare/stew ~/.qmail-fare-stew stew fare.myvirt.com
```

This creates three lists, one in each domain: *scrod@fish.myvirt.com*, *duck@fowl.myvirt.com*, and *stew@fare.myvirt.com*. This scheme scales up very well, easily handling a hundred domains each with a hundred lists. (Whether one host could handle the traffic for 10,000 lists is another question, although if the per-list traffic is modest and the computer is fast, the performance could be fine.)

One problem is that all of the .*qmail* files are in the home directory, and each list has four .*qmail* files, so that's 40,000 files in one directory, which most Unix systems won't handle well. If the lists are moderated or digested, it could be as many as 80,000 files. A small change to the virtual domain setup solves the problem by putting each domain's .*qmail* files in a separate directory:

```
fish.myvirt.com:lists-fish/q
fowl.myvirt.com:lists-fowl/q
fare.myvirt.com:lists-fare/q
```

Now the .*qmail* file for *scrod@fish.myvirt.com*, rather than being .*qmail-fish-scrod*, is .*qmail-fish/q-scrod*. Create directories .*qmail-fish*, .*qmail-fowl*, and .*qmail-fare*, each of which contains the .*qmail* files for a single domain with names like *q-scrod*, *q-scrod-default*, *q-scrod-return*, and *q-scrod-return-default*. Or if you want to put the .*qmail* files in the same directory as the list directories, rather than creating separate directories, just symlink the names:

```
ln -s fish .qmail-fish
ln -s fowl .qmail-fowl
ln -s fare .qmail-fare
```

I prefer this last approach. With a hundred lists, the domain's directory has a hundred list directories each with between 400 and 800 .*qmail* files, depending on list configuration, which is still a very manageable number.

Sending Mail to and Testing an Ezmlm List

To send mail to an ezmlm list, just send a message to the list's address. If you've used –u and haven't subscribed yourself, the message should bounce back with an error saying Sorry, only subscribers may post. Now subscribe to your list by sending mail to the list's subscription address. If the list is *fishing@example.com*, the subscription address is *fishing-subscribe@example.com*. Ezmlm should respond to your request with a confirmation message including a return address with a long random string to deter signup forgery. Respond to that message, and you should get a welcome message confirming that you're on the list. Now send another message to the list itself, which should show up shortly in your mailbox. You can check that it came through ezmlm by looking at the message headers that should include headers such as Mailing-List: and List-Post:. Now the list is ready to go, and anyone can subscribe and post to it. Unsubscribing works just like subscribing, so to get off the list, write to *fishing-unsubscribe@example.com* and respond to the confirmation message.

If you created a digest version of the list, the digest acts like a separate list whose name is the list name with -*digest* added, such as *fishing-digest@example.com*. Subscriptions work the same way, *fishing-digest-subscribe@example.com* and *fishing-digest-unsubscribe@example.com*. Subscribers to either version of the list post messages to *fishing@example.com*. The list of subscribers to the main list and the digest are kept separately so it's possible and occasionally useful to subscribe to both the regular list and the digest.

If you made the list moderated, you have to add the moderators' addresses using ezmlm-sub before anyone can post to the list. (See the next section.) Whenever someone posts a message to the list, the message is forwarded to all of the moderators in a message with instructions containing two return addresses, one to accept the message and one to reject it.

Configuring and Maintaining an Ezmlm List

Ezmlm comes with a long list of programs, some intended to be run from qmail when mail arrives, some to be run by list managers, and in a few cases, either way. To add addresses to a list, use ezmlm-sub:

```
$ ezmlm-sub ~/fishing mary@example.com fred@myvirt.com
```

For lists that allow posts only by subscribers, the subdirectory *allow* contains additional addresses that are allowed to post to the list, typically variant versions of subscriber addresses:

```
$ ezmlm-sub ~/fishing/allow mary.nade@example.com
```

If a list has a digest version, the digest subscribers are stored in the subdirectory *digest*:

```
$ ezmlm-sub ~/fishing/digest edgar@example.org
```

If a list is moderated, the moderators are stored in the subdirectory *mod*:

```
$ ezmlm-sub ~/fishing/mod jane@myvirt.com
```

(The list of moderators is unrelated to the list of subscribers. If a moderator should be subscribed to the list, add the address separately to the list and the moderator list.)

To take people off a list, use ezmlm-unsub:

```
$ ezmlm-unsub ~/fishing mary@example.com          # leave the list
$ ezmlm-unsub ~/fishing/allow mary.nade@example.com # alternate address, too
$ ezmlm-unsub ~/fishing/digest edgar@example.org  # leave the digest
$ ezmlm-unsub ~/fishing/mod jane@myvirt.com       # stop moderating
```

The boilerplate messages used by ezmlm for subscription request responses, bounce probes, and so forth are kept in files in the *text* subdirectory of the list directory. The standard messages aren't bad, but to customize them for a particular list, just edit the text files. The files contain codes like <#l#> for the list name that are expanded each time one of the boilerplate messages is sent.

Addresses that bounce are automatically tracked. If an address bounces consistently, ezmlm sends a final probe message and, if the probe bounces, removes the address from the list. In most cases, the bounce management works completely automatically. The only exception is for remote mail systems that mangle the VERP envelope return address so that ezmlm cannot figure out what address is bouncing.

Other Ezmlm Tricks and Features

Ezmlm has provisions for list administration by email for managers without shell access; for message archives, including both mail-based and web-based indexes and retrieval; and a wide variety of other list options, such as rejecting some or all MIME attachments and adding boilerplate text to messages or digests. Ezmlm, like qmail, is built from a collection of small programs run from shell scripts, so even if a particular feature isn't present, it's often possible to adapt the existing programs to do what you want.

For further information, consult the included documentation, which includes manpages for all 30 ezmlm programs, as well as *http://www.ezmlm.org* where there is both a FAQ and a 30-page printable manual.

Using Other List Managers with Qmail

Although ezmlm is the list manager most often used with qmail, any list manager that's written to work with sendmail can easily be adapted to work with qmail. The most popular freeware packages are GNU Mailman, which has qmail config advice in *README.QMAIL*, and the Majordomo2 list manager, which has qmail support for lists in virtual domains built-in.*

Incoming Mail to List Managers

Mail sent to a list manager includes both the messages for the lists and the administrative mail to *--request* addresses and the like. Systems with a small number of lists usually put sendmail alias entries for all of the entries into */etc/aliases*. That also works with qmail, but can get unwieldy as the number of lists grows and if there are collisions between list names and usernames. Systems with lots of lists usually put the lists into virtual domains. Sendmail handles virtual domains differently from qmail, so the setup for qmail has to be a little different. List manager software is usually set-uid because it would difficult to control the UID for programs run from sendmail's */etc/aliases*. With qmail, the virtual domain(s) for the list manager should belong to the list manager user, removing the need for set-uid except perhaps on CGI scripts for web interfaces. The individual list and administrative addresses can each be a *.qmail* file, or it might be easier to put them all in one file and use *fastforward* as described in Chapter 12.

---

* Majordomo1 is obsolete, and anyone thinking of using it should use majordomo2 instead. The commercial packages such as LISTSERV and Lyris include their own SMTP engine so they can run in parallel with qmail on a different virtual IP address, but they don't connect to qmail, or any other local MTA, directly.

Outgoing Mail from List Managers

List managers can hand mail to the MTA in two ways, by calling sendmail or SMTP. Using sendmail makes sense for administrative mail sent to a single recipient. It's a problem for list mail because the operating systems set a maximum total argument size in a call to sendmail or any other program, typically 64 K characters, which would limit lists to under 4,000 names. To get around this limit, the list manager can break the list up into sections and call sendmail multiple times or, more often, open an SMTP session to localhost, which permits an unlimited number of RCPT TO recipients. Either of these techniques works with qmail, although of course calling *qmail-queue* directly works better if a list manager has code to support it.

Some list managers can sort recipient addresses by domain and pass all the addresses in a domain together. This speeds up sendmail, which does domain or MX sorting internally, but doesn't help qmail. In fact, it can lead to somewhat unfortunate behavior; if qmail processes a message with a hundred recipients all in the same domain, it will open a large number of SMTP connections to that domain's mail server, which system managers misinterpret as an attempt to overload their system. If you can prevent your list manager from sorting its addresses by domain, do so.

Sending Bulk Mail That's Not All the Same

Qmail does a magnificent job of sending identical copies of a single message to thousands of recipients.[*] It does a considerably less magnificent job of sending thousands of messages all of which are different each to a single recipient. The overhead of passing a message to *qmail-queue*, storing it in the *queue/todo* directory, then moving it into the delivery queue, is substantial. When large numbers of messages arrive quickly, *qmail-send* can fall behind to the point where it's so busy dealing with injected mail it doesn't schedule deliveries as fast as it should, the so-called "silly qmail syndrome." The big-todo patch discussed in Chapter 16 helps somewhat, but the fastest way to deliver lots of unique messages is to avoid asking qmail to deal with them in the first place. To test this theory out, I wrote a small Perl module Qspam, available as *http://www.iecc.com/Qspam.pm*, to send lots of unique messages fast.

The program sending the mail starts by calling qspam_start(N, &donefunc), where N is the number of deliveries to handle at once (analogous to *concurrencyremote*) followed by a callback routine that's called each time a delivery attempt finishes. To send a message, the program calls qspam_send("to", "from", mfile, code), where to and from are the envelope addresses, mfile is the name of a file containing the entire message to send, headers and body, and code is an optional code string that identifies

---

[*] Identical except for the VERP envelope, of course.

the message. When the delivery is done, it calls the callback as donefunc(mfile, code, resultflag, resultmsg) where mfile and code are from *qspam_send*, and resultflag is "y" if the message was delivered, "n" if the delivery failed (in which case resultmsg is the error message), or a null string if the delivery was deferred until later. At the end of the program, *qspam_flush()* waits for all of the delivery attempts to complete.

How does this all work? Qspam_send forks and calls *qmail-remote* to deliver the message. The module keeps a table of all of the deliveries in progress and won't start more than the delivery limit at once. When an instance of *qmail-remote* completes, if it either delivered the mail or got a permanent error, the delivery is done. If there was a temporary error, Qspam forks again to call *qmail-queue* to use the standard qmail delivery scheme, which always succeeds (from Qspam's point of view). Because *qmail-remote* can't deliver local mail, qspam_send checks the delivery address of each message against *locals* and *virtualdomains* to see if an address is local, and if so calls *qmail-queue* immediately. In practice, most remote delivery attempts succeed or fail on the first try, so only a small fraction of the messages need to be queued. Some mail is accepted by the remote MTA only to be bounced back later, and qmail returns its usual bounce messages if a queued delivery eventually fails, so the application needs to use envelope return addresses that can be handled by a companion bounce processor, just like list mail sent directly through qmail.

Although Qspam wasn't written for maximum efficiency (it opens and closes temporary files rather than using pipes), it's pretty fast. On a modestly sized PC sending lightly customized mail to a list of several thousand users selected from a MySQL database, it has no trouble keeping 100 simultaneous deliveries going at once. The entire application is written in Perl, but it spends nearly all of its time waiting for *qmail-remote* processes to finish so there's little reason to rewrite it to be faster. This approach, try one delivery attempt before queueing, has proven to be a simple but effective way to handle customized list mail.

CHAPTER 15

The Users Database

In Chapter 10, we saw that local deliveries all look up the mailbox in qmail's users database to determine both where to deliver a message, and what user and group ID and home directory to use when making the delivery. Although the most common setup of users is to deliver to the users in */etc/passwd*, the users database is considerably more flexible than a mere mirror of the password file.

The users database maps each local address to a set of user data including:

- Username
- Numeric user ID
- Numeric group ID
- Home directory
- Character to separate parts of a subaddress, usually a dash
- Extension, used to find an appropriate qmail file

The *qmail-lspawn* program changes to the user and group ID and home directory before starting a delivery, then uses the separator character and extension to locate a *.qmail* file to control the delivery, as covered in Chapter 10.

If There's No Users Database

If you don't create a users database, qmail calls *qmail-getpw*, which implements a default mapping from login users to qmail users for each local delivery. It takes the local part, passed as its argument, and looks that up using the standard *getpwnam()* routine. If the user exists and meets some safety criteria (discussed in a moment), it returns user information for the user, uid, gid, and home directory from the password file, and null dash and extension. If the name is of the form *user-extension* and the username exists, it returns the user information with the dash being a literal dash and the extension the part of the local part after the dash. If the user doesn't exist, it falls back to the default user *alias* with the dash being a dash and the extension being the entire local part, so in that case the delivery is controlled by *~alias/.qmail-localpart.*[*]

To avoid security problems, *qmail-getpw* only returns user information if a user account has a nonzero uid (isn't the super-user), and the account's home directory exists, is readable, and belongs to the user. It also ignores any account with capital letters in the name or with a name more than 32 characters long.

Do You Need a Users Database?

Experienced qmail users have widely varying opinions about whether to create a users database. I've always used one, but my system has only a handful of shell users and (mostly for historical reasons) many mail-only users with addresses in the same domain as the shell users. A more typical system either has a lot of shell users, nearly all of whom receive mail, or runs a system where all the addresses are in virtual domains controlled by a few dedicated user IDs. If the list of users in your passwd file is nearly the same as the list of addresses that should get mail, you may be happier with no users database so users can get mail as soon as they're added to the passwd file.

A setup with a users database is somewhat faster, because a lookup in the users CDB is faster than running *qmail-getpw*, and marginally more secure, because *qmail-getpw* depends on the system *getpwnam()* library routine, which can be complex and fragile. But unless you're trying to squeeze every bit of speed out of a mail server, the more compelling argument is what you find more convenient.

Making the Users File

The format of */var/qmail/users/assign* is fairly simple. It's a sequence of lines with two slightly different formats, one for an exact match and one for wildcards. An exact match line starts with an equals sign:

```
=local:user:uid:gid:homedir:dash:ext:
```

This means that mail to address `local` is delivered to `user` with user and group IDs `uid` and `gid` and home directory `homedir`, using a qmail file named *.qmail dashext*. (Usually dash and ext are null.)

A wildcard line starts with a plus sign:

```
+loc:user:uid:gid:homedir:dash:pre:
```

---

[*] You can replace the dash with another character by adjusting the contents of *conf-break* at the time you build qmail.

In this case, any address that starts with loc is handled by the given user, with pre inserted in front of the rest of the address to determine the name of the qmail file. (In this case dash is usually a dash, and pre is usually null.)

Here's a snippet from a real *assign* file:

```
+:alias:121:105:/var/qmail/alias:-::
=carol:carol:108:102:/usr/home/carol:::
+carol-:carol:108:102:/usr/home/carol:-::
```

In this case, mail to carol is handled by the second line, and delivered using */usr/home/carol/.qmail*, while mail to carol-ina is handled by the third line and delivered using */usr/home/carol/.qmail-ina*. Any address not starting with carol is handled by the first catchall line so that mail to, say, fred is delivered using */var/qmail/alias/.qmail-fred*. Note the hyphen in the third line in carol-, so that line matches any of carol's subaddresses, but not plain carol.

Usually the list of users in *assign* is more or less the same as the list in */etc/passwd*, so qmail provides the *qmail-pw2u* utility to create your *assign* file. I use this *Makefile* to control the process:

```
cdb:        assign
        ../bin/qmail-newu

assign: /etc/passwd append exclude
        cp assign assign.old
        ../bin/qmail-pw2u < /etc/passwd > assign
```

When creating *assign*, *qmail-pw2u* uses approximately the same rules as *qmail-getpw*, ignoring any users that have a zero uid, don't own their home directory, or contain capital letters. For each user, the output contains two lines, with the username, user and group IDs, and home directory from the password file, as in the "carol" example.

Several command-line flags to *qmail-pw2u* modify the default behavior and are documented in the manpage, but I've never found the flags very useful. The only ones I've ever used are -h, fail if a user's home directory doesn't exist, and -c, change the separator character from a hyphen to something else, usually a plus sign for compatibility with the subaddressing in sendmail and postfix. What is useful is a set of auxiliary files in */var/qmail/users* that modify the generated *assign* file:

exclude
> A list of users to omit, either because they shouldn't get mail or because their mail setup isn't the default. It should include accounts such as bin, daemon, and uucp that don't have human readers to read the mail. (You can and should create qmail files in *~alias* to forward mail sent to any of those addresses that are likely to get interesting mail, of course.)

include
> A list of users to include. If this file exists, only users in the file have lines generated in the output.

append
> The contents of this file are literally appended to the output. This is usually a combination of mail-only users not in the password file and modified info for specially handled users, e.g., users that don't use subaddresses.

mailnames
> Mail aliases. A line of the form *jim:jim:james:jimmy* makes the second and subsequent fields aliases for the first, and creates a pair of output lines for each alias. Note that if the username doesn't appear as one of the aliases, there will be no entries for the user itself. Most system managers prefer to use *.qmail* files in *~alias* or entries in */etc/aliases* instead.

subusers
> Users implemented as subaddresses of other users. A line of the form *jim:fred:jf:* creates a pair of lines so that mail to *fred* is treated as mail to *jim-jf* and mail to *fred-ext* as mail to *jim-jf-ext*. Except for the simplest setups, again I prefer qmail files in *~alias* or entries in */etc/aliases*.

Assuming you use the *Makefile* shown previously, you just need to run *make* in */var/qmail/users* every time to add or delete a user to or from the password file. Qmail rechecks *cdb* for every local delivery so there's no need to restart qmail.

How Qmail Uses the Users Database

Once you've created the users database, qmail checks it for each local delivery. First it checks for an exact match of the mailbox as a nonwildcard address. If that doesn't work, it tries for the longest match against a wildcard, starting with the full mailbox and shrinking a character at a time until there's a match. (To speed up this process, *qmail-newu* makes a list of the final characters used by all the wildcard entries and stores it in the CDB file. When looking up a mailbox, *qmail-lspawn* only checks substrings where the last character of the substring is one of those final characters.) The wildcard match always succeeds, either against one of the subuser entries, or else against the default wildcard entry created by *qmail-newu,* which looks like this:

```
+:alias:uid:gid:/var/qmail/alias:-::
```

Once *qmail-lspawn* has the user data, either from the database or from *qmail-getpw*, it changes to the user ID, group ID, and home directory, then runs *qmail-local* to read the *.qmail* file and perform the delivery.

Typical Users Setup

The simplest arrangement makes a qmail user for all of the live users in the passwd file. In that case, in */var/qmail/users* create an *exclude* file that lists all of the passwd entries that don't correspond to people, such as root, bin, daemon, uucp, ftp, and lpd. Then create a *Makefile* as described earlier in this chapter, and as the super-user type make. This creates a CDB with an entry for all of the un-excluded users.

Having excluded root, bin, and so forth from your users file, be sure to arrange for mail sent to those addresses to be delivered somewhere, because daemons tend to send reports to those addresses. Either create individual qmail files like *~alias/.qmail-root* or, if you use *fastforward*, put the instructions in */etc/aliases*.

Adding Entries for Special Purposes

If your system acts as a mail server for more than the people with shell accounts, you'll probably want to add some entries to the users database.

Adding a Few Mail-Only Accounts

In many cases, a host serves a mix of shell and mail-only accounts. If the number of mail-only accounts is small, it's not worth installing an entire virtual domain POP system. To handle my mail-only users, I created a user *maildrop* that owns all of the Maildirs for the mail-only users. Each user has a Maildir, so that if fred is a mail-only user, his Maildir is *~maildrop/fred/* and his mail is delivered via *~maildrop/.qmail-fred*, which contains either just the name of the Maildir, *./fred/*, or more likely a call to procmail to filter out viruses and spam before delivery. Fred is a subuser of mail-drop, so his address would be *maildrop-fred* rather than *fred*. To make his plain address work, you can forward his mail via a qmail file *~alias/.qmail-fred* or an entry in */etc/aliases* forwarding to *maildrop-fred*. Or what I do is to use the *subusers* file, with entries like this:

```
fred:maildrop:fred:
```

(Also modify the *Makefile* to add *subusers* to the end of the line starting with `assign:`, so that it rebuilds the users database if the subusers file changes.) This has exactly the desired result, to treat mail to *fred* as though it were addressed to *maildrop-fred*. It also routes subaddressed mail, so if you want Fred's subaddresses to work, you should create *~maildrop/.qmail-fred-default*, which in a simple case can be a link to *.qmail-fred* to deliver all of fred's subaddressed mail the same as his regular mail.

You must also arrange for the POP server to know about the mail-only users. See Chapter 13 for advice on doing so.

Preparing for the POP Toaster

If you have a more complicated mail setup, you may want to add a few custom lines to the users database by putting them in *append*. If you run a POP toaster, a mail server for POP users with mailboxes in virtual domains, and the user mailboxes belong to user pop, but you want to put the mailboxes in */var/popmail* rather than in *~pop*, just add a line like this to *append*:

```
+popmail-:popmail:111:222:/var/popmail:-::
```

(Use the user and group IDs for *pop* rather than 111 and 222, of course.) Once you've rebuilt the users database, any mail addressed to *popmail-something* will be delivered via */var/popmail/.qmail-something* or */var/popmail/.qmail-default*, running as user pop. I find this a convenient way to work, so I can put files of software and notes to myself in pop's home directory, and keep the mailboxes on a separate large filesystem.

## CHAPTER 16

Logging, Analysis, and Tuning

Although qmail performs well in its standard configuration, it's often possible to tune it to work better, particularly for very large or very small installations.

What Qmail Logs

Qmail logs quite a lot of information about what it's doing, although it can be daunting to collect it all together. If you're using daemontools, each daemon has its own set of logs, kept in a rotating set of log files maintained by *multilog*, usually with a TAI64N timestamp (see the following sidebar "TAI64 Time Stamps"). The *qmail-send* process logs each message queued and each delivery attempt. The *qmail-smtpd* process logs each incoming SMTP connection, although it won't describe what happened during the connection. *tcpserver* logs every connection denied due to entries in the connection rules file, and *rblsmtpd* logs every connection it blocked due to a DNSBL entry. If you use QMAILQUEUE to run other programs at SMTP time, anything they send to stderr is logged, and if you've added other patches to *qmail-smtpd*, anything they write to stderr is logged, too.

A system can be set up to do logs analysis on the fly, every time *multilog* switches to a new log file or once a day in a batch. It often makes sense to combine the two, doing some work at switching time and the rest daily. Although it's usually more convenient to keep the logs for each application separate, it's not hard to create combined logs for analysis or just to keep around in case someone needs to look at them later. If a set of logs from different programs all have TAI64N timestamps, merge them using the standard sort program *sort -m*. TAI64N timestamps are fixed-length hex strings, so merging them in alphanumeric order is the same as date order.* Once they're merged, *tai64local* can make the timestamps readable by people. So to merge

---

* Well, unless your system uses EBCDIC rather than ASCII. Unless you're running an obscure mainframe Unix version from the 1970s, it doesn't, so we won't worry about it.

---

a set of log files, all of which have the standard multilog TAI64N names that start with an at-sign:

```
sort -m \@* | tai64nlocal > merged-log
```

TAI64 Time Stamps

TAI stands for International Atomic Time, an extremely precise standard maintained by the International Bureau of Weights and Measures (BIPM). The BIPM is in France, so the acronyms are for Temps Atomique Inernational and Bureau International des Poids et Measures. Dan Bernstein noted that Unix has no generally accepted way to store times at a granularity of less than a second, and the standard 32-bit timestamps can't represent times before 1970 or after 2038, so he devised a new set of TAI-based timestamp conventions for his logs.

A TAI64 label is a 16-digit hex number that represents a 64-bit number of seconds. 4000000000000000 is the beginning of 1970, the same time as a zero Unix timestamp. Smaller or larger numbers represent earlier or later times. A TAI64N label is a timestamp in nanoseconds represented as a 12-digit hex number, which is a TAI64N label followed by another four-digit hex number representing the number of nanoseconds within the second. TAI64N labels are conventionally preceded by an @ sign, like @400000003ff4ccf806d0f4fc. The *multilog* program can prefix TAI64N timestamps to each line of the information that it logs, and *tai64nlocal* translates those timestamps to readable dates and times.

See *http://cr.yp.to/libtai/tai64.html* for more detail.

Collecting and Analyzing Qmail Logs with Qmailanalog

The qmailanalog package extracts statistics from the logs created by *qmail-send*. It consists of *matchup*, which preprocesses the qmail logs; some scripts such as *zoverall* and *zddist*, which collect and print statistics; a second set of scripts, such as *xsender*, for picking out subsets of messages to analyze; and a few other auxiliary programs and scripts. The only C programs are *matchup* and *columnt*, an auxiliary program that neatens up the columns in the reports. Everything else in the package is short awk or shell scripts that are not hard to edit.

Using qmailanalog is more painful than it should be because it expects its input log files to use an older decimal timestamp format used by the now obsolete *splogger* and *accustamp* rather than the TAI64N format used by *multilog*. I have a patch to *matchup* to translate TAI64N to the older format as the logs are read at *http://www.iecc.com/ qmailanalog-date-patch*. The rest of the discussion here assumes that *matchup* has that patch. To build the qmailanalog package, download the current version (0.70 as of this writing) from *http://cr.yp.to*, download and apply the patch, do the usual *make*, then become super-user and make setup check. Normally qmailanalog installs itself in */usr/local/qmailanalog*. To change the installation directory, edit *conf-home*. The setup instructions advise against installing the programs in */usr/local/bin* because some of the names may collide with other unrelated programs.

To use qmailanalog, first you pass the raw logs through *matchup* to create a condensed file with one line per message and one line per delivery. Then the analysis scripts read the condensed files and produce reports. *matchup* writes both the condensed file and a second file listing messages that haven't been completely processed. The next time *matchup* runs, it needs that second file to pick up where it left off. The condensed file is written to standard output, and the second file to file descriptor 5.

Log Analysis at Rotation Time

The condensed files produced by *matchup* are about half the size of the raw qmail logs and *matchup* is fairly fast, so it makes sense to call *matchup* from *multilog* to create the condensed logs each time it switches log files, as shown in Example 16-1.

Example 16-1. Qmail log run with analysis

```
1. #!/bin/sh
2.    exec setuidgid qmaill \
3.    multilog t s4000000 \
4.    !'cat /dev/fd/4 - | /usr/local/qmailanalog/bin/matchup' \
5.    ./main
```

Line 4 in this modified run file creates the condensed logs, using the short quoted shell script as the log processor. Because *matchup* was written before *multilog*, their file descriptor conventions almost, but not quite, agree with each other. When multilog runs the log processor, it opens the existing log file as standard input and as a file of saved data from the previous run on file descriptor 4. The standard output is saved as the old log file, named with the current TAI64N timestamp, and any output on file descriptor 5 is stored away for the next time the processor runs. Although *matchup* does write information about partially processed messages to file descriptor 5, the next run reads that information from the previous run from the standard input along with the next log file. Hence use cat /dev/fd/4 - to read from the two file decriptors and pipe it all to *matchup*. The result of all of this is a set of condensed log files in */service/qmail-send/log/main*.

Log Analysis Once a Day

It's equally possible to do the log analysis once a day from *cron* or */etc/daily*. If the original logs have to be saved, you should do all of the processing at once. In this case, be sure that the file rotation options for *multilog* make the log files it creates large enough and that it saves enough of them to keep a full day's log files. I use "s 4000000" so that each log file is up to four megabytes or a total of 40 MB before *multilog* starts overwriting them.

Example 16-2, to be run once a day, saves the logs as *qmail-send.yyyymmdd* and a preprocessed version as *qmail-summary.yyyymmdd*.

Example 16-2. Daily log save and analyze

```
1.   #!/bin/sh
2.   cd /var/log                   # or wherever logs are archived
3.   a=$(date +'%Y%m%d')           # yyyymmdd
4.   svc -a /service/qmail-send/log # force log rotation
5.   sleep 5                       # give rotation a moment to happen
6.   cat /service/qmail-send/log/main/@* > qmail-send.$a
7.   cat qmail-send.yesterday qmail-send.$a | \
8.    /usr/local/qmailanalog/bin/matchup > qmail-summary.$a 5>qmail-send.tomorrow
9.   mv qmail-send.tomorrow qmail-send.yesterday
10.  gzip qmail-send.$a  qmail-summary.$a  # log files are big, save space
```

The file of incompletely processed deliveries is saved to *qmail-send.tomorrow*, then it is renamed to *qmail-send.yesterday* for the next run. This creates a new pair of log files every day, so you need some provision for deleting old logs now, e.g., to delete logs over a month old:

```
$ find . \( -name qmail-send.[0-9]* -name qmail-summary.[0-9]* \) \
    -mtime +30 -exec rm { } \;
```

Getting Statistics with Qmailanalog

Once the summary files are created, you can run the various summary scripts, all of which have names starting with *z*, to get mail system statistics. All of the scripts read the summary file from their standard input:

```
# Summaries created at rotation time log directory
$ cat /service/qmail-send/log/main/@* |
    /usr/local/qmailanalog/bin/zoverall
# Daily summaries in /var/log
$ gzcat /var/log/qmail-summary.yyyymmdd.gz |
    /usr/local/qmailanalog/bin/zoverall
```

The most useful report is *zoverall*, which as its name suggests produces overall statistics. Example 16-3 is from my main mail server, which hosts some mailing lists, a few dozen personal mailboxes, and the abuse.net message forwarding service.

Example 16-3. A zoverall report

```
Basic statistics

qtime is the time spent by a message in the queue.

ddelay is the latency for a successful delivery to one recipient---the
end of successful delivery, minus the time when the message was queued.
```

Example 16-3. A zoverall report (continued)

```
xdelay is the latency for a delivery attempt---the time when the attempt
finished, minus the time when it started. The average concurrency is the
total xdelay for all deliveries divided by the time span; this is a good
measure of how busy the mailer is.

Completed messages: 56013
Recipients for completed messages: 65158
Total delivery attempts for completed messages: 66940
Average delivery attempts per completed message: 1.19508
Bytes in completed messages: 309400658
Bytes weighted by success: 349381796
Average message qtime (s): 31.3781

Total delivery attempts: 75035
  success: 66080
  failure: 974
  deferral: 7981
Total ddelay (s): 2353455.027418
Average ddelay per success (s): 35.615240
Total xdelay (s): 437123.420922
Average xdelay per delivery attempt (s): 5.825594
Time span (days): 0.631722
Average concurrency: 8.00874
```

In this case, the summary file covers about 15 hours (0.631 days), long enough to be interesting but perhaps not typical of a full 24-hour period. The system is moderately busy with an average of eight messages in transit at once, and the average message dealt with in 31 seconds and the average delivery taking about 35 seconds. (This is unusually slow, probably because abuse.net sends messages to very overloaded recipient hosts via long international links.) This system is configured to permit 110 remote deliveries at a time, but the average concurrency is only 8, so increasing the maximum probably wouldn't make much difference.

Another useful summary is *zsuids*, summary by numeric sender ID, as shown in Example 16-4.

Example 16-4. Log summary by sender user IDs

```
One line per sender uid. Information on each line:
* mess is the number of messages sent by this uid.
* bytes is the number of bytes sent by this uid.
* sbytes is the number of bytes successfully received from this uid.
* rbytes is the number of bytes from this uid, weighted by recipient.
* recips is the number of recipients (success plus failure).
* tries is the number of delivery attempts (success, failure, deferral).
* xdelay is the total xdelay incurred by this uid.
```

mess	bytes	sbytes	rbytes	recips	tries	xdelay	uid
21	27319	27319	27319	21	21	3.736360	0
13	25340	25340	25340	13	13	9.240442	9

Example 16-4. Log summary by sender user IDs (continued)

1608	6597028	30396182	31342313	6143	7233	129119.309333	85
27052	156054190	167640496	168084828	30104	30392	53368.913426	120
113	1552110	1552110	1552110	113	119	120.743584	121
838	7325053	7256425	7325053	838	900	2406.317767	124
4	18179	18179	18179	4	4	64.632176	130
233	1113023	1208518	1210043	299	308	3266.386563	143
1955	6336818	8803216	8968141	2714	2758	20493.535539	162
1028	6983187	6985508	7248128	1120	1155	4744.157863	166
23060	123111117	125207318	129722143	23698	23945	87628.298410	170
24	224755	224755	224755	24	24	11.962693	172
64	32539	36430	36430	67	68	327.511405	32767

In this system, user 85 is majordomo, so most of its messages are to mailing lists. (Note that it sent 1608 messages to 6143 recipients, an average of almost four recipients per message, which is very high.) User 120 is qmaild, which is considered responsible for all mail arriving via SMTP. User 162 is the spam trap, sending out many semiautomatic abuse reports; user 166 is the POP toaster for the individual mail users; and 170 is abuse.net, forwarding third-party messages. It's easy to see that abuse.net accounts for the largest part of the mail traffic, followed by majordomo, the POP toaster, and the spam trap with about equal traffic.

Another level of filters makes it possible to look at just mail to or from a particular address. Use *xsender* to pick out just mail sent from a particular address:

```
# assume /usr/local/qmailanalog/bin is in $PATH
$ cat qmail-summary | xsender fred@example.com | zoverall
```

Use *xrecipient* to pick out mail just to a particular address. The summary file prefixes each address by local. or remote., depending on whether deliveries are local or remote, and virtual addresses are expanded out to the full local address:

```
# assume /usr/local/qmailanalog/bin is in $PATH
# local user
$ cat qmail-summary | xrecipient local.fred@example.com | zoverall
# virtual user
$ cat qmail-summary | xrecipient local.myvirt-fred@myvirt.com | zoverall
# remote user
$ cat qmail-summary | xrecipient remote.fred@domain.com | zoverall
```

There's also *xqp* to pick out particular message numbers, which I don't find very useful.

The full set of analysis programs includes:

zddist

Reports a percentage distribution showing how long mail deliveries take. If 90% of deliveries aren't done within a few seconds, there's probably a network problem.

zdeferrals

Reports delivery deferrals with reasons and can be useful if there are particularly recalcitrant remote hosts.

zfailures

Reports delivery failures with reasons, if you want to see all the bounce messages.

zoverall

Overall summary.

zrecipients

Summarizes all deliveries by recipient, with message counts and sizes.

zrhosts

Summarizes remote deliveries by recipient hosts, with counts and sizes.

zrxdelay

Summarizes deliveries by recipients, sorted by how fast mail to them is delivered.

zsenders

Summarizes messages by envelope sender, with counts and sizes.

zsendmail

A log report that is similar to sendmail's log report, for people who like that sort of thing.

zsuccesses

All successful deliveries, with the log messages and delivery delays.

zsuids

Summarize by numeric user ID.

It can be enlightening to run these programs from time to time to see if there are senders or recipients with inexplicably large amounts of mail, remote hosts that consistently reject large amounts of mail, or other anomalies.

Analyzing Other Logs

There's nothing like qmailanalog for the *qmail-smtpd* logs, mostly because the useful information in them varies so much depending on what auxiliary programs and what patches are in use. I've written some Perl scripts that read through the logs and count the rejection messages for each DNSBL in use, but they rarely reveal anything interesting beyond the dismayingly large amount of spam that's showing up at my mail servers.

Tuning Qmail

More often than not, qmail doesn't need any tuning. It's designed to work well on typical Unix systems. For local deliveries, qmail is usually disk-bound, because it syncs files and directories to disk to avoid losing mail if the system crashes. Although it's possible on some systems to set filesystem parameters to subvert the syncs, that's usually a poor economy. If you want your local mail delivered faster, get a faster disk.* If your system has a lot of unusually slow local delivery programs, or it runs really slow spam filters (Spamassassin can fall into that category), it's possible that local deliveries could be CPU-bound. The easiest way to find that out is with a utility like *top* that shows what's running. Much of the slowness in slow spam filters is due to DNSBL lookups, which are in fact network bound. Modern CPUs are so fast that it's a rare mail system that is even occasionally compute-bound.

Remote deliveries are invariably network-bound. If the goal is to deliver mail as fast as possible, crank the concurrency up as high as possible. Looking at the *zoverview* results, it completed deliveries of 309400658 to 65158 recipients, for an average of a little under 5 Kbps per message. The average xdelay was 5.8 seconds, so each delivery was sending under 1 Kbps. This system happens to be on a T1 line, which can transmit 192 Kbps (that's 1.5 megabits divided by 8 bits per byte). So if each delivery sends 1 Kbps and the channel is 192 Kbps, it takes about 192 simultaneous deliveries to fill up the T1. Note that the ddelay, the time from when a message enters the queue to when a delivery finishes, is 35 seconds, while the average xdelay, the time from the beginning to end of a delivery, is only 5 seconds, which means messages wait 30 seconds to get a delivery slot. The mail traffic on this system is very bursty; a message comes in for a majordomo list and is queued for delivery to the 900 members of the list. The remote concurrency is 110, so the 110 slots immediately fill up and the other 790 deliveries have to wait for slots to be available as deliveries finish. Increasing the concurrency speeds overall deliveries. (I don't do this, because there are web and other servers on the network, and I don't want to squeeze them out every time there's a mailing list message.)

These numbers are fairly typical; if the channel ran at an Ethernet-like 10 megabits, the useful concurrency would be over 1000. Of course, most networks aren't entirely dedicated to email, but these sorts of estimates remain useful for setting up a system to use as much email bandwidth as the system manager wants to use.

Tuning Small Servers

Usually the only tuning needed on a small server is to adjust *concurrencylocal* and *concurrencyremote*. On very small systems with slow deliveries (Spamassassin run from procmail), it may be useful to decrease *concurrencylocal* to limit the hit on system performance from a lot of incoming mail, at the cost of slower deliveries. Set *concurrencyremote* using 1 K per second per delivery so that, for example, a DSL connection with 256 Kbits/sec of outbound bandwidth is 64 Kbytes/sec, so it would make sense to set *concurrencyremote* to 64 to use all of the bandwidth or to 32 to use up to half of it.

---

* If you haven't priced 15K RPM SCSI disks or 10K RPM ATA disks on eBay, you may be amazed how cheap they are. Be sure to get a drive cooler, too.

Tuning Large Servers

Large servers can be tuned and patched to increase the concurrency past what's normally possible. All of the necessary patches are at *www.qmail.org* in the section "Patches for high-volume servers."

For systems with a very large number of injected messages, the big-todo patch improves performance. In qmail's mail queue, most of the queues are divided into 23 subdirectories, with the files distributed pseudo-randomly into the 23 directories, but incoming mail goes into a single *todo* directory. If mail is injected at a high enough rate, the *todo* directory becomes inefficiently large and *qmail-send* falls behind. The big-todo patch by Russ Nelson and Charles Cazabon splits *todo* and the parallel *intd* directory into 23 subdirectories. The patch changes the format of *todo* but not the rest of the queue, so to install it without losing mail, you must ensure that nothing's queued in *todo*. After applying big-todo and rebuilding, use svc -td to stop *qmail-smtpd* and stop any local daemons likely to inject mail, then use svc -td to stop *qmail-send*, then make setup check to install the patched qmail, and use svc -u to restart *qmail-send* and *qmail-smtpd*.

An alternative, more complex, big-todo patch by André Oppermann is available at *http://www.nrg4u.com/*. (Look for the "silly qmail syndrome" patch.) It was written for use with *qmail-ldap*, described in Chapter 13, but it works equally well with regular qmail. It splits the *qmail-send* daemon into two separate processes, *qmail-todo*, which processes newly queued messages, and *qmail-send*, which schedules local and remote deliveries. This patch doesn't change the queue file format, so it can be installed merely by building the patched version, stopping qmail, make setup check to install the new version, and restart qmail. Normally I prefer simpler patches to more complex ones, but in this case, the Oppermann patch does a better job of dealing with a lot of incoming mail, so it's a better choice for systems busy enough that todo is an issue.

Normally qmail is built with a maximum delivery concurrency of 120 local deliveries and 120 remote deliveries. For large servers on fast networks, that's nowhere near enough remote deliveries. To raise the concurrency limit to 255, edit *conf-spawn* and change the 120 to 255, and recompile. This doesn't change the queue format, so to install it, stop *qmail-send*, install, and restart *qmail-send*. You don't need to stop *qmail-smtpd*.

If you need concurrency of more than 255, another patch found at www.qmail.org increases the maximum concurrency to 65,000. As distributed, the components of qmail pass delivery numbers to each other as single bytes. This patch changes them to pass the components as two-byte numbers. It doesn't change the queue format, so to install it, apply the patch, rebuild qmail, stop *qmail-send*, install the patched version, and restart *qmail-send*. The patch sets the concurrency limit to 1,000, which should be enough for most systems. As the patch file notes, if the concurrency limit is 1,000 and a message has 1,000 recipients in the same domain, qmail might try to open

1,000 simultaneous connections to the same server, which managers of some recipient systems might misinterpret as a denial-of-service attack. It's not likely in practice unless you happen to have a mailing list with all of the recipients in the same domain. (Recall that deliveries are made in random order, so a list with 1000 recipients in each of 10 domains does about 100 deliveries at time to each of the 10 domains.)

The final patch for large systems makes the queue bigger. If your system sends a lot of mail that takes a long time to deliver, you may need to enlarge the queue directories. Most Unix filesystems perform poorly with more than 1,000 files in a directory, so the default 23-way split will have trouble with more than 23,000 queued files. If you find yourself in this condition, the code change is easy; just edit *conf-split* to a larger prime number (at least as great as 1/1000 of the number of queued files you expect) and rebuild. But this changes the queue format, so the new version won't work with the existing queued files. Qmail.org tells how to make a smooth transition: before changing the split, stop qmail, move the existing set of qmail files from */var/qmail* to */var/qmail2*, edit *conf-qmail* to refer to */var/qmail2*, and build and install a new temporary copy of qmail with make setup. Run /var/qmail2/rc to start up the temporary version, which will continue delivering mail out of the old queue. Now change *conf-qmail* back to */var/qmail*, edit *conf-split* to increase the split, build and install it with make setup, and restart qmail. All future mail will be handled by the new copy of qmail. After a week or so all the mail in the old copy of qmail will be delivered, at which point you can kill off the *qmail-send* started from */var/qmail2/rc* and delete */var/qmail2*.

Tuning to Deal with Spam

The vast amount of spam sent from forged return addresses to nonexistent recipients causes correspondingly vast numbers of bounces and doublebounces when qmail bounces the spam and finds that it can't deliver the bounce to the nonexistent return address. Because nearly all doublebounces are now due to spam, there's little point in doing anything with them. To throw them away, change the configuration file *doublebounceto* to *nobody*, and if you haven't already done so, create *~alias/.qmail-nobody* containing a single comment line to throw the mail away. (The file can't be empty, because that's treated as a default delivery, but just # will do.)

This still queues and delivers doublebounces. To throw them away without queueing them, apply the small patch at *http://www.qmail.org/doublebounce-trim.patch*, which adds a special case to *qmail-send* so that if *doublebounceto* contains a blank line, doublebounces are just discarded.

Looking at the Mail Queue with qmail-qread

It's not a bad idea to look at the contents of your mail queue every week or two just to see if there's anything strange. The two utility programs to do that are *qmail-qstat* and *qmail-qread*.

For a two-line summary of your queue, run *qmail-qstat* as the super-user:

```
messages in queue: 21
messages in queue but not yet preprocessed: 0
```

The first line is the number of messages that have been queued but not delivered yet. On most systems the number should be small, less than a hundred. If your system hosts mailing lists, the number of messages can reasonably be larger because each list message stays in the queue until every recipient address is either delivered or bounces, and on any list of significant size, there will be a few addresses that have gone bad but take a long time to bounce.

The number of messages not preprocessed should always be zero or close to it. If you have many messages waiting to be preprocessed, it means that qmail can't deliver the mail as fast as it's arriving. If you have a very large mail system you may need to install one of the big-todo patches discussed earlier in this chapter. If not, you should look at the queue in more detail and see what's clogging it up. There's no convenient tool to look at the waiting messages, but if you simply look at the files in *queue/todo* with *more*, you can easily make out the envelope information for each message. The text of the message is stored in a file in a subdirectory of *mess* with the same filename as the *todo* file. To find the message that goes with *todo/123456*, the easiest approach is more mess/*/123456. Don't change or delete files in any of the queue directories while qmail is running, because *qmail-send* does not expect to have files changed or deleted while it's running.

To look at the messages in the queue, run *qmail-qread*, also as super-user. If you don't use mailing lists, its report will probably be quite short, while if you do use lists, it can be enormous. On the host I use for individual user mail, its output is about 50 lines, while on the mailing list host, its output is over 29,000 lines, because the qread output contains a line for every recipient of every message including the ones that have already been delivered, which with mailing lists can add up fast.

```
30 Dec 2003 20:49:34 GMT  #1222959  2113  <mary@example.com>
   done  remote  aaron@myvirt.com
         remote  zelda@somewhere.aq
 4 Jan 2004 04:18:44 GMT  #1223051  11419  <>
         remote  user1@bogus.com
```

In this qread output, the first message from mary@example.com has been delivered to aaron@myvirt.com, but not yet to zelda@somewhere.aq. The second message, which is a bounce because it has a null sender, has not yet been delivered to user1@bogus.com. Deliveries to local recipients say local rather than remote. If some of the deliveries have failed, the report will say bouncing. The number after the # sign in each report is the message number in the queue, so you can find the file for the second message with more mess/*/1223051. The number after the message number is the size of the message in bytes.

When looking at the queue content for hosts with mailing lists, it is useful to leave out the addresses that are done:

```
# /var/qmail/bin/qmail-qread | grep -v 'done'
```

On my list host, that gets the report down from 29,000 lines to 1500.

The results of qread are rarely very interesting, but when they are, if say you see a whole lot of large messages queued to addresses that you don't recognize, they can be the key to tracking down otherwise hard to detect problems.

## CHAPTER 17

Many Qmails Make Light Work

Qmail is well-suited for environments with multiple computers working together, as well as multiple copies of qmail dividing up work in various ways. This chapter starts by looking at the aspects of qmail useful for multiple operation and then explains some common applications.

Tools for Multiple Computers and Qmail

Here's a quick rundown of the tools in our multisystem toolbox.

Multiple Copies of Qmail

Normally, all of qmail is installed in */var/qmail*. That directory is specified at build time in *conf-qmail*. If you change the contents of *conf-qmail* to, say, */var/qmail2* and rebuild and install qmail, you'll create a complete second copy of qmail along with its queue directories. You can send mail into it using */var/qmail2/bin/qmail-queue* or any of the programs that call it, such as */var/qmail2/bin/forward*, or by using *tcpserver* to run a SMTP service with */var/qmail2/bin/qmail-smtpd*. Outbound mail works normally, although you can control it using the standard mechanisms such as *concurrencyremote* and *smtproutes*.

Remember that qmail's queue cannot be on a shared or remote disk; a single local copy of *qmail-send* has to manage each queue.

To pass mail for particular domains from one copy of qmail to the other, you can use either SMTP or *virtualdomains*. To use SMTP, set up a SMTP daemon for the second copy of qmail on localhost (127.0.0.1), but listening on port 26 or any other unused port. Then in the *control/smtproutes/* in the first copy, route the mail for each domain to that SMTP daemon:

```
bad.example.com:localhost:26
```

To route using virtual domains, add *virtualdomain* entries to assign all the domains to a pseudo-user called qmail2:

```
example.com:qmail2
myvirt.com:qmail2
```

Then in *~alias/.qmail-other-default*, forward the mail to the other copy of qmail:

```
| /var/qmail2/bin/forward "$DEFAULT@HOST"
```

The qmail2 version of *forward* will use the qmail2 version of *qmail-queue* to queue the mail in the second copy of qmail. If you've applied the QMAILQUEUE patch, you can set QMAILQUEUE to */var/qmail2/bin/qmail-queue* in any command that queues mail to force the mail into the second copy of qmail.

mini-qmail

mini-qmail is a stripped-down qmail package. It uses QMQP, a faster and simpler scheme than SMTP, to send all mail to another host running regular qmail. Because *mini-qmail* makes neither local nor remote mail deliveries, and has no mail queue (all mail is sent to the QMQP server immediately), it's useful on client hosts in a mail cluster. The details of setting up *mini-qmail* are discussed later in this chapter.

Shared Mail Folders

Maildir format mailboxes can safely be shared read/write using NFS. Each message is written as a separate file, so the hosts creating the files use their hostnames as part of the files they create to avoid name collisions, and NFS does a reasonably good job of making file rename operations atomic; delivery to and retrieval from remote Maildirs works well. This means that one host can deliver the mail into a mailbox and another can pick it up, such as when one is the SMTP server and the other is the POP server. Or several hosts can use a shared Maildir as a gateway to a single host or service.

Sharing mboxes is much less reliable, because it depends on the NFS lock daemon to keep multiple writers in sync. People who share mboxes via NFS usually regret having done so.

Multi-Host POP Toasters

If you use vpopmail, described in Chapter 13, it's straightforward to expand to multiple mail servers for both incoming and outgoing mail. The mail system uses three conceptual parts: the SMTP server(s), the POP server(s), and the mail store. In the simplest case, all three parts reside on a single computer, but it's equally workable to put them on separate computers. The mail store resides on one or more computers running NFS servers, and the SMTP and POP servers mount the NFS partition. The SMTP servers receive the mail and deliver it to the mail store, and the POP servers retrieve user mail from the mailstore. Because Maildirs don't require file locking to work correctly, NFS with all its faults is quite adequate for a reliable system. If there's a single POP server, the CDB user database can reside on the POP server (where it can be updated as needed) with the SMTP servers having read-only access. Or better, build vpopmail using MySQL to keep the user database. All of the hosts can access a single MySQL database to track users, mail quotas, and POP-before-SMTP data. If that becomes a bottleneck, MySQL has built-in database mirroring so that there can be a local copy of MySQL on each server that needs it, mirroring the master database, with all updates fed back to the master. This is a very flexible design that should scale to a huge number of mailboxes and servers.

Another alternative for a multi-host system is *qmail-ldap*. Either it can use NFS for deliveries from multiple SMTP servers to user mailboxes, or the servers can be configured as a cluster in which each user entry in the LDAP database assigns the user's mailbox to a single server. The SMTP servers use QMQP to pass mail that arrives on the wrong server to the right one. Normally, users' MUAs are configured to log into their home server to pick up mail, but if a user logs into the wrong server for POP or IMAP, the session is transparently forwarded to the right one. It's all pretty slick.

Setting Up mini-qmail

Installing *mini-qmail* requires two steps: installing a QMQP server or two, and then installing the *mini-qmail* QMQP client.

Setting Up a QMQP Server

If you already have an SMTP server running, setting up QMQP is easy, because its configuration is much simpler. The only pitfall is that QMQP has no relay protection at all, so you have to make sure that only your own QMQP clients connect to the servers. QMQP doesn't queue, which means that clients discard mail if they can't deliver it to a server immediately, so you should set up at least two QMQP servers if possible.

First, create the rules file to permit connections only from your network. Create */var/qmail/rules/qmqprules.txt*:

```
# only allow connections from our network
:deny
172.16.42.:allow
```

Replace the 172.16.42. line with your own network range(s), of course. If you created a *Makefile* for your SMTP rules file, add the QMQP rules file to it, too, and then run *make* to create *qmqprules.cdb*:

```
default: smtprules.cdb qmqprules.cdb

smtprules.cdb: smtprules.txt
        cat $> | /usr/local/bin/tcprules $@ smtprules.tmp

qmqprules.cdb: qmqprules.txt
        cat $> | /usr/local/bin/tcprules $@ qmqprules.tmp
```

Now it's time to create the directories for the QMQP service:

```
# mkdir /var/qmail/supervise/qmail-qmqpd
# mkdir /var/qmail/supervise/qmail-qmqpd/log

# mkdir /var/qmail/supervise/qmail-qmqpd/log/main
# chown qmaill /var/qmail/supervise/qmail-qmqpd/log/main
```

And create */var/qmail/supervise/qmail-qmqpd/run*:

```
1. #!/bin/sh
2. limit datasize 3m
3. exec tcpserver \
4.     -u000 -g000 -v -p -R \
5.     -x/var/qmail/rules/qmqprules.cdb 0 628 \
6.         /var/qmail/bin/qmail-qmqpd 2>&1
```

In line 4, use the values on your system for *qmaild*. Note on line 5 that the service is running on port 628. Finally, create */var/qmail/supervise/qmail-qmqpd/log/run*. It's identical to its smtpservice equivalent:

```
#!/bin/sh
exec setuidgid qmaill \
    multilog t s4000000 ./main
```

Once you have all the files created, symlink the *supervise/qmail-qmqpd* directory so *svscan* starts it up:

```
# ln -s /var/qmail/supervise/qmail-qmqpd /service
```

If you look at *log/current* you should see the initial tcpserver status line:

```
tcpserver: status: 0/40
```

If you're using more than one QMQP server, repeat this exercise on the other server(s). If you use the same directory structure on each server, you might be able to use cp -Rp to copy the whole thing over rather than recreating each file and directory by hand.

Setting Up QMQP Clients

Once you have the server set up, the QMQP client is easy. *mini-qmail* does no queueing and no local delivery, so what little it does do all runs as whatever user calls it. As a result, you don't need to define any user or group IDs, nor do you need to create the queue or *~alias* directories. Usually the easiest thing to do is to build qmail on the server, then copy the pieces to the QMQP client machines.

All of the QMQP files are read-only, so if you have multiple client systems, all of these files can be shared except for *idhost*, which must have different contents for each host.

What you should install includes:

- In */var/qmail/bin*, include *qmail-qmqpc* and *qmail-inject* (or *new-inject*, linked to *qmail-inject*). You should also install the *sendmail* program, and if you plan to use them, other programs including *forward*, *predate*, *datemail*, *mailsubj*, *qmail-showctl*, *maildirmake*, *maildir2mbox*, *maildirwatch*, *qail*, *elq*, and *pinq*. If you want, install all of the usual programs in */var/qmail/bin* and delete *qmail-queue*, the one program that's not used.

- Symlink *qmail-qmqpc* to *qmail-queue*, so that all injected mail is sent out using QMQP. Also, as on full qmail systems, install qmail's version of sendmail as described in "Sendmail Switching Systems" in Chapter 5.

- In */var/qmail/control*, copy the files *me*, *defaultdomain*, and *plusdomain* from the QMQP server. Create *idhost* with the name of the QMQP client to be used in message IDs. Create *qmqpservers* with the numeric IP addresses of the QMQP servers, one per line. (Use IP addresses, not domain names.)

Once these files are installed, and assuming you've started your QMQP servers, you should be able to send mail using *Mail* or any other mail application. Send yourself a message, make sure it's delivered, and check that it includes a header like this one:

```
Received: from client.example.com (172.16.42.201)
  by server.example.com with QMQP; 13 Feb 2003 01:37:41 -0500
```

The QMQP client produces no logs at all, but you can check the logs on the QMQP server to see what incoming connections have occurred.

Using QMQP

QMQP has three common uses: on a cluster of machines with a mail smarthost, on a network firewall, and for load-sharing with mailing lists.

Using a smarthost

On a network with multiple machines, it usually makes sense to use one or two of them as the mail hosts. That makes the mail system easier to administer, because you only have to manage the configuration on the mail hosts. The rest of the hosts, even if they're doing only one thing, such as running a database or serving web pages, usually send out a little bit of mail with status reports, logs of daily cleanup jobs, and the like. On the machines that aren't mail servers, install *mini-qmail*, being sure to install qmail's version of sendmail to catch all the mail sent by daemons and *cron* jobs. Be sure to disable any startup scripts that attempt to run sendmail as a daemon, because the *mini-qmail* version of sendmail doesn't do that.

Setting up a mail firewall

If you have a firewall or bastion host separating your internal network from the outside world, good security design mandates that you run as few services on the bastion host as possible. If that host is the only one visible to the outside world, it has to run an SMTP daemon, but you can use *mini-qmail* to pass incoming mail directly to the smarthost, minimizing the processing on the bastion host.

On that host, install *mini-qmail* and *ucspi-tcp*. Set up *tcpserver* and *qmail-smtpd* in the usual way described in Chapters 3 and 4. In */var/qmail/control*, create the files *me* with the name of the host, *rcpthosts* with the domain names for which the host receives mail, and *qmqpservers* with the address of the internal mail host. You can also create *databytes* if you want to limit the size of incoming messages.

Even though this setup provides no queueing on the bastion host, if the internal mail host doesn't respond to QMQP when an incoming message arrives, *qmail-qmqpc* (masquerading as *qmail-queue*) will fail, and that will make *qmail-smtpd* fail with a 451 temporary error, which should make the sending host hold on to the message and try it again later.

In most cases, you'll want to do some spam filtering at the gateway using DNSBLs and perhaps *qmail-filter*. See Chapter 9 for details.

Mailing list load sharing

Mailing list software needs a specialized kind of load sharing. A typical mailing list message is delivered to the list manager program, which validates it in various ways, and then remails it to the potentially very large set of addresses on the list. Most list managers also have management interfaces that accept commands via email or a web page to add and remove list members, create and reconfigure lists, and otherwise maintain the lists. It makes sense to run the list management software on one host or set of hosts, and the mail deliveries on another. Fortunately, this is really easy to arrange.

For list managers that interface directly to qmail (ezmlm/ezmlm-index and majordomo2 at this point), outgoing list mail is sent by running *qmail-queue*. To move the delivery work to another computer, it needs only to run *qmail-qmqpc* rather than *qmail-queue*. Ezmlm supports this directly; if the list's directory contains the file *qmqpservers*, outgoing mail uses QMQP. If *qmail-qmqpc* is patched appropriately (the patch comes with ezmlm-idx), it can read the list of QMQP servers from that file rather than the default in */var/qmail/control/qmqpservers*. Majordomo2 has no direct support for QMQP, but because it's written in Perl, it takes about 10 seconds to find the place in the file *QQEnvelope.pm* that refers to *qmail-queue* and change it to *qmail-qmqpc*. I use a two-host majordomo2 setup, and it works very well for me.

Other list managers that aren't aware of qmail either inject mail with sendmail or via SMTP. For mail sent by SMTP, merely configure the package so that the SMTP connection is to the other computer rather than to localhost. Most packages don't send list mail via sendmail due to the argument size limits, using it only to send administrative messages to single users that don't put a lot of load on the mail system. If you do want to reroute the mail injected by sendmail, and you've installed the QMAILQUEUE patch, you only need to ensure that the QMAILQUEUE environment variable is set to /var/qmail/bin/qmail-qmqpc whenever the list package runs, something like this:

```
#!/bin/sh
export QMAILQUEUE=/var/qmail/bin/qmail-qmqpc
exec /usr/lib/listmanager "$@"
```

## CHAPTER 18

A Compendium of Tips and Tricks

The good thing about qmail is that there are simple ways to perform a wide variety of mail handling tasks, even though qmail doesn't have as many task-specific features as other MTAs. The bad thing is that the simple ways are often a less than obvious combination of more basic qmail features. Here is a list some common problems, and some of those tasks and combinations.

Qmail Won't Compile

You have unpacked the qmail sources and typed make, but it won't compile. If you're receiving error messages about errno, you've run into a compatibility problem between qmail and recent versions of the GNU C library. The fix is very simple. See the sidebar "Building with Recent GLIBC and Fixing the errno Problem" in Chapter 3.

(This is the number one question on the qmail mailing list, so frequent that there's an autoresponder that mails back the answer to any message that contains the word "errno".)

Why Qmail Is Delivering Mail Very Slowly

If qmail seems to wait about half a minute to do anything when you inject mail, the problem is almost certainly that the *lock/trigger* file used to communicate between *qmail-queue* and *qmail-send* is messed up. That file should be a named pipe:

```
# ls -l /var/qmail/queue/lock/trigger
prw--w--w-  1 qmails  qmail  0 Nov  7 03:02 /var/qmail/queue/lock/trigger
```

If it's a regular file or anything other than a pipe, you have a problem. Fortunately, it's a problem that's easy to fix:

```
# svc -td /service/qmail-send   # shut qmail down for a minute
# tail -f /service/qmail-send/log/main/current
# # wait until the log says that it's exited
# rm /var/qmail/queue/lock/trigger  # remove bogus trigger
```

```
# cd wherever you built qmail from source
# make setup check    # recreates all the crucial files including trigger
# svc -u /service/qmail-send    # restart qmail
```

This is the second most frequently asked question on the qmail mailing list, and tends to get aggrieved responses pointing out that the answer is in the archives about a hundred times. So don't ask it, because now you know the answer.

Stuck Daemons and Deliveries

Some of the most frustrating problems are due to background daemons that don't do what they're supposed to do. Fortunately the daemontools package makes daemon debugging relatively straightforward.

Daemons Won't Start, or They Start and Crash Every Few Seconds

Starting a daemon under *svscan* and *supervise* is simple in concept, although the details can bite you. The super-daemon is started at system boot time by running */command/svscanboot*. It runs *svscan* to control daemons and the useful but obscure readproctitle, which takes any error messages from *svscan* and puts them into its command area so that ps will show it.*

Every five seconds *svscan* looks at all of the subdirectories of */service* and starts up a *supervise* process on any that don't have one running. In the usual case that the sub-directory in turn has a subdirectory called *log*, it starts a second *supervise* process in the subdirectory and pipes the output from the first process to the second.

When *supervise* starts up a daemon, it runs the file *run* in the daemon's directory. That file has to be a runnable program that either is or, more commonly, exec's the daemon itself. That means that *run* has to have its execute bits set and, if it's a shell script, start with #!/bin/sh so that it's runnable. If either of those isn't the case, there is a failed attempt to start the daemon every five seconds. A ps 1 that shows readproctitle should reveal the error messages and give hints about what needs to be fixed.

The *run* script generally sets up the program environment and then exec's the actual daemon. If you become super-user and type ./run, the daemon should start. If that works, the daemon still doesn't start, and you don't use full program paths in the *run* file, the problem is most likely that the search path that *supervise* uses isn't the same as the one you're using. Look at */command/svscanboot* to see the search patch that it uses. Most notably, it does not include */var/qmail/bin* unless you edit the file yourself to include it.

---

* This odd way of displaying error messages is intended to work even in the presence of serious configuration screwups like disks that should be mounted but aren't and directories that are supposed to be writable but aren't.

Nothing Gets Logged

Sometimes the daemon runs but nothing's going into the log files. This generally is due to either file protection problems or an incorrect set of *multilog* options. The usual way to run *multilog* is to create a subdirectory called *main* in which it rotates log files. It's safer to run daemons as a user other than root, so when possible, use qmaill, the qmail log user. A common error is to forget to change the ownership of the log file directory to qmaill (or whatever the log user is). When *multilog* starts successfully, it creates a *current* log file in the directory, so if there's no *main/current*, the most likely problem is directory ownership or protection.

If *multilog* is running but there's nothing logged, the most likely problems are that the daemon isn't sending anything to log, or that *multilog*'s options are telling it to discard everything. Because the daemon and the logger are connected with a regular Unix pipe, only messages sent to the daemon's standard output go to the logger. In particular, anything sent to standard error shows up in readproctitle, not the log. If, as is usually the case, you want to log the errors a daemon reports, just redirect the error output to the standard output in the *run* script with the standard shell redirect 2>&1. (That redirect is at the end of just about every *run* script example in this book.)

If the daemon is a program originally intended to run as a standalone daemon rather than under daemontools, it probably sends its reports to syslog, not to standard output or standard error. In most cases, there is an option to send messages to stdout or stderr.

If you are using *multilog* options to select what to log, be sure that you're selecting what you think you are. In particular, its pattern language resembles shell wildcards but is in fact considerably weaker because it doesn't move ahead or back up on a failed match. (Patterns do resemble shell wildcards closely enough that they should always be quoted to keep the shell from messing with them.) The pattern must match the whole line, and stars stop matching the moment they see the following character in the pattern. If a pattern is, say, +'+*: status: *', it will match one: status: two, but it will not match one: two: status: three, because the star will stop at the first colon and won't look for the second one. If the pattern didn't have the star at the end, it wouldn't match anything useful because it wouldn't match any lines with anything after the status:. In practice, most log file messages have a pretty simple syntax, and it's not hard to come up with adequate patterns if you keep in mind the limitations of the pattern-matching language. For debugging, start with no patterns to be sure that the stream of messages going into the log files contains what you expect, then add one or two patterns at a time and restart *multilog* with svc -t and see what's going into *main/current* each time until it looks right.

Daemons Are Running but Making No Progress

One of the most baffling problems occurs when the daemon seems OK, the logger seems OK, but the daemon's not doing anything. What's wrong? Usually the problem is that the disk to which the log files are written has filled up or is mounted read-only. Because *multilog* is designed not to lose any log data, if it can't write to the disk, it just waits and retries until it can. This means that the pipe between the daemon and *multilog* fills up and the daemon stalls waiting to be able to write to the pipe. The solution is to delete some files and fix whatever it was that filled up the disk so it doesn't happen again. If the disk is full of files written by various *multilog* loggers, adding or adjusting s and n options to set the maximum size and number of log files can help.

Mail Rejected with Stray Newline Reports

The SMTP spec says that the way that each line of text in an SMTP session ends is with a carriage return/line feed pair (0d 0a in hex or \r\n in C.) Some buggy MUAs and MTAs only try to send mail that contains linefeeds with no preceding carriage return. Qmail's SMTP daemon normally rejects such mail with a log message like Stray newline from 10.2.3.4 because there's no way to tell whether the bare linefeed is just missing a carriage return or it's some kind of malformed binary data.

If you're seeing stray newline entries in your logs and you're reasonably sure that they're being sent by MTAs or MUAs that intend them to be handled as an end-of-line, use the *fixcrio* program from the ucspi-tcp package to placate the SMTP daemon. Modify the *run* script for *qmail-smtpd* so that it pipes mail through *fixcrio*, as shown in Example 18-1:

Example 18-1. SMTP daemon that forgives stray newlines

```
1. #!/bin/sh
2. limit datasize 3m
3. exec tcpserver \
4.     -u000 -g000 -v -p -R \
5.        0 25 \
6. /usr/local/bin/fixcrio | /var/qmail/bin/qmail-smtpd" 2>&1
```

Line 6 is the modified one, starting up *fixcrio* and *qmail-smtpd*. When *fixcrio* runs, it passes the input and output of *qmail-smtpd* through pipes so it can add missing carriage returns in front of newlines as needed. In the longer run, see if you can persuade your correspondents to upgrade their SMTP clients to newer, less buggy versions.

Mail to Valid Users Is Bouncing or Disappearing

If you use *users/assign* as described in Chapter 15, a common mistake is to add a user to the system without updating the *users* file. Fortunately, this oversight is easily remedied:

```
# cd /var/qmail/users; make
```

Mail Routing

Qmail lets you build very complex routing strategies on top of its three basic delivery paths: local, virtual, and remote.

Sending All Mail to a Smarthost

If your qmail system has a full-time Internet connection, route all mail to a smarthost with a default entry in *smtproutes*, e.g., `:mail.myisp.com`. If you have a dialup or other intermittent connection, use a default virtual domain to route all outgoing mail into a Maildir, then when you connect to your ISP, use *maildirsmtp* to take the mail out of the directory and send it to the smarthost. See Chapter 11.

If you have a few locally connected systems to which you can send mail directly, you can also put specific entries for them in *smtproutes*, overriding the smarthost default. If you use *virtualdomain* delivery, you also need not-virtual entries for each of them in *virtualdomains*, e.g., `nearby.com:`. See Chapter 12.

Treating a Few Remote Addresses as Local

If you have local users who use addresses at another system as their return address on mail, you can "short circuit" mail to them and handle mail to them as local, by creating individual address *virtualdomains* entries for them. See Chapter 12.

Slowing Mail Delivery to Certain Domains

Some mail servers have an unfortunate habit of accepting more incoming SMTP connections than they can handle, and then collapsing. The simplest way to limit the number of connections to a server is to route all the mail destined to it into a Maildir using lines in *virtualdomains*, then run *maildirserial* from *cron* to deliver the mail one at a time. Another approach is to install two copies of qmail, the main one with the usual high concurrencyremote level, and a second one with a very low concurrencyremote level of 5 or so. Then in the main system, for any domains that need to be fed mail slowly, use either virtual domains or *smtproutes* to hand mail for those domains to the secondary copy of qmail. See Chapter 17.

Local Mail Delivery Tricks

Even though qmail's local mail delivery design is pretty simple, it still has the flexibility to handle all sorts of situations.

Using a Subaddress Separator Character Other than Hyphen

Some people prefer to use a plus sign rather than a hyphen in subaddresses, so they like *carol+prunes* rather than *carol-prunes*. If you can't persuade them that their life will be easier if they use a hyphen like everyone else, it's not hard to arrange if you use *users* for local mail delivery. Create */var/qmail/users/assign* if it doesn't exist yet, and then in the user's wildcard entry, change the first hyphen to a plus:

```
+carol-:carol:108:108:/home/carol:-::
```

```
+carol+:carol:108:108:/home/carol:-::
```

Then run *qmail-newu* to rebuild the users database. That's all it takes. The plus sign only affects the separator between the name and extension, not the name of *.qmail* files, which will still be *.qmail-prunes* in this case, nor the character that separates subextensions.

In the usual case that the users file changes from time to time as the password file is updated, put the user's name in *exclude* and put the two lines for that user (the modified line that starts with a plus and the unmodified line that starts with an equals sign) in *append* so they'll be included automatically each time *qmail-pw2u* runs.

Customized Bounce Messages for Virtual Domains

Often a virtual domain belongs (logically at least) to a different organization than the main domain on the mail server. When mail to a bad address at the virtual domain bounces, it is nice to give an error specific to that domain. Say the domain *myvirt.com* is routed to the *myvirt* user. If addresses in that domain are handled by individual *.qmail* files, anything that lands in *.qmail-default* is a bad address, easily handled by *bouncesaying*:

```
| bouncesaying "Not a valid user at myvirt.com.  Call 617-637-VIRT for information."
```

If addresses are handled by an alias file created by *setforward*, set -p to tell *fastforward* not to fail on an unknown address so you can handle it yourself. Put these two lines in *.qmail-default*:

```
| fastforward -p myvirt.cdb
| bouncesaying "Not a valid user at myvirt.com.  Call 617-637-VIRT for information."
```

Delivering Mail on Intermittent Connections

If your qmail system is a hub host for remote systems that connect intermittently by dialup, it is straightforward but messy to deliver the mail while the remote systems are connected.

One approach is to create a flag file in a known directory when a host connects and delete the file when the host disconnects. Then run a script periodically from *cron* that loops over all of the flag files to push out mail to currently connected hosts.

To flesh out this example, assume there are three dialup hosts called red.example.com, blue.example.com, and green.example.com. Create *virtualdomains* that give them different virtual domain prefixes:

```
red.example.com:alias-dial-red
blue.example.com:alias-dial-blue
green.example.com:alias-dial-green
```

You can put all of the *alias-dial* mail into one Maildir since the Delivered-To: prefixes keep them separate. To put all the mail for the three hosts into *~alias/dialmail/*, create *~alias/.qmail-dial-default* containing the line ./dialmail/.

To track the currently connected hosts, put the flag files into *~alias/dialflags* and have the dialup connection script create a file with the host's simple name (red, blue, or green) in that directory containing the host's current IP address. Then run this script from *cron* to push out the mail to whichever hosts are currently connected:

```
#!/bin/sh
#  run this every 15 minutes from cron to push out the mail

cd /var/qmail/alias/dialflags

for hn in *
do
   ip=$(cat $hn) # IP address in the flag file

   setlock ../$hn.lock \  # lock deliveries to this host
       maildirsmtp /var/qmail/alias/dialmail \
          alias-dial-$hn- $ip my.example.com 2>&1 |
       splogger serial
done
```

If you also want to push out any waiting mail as soon as a host connects, also put a call to *maildirsmtp* into the host's connection script. Be sure to use the same lock file to avoid confusion if the *cron* job happens to run at the same time. If you add another host called purple, you only need to add another line to *virtualdomains*:

```
purple.example.com:alias-dial-purple
```

The remote hosts can use a similar setup to forward their mail to the main host, using a single smarthost entry in *virtualdomains*. See the discussion of serialmail in Chapter 11.

Limiting Users' Mail Access

Some organizations grant different amounts of access to email to different users. In particular, some are allowed to send mail outside the organization and some can't.

There are a lot of different ways to set this up, but one of the simplest to set up is to create two parallel copies of qmail on the same host, one for restricted users and one for general users. Following the instructions in Chapter 17, create two instances of qmail; the regular one for unrestricted users and incoming mail in */var/qmail*, and the restricted one in */var/rqmail*. Create accounts for all of the users so that every user has a mailbox, and set up a POP (and IMAP if you want it) server.

Set up SMTP daemons for both instances on separate IP addresses, and set up the users' PCs so that the restricted users send their outgoing mail to the restricted server and the unrestricted users to the general server. To keep the restricted users from sending any mail through the general server, add their addresses to */var/qmail/ control/badmailfrom*. To keep them from sending external mail from the restricted server, put this line to fail all remote deliveries into */var/rqmail/control/smtproutes*:

```
:[127.0.0.0]
```

(This is a deliberately bad address that will refuse all connections.)

Another approach that's a little harder to set up but easier to administer is to use a single copy of qmail but to check the mail as users send it. If you use the old-fashioned fixup scheme described at the beginning of Chapter 7 to handle injected mail, you can check whether a user is allowed to send external mail in the fixup script. Modify *~alias/.qmail-fixup-default* to something like this:

```
| bouncesaying 'Permission denied' [ "@$HOST" != "@fixme" ]
| ./checkrestrict
| qmail-inject -f "$SENDER" -- "$DEFAULT"
```

Example 18-2 checks whether the sender is in a list of authorized users.

Example 18-2. checkrestrict script for .qmail-fixme

```
#!/bin/sh
# inherit $SENDER and $DEFAULT from the .qmail file

  case "$DEFAULT" in
      *@example.com) # our domain, always permitted
          exit 0 ;;
      *@*) # external address
          if egrep -q "^($SENDER)$" authorized-users
          then
              exit 0
          else
              bouncesaying "You cannot send external mail."
          fi ;;
      *) # local mail, always permitted
          exit 0 ;;
  esac
```

This script needs to be ruggedized a little, because mail from user fred might have a sender of *fred* or *fred@example.com* depending on how his mail program is set up, and a local recipient address might be *mary@EXAMPLE.COM* in uppercase, but the checking remains quite simple.

If you use *ofmipd*, you can't easily use the fixup trick, but assuming you've applied the QMAILQUEUE patch, you can run *qmail-qfilter* and use a similar script that checks $QMAILUSER and $QMAILRCPTS and returns an exit code of 31 to reject the mail or 0 to permit it. (Remember that if you accept the mail, you have to copy the message from stdin to stdout, too, or the message you accept will always be empty.) Call the checking program, which can most easily be write in Perl or Python, */var/qmail/bin/checkauth*, then create this script called */var/qmail/bin/authfilter* to run it. See Example 18-3.

Example 18-3. Run injected mail through authorization checker

```
#!/bin/sh
# check incoming mail

exec /var/qmail/bin/qmail-qfilter \
    /var/qmail/bin/checkauth
```

Then set QMAILQUEUE to */var/qmail/bin/authfilter*. If you provide web mail for your users, be sure to set QMAILQUEUE when running the web mail application so it also calls the filtering script to check whether a user is allowed to send mail.

Adding a Tag to Each Outgoing Message

Some organizations want to add a footer to every message with text that identifies the company, includes disclaimers, or makes implausible claims about the legal status of messages. This is another problem that's easily solved with *qmail-qfilter*, in this case so easily that it doesn't even need a program of its own, just a two-line script I'll call *addtag*, as shown in Example 18-4.

Example 18-4. addtag script to add a tag to messages

```
#!/bin/sh
exec /var/qmail/bin/qmail-qfilter \
    cat - /etc/mailtag
```

Put the tag in */etc/mailtag*, and set QMAILQUEUE to run the tagging script in *ofmipd* and anywhere else that mail is injected. If local programs inject mail with sendmail, you might want to rename */var/qmail/bin/sendmail* to *realsendmail* and put this in its place:

```
#!/bin/sh
QMAILQUEUE=/var/qmail/bin/addtag exec /var/qmail/bin/realsendmail "$@"
```

If you use the older fixup approach to inject mail, you can add the tag in *.qmail-fixup-default*, as shown in Example 18-5.

Example 18-5. .qmail-fixup that adds a tag

```
| bouncesaying 'Permission denied' [ "@$HOST" != "@fixme" ]
| cat - /etc/mailtag | qmail-inject -f "$SENDER" -- "$DEFAULT"
```

Logging All Mail

Some organizations need to log all email passing in or out of their system. An obscure feature called QUEUE_EXTRA makes this quite straightforward. Every time *qmail-queue* enqueues a message, it adds the string QUEUE_EXTRA to the recipient addresses. Normally that string is empty, but you can edit *extra.h* in the qmail source code to be whatever you want. The usual change (recommended in the qmail FAQ) is to make it add a recipient called *log* to each message. Change QUEUE_EXTRA to be the exact string to add to the recipient string including the leading T and trailing null, and set QUEUE_EXTRALEN to be the length of the string. Then rebuild and reinstall qmail. See Example 18-6.

Example 18-6. Code in extra.h to copy everything to log

```
#define QUEUE_EXTRA "Tlog\0"
#define QUEUE_EXTRALEN 5
```

Now every message will be copied to the address *log*, so you can create *~alias/.qmail-log* to save the mail:

```
./logmaildir/
```

The *.qmail* file must save the mail but cannot forward it. Why not? Because forwarding mail invokes *qmail-queue* again, which will redeliver the mail to *log*, creating a nasty mail loop.

Setting Mail Quotas and Deleting Stale Mail

Because qmail's mailboxes are normally in each user's home directory, any quota scheme that applies to the user's files automatically includes the file(s) in the mailbox. For many purposes, this is all the mail quota that's needed. You may want to apply Jeff Hayward's quota exceeded patch to *qmail-local* that recognizes an over quota error and treats it as a hard error so mail is bounced back to the sender, rather than a soft error so mail stays in the queue.

For POP toasters, the vpopmail package discussed in Chapter 13 includes code to enforce mail quotas. If you build your own simpler POP-only system, use the *mailquotacheck* script in *.qmail* files to check quotas as mail is delivered. (All these have links at www.qmail.org.)

You may also want to set a policy for stale mail, so that mail is deleted from the server after some period of time. If you use Maildirs, this is very easy to implement, because each message is in a separate file with a timestamp. In each Maildir, messages in the *new* subdirectory haven't been read, and messages in *cur* have been read and left on the server. My policy is to delete unread mail after a month, on the theory that if you don't look at your mail once a month, you'll probably never look at it at all, and to delete read mail after three months. This is easily arranged with a

---

couple of shell commands to run every day or every week. While you're at it, you might as well delete mail that's been marked deleted (the T flag in the filename) or moved into the Trash subfolder. If all the user directories are under */home*:

```
cd /home
{
    # unread mail over a month old
    find /home/*/Maildir/new -type f -mtime +30 -p
    # read mail over three months
    find /home/*/Maildir/cur -type f -mtime +90 -p
    # any mail marked deleted
    find */Maildir -type f -name "*:2,*T*" -print
    # any mail in Trash/new or cur
    find */Maildir/.Trash/??? -type f -print
} | xargs -t rm
```

If your Maildirs are somewhere else, modify the find commands appropriately to look where they are. By adding a few more commands, you can add policies like deleting mail from a spam subfolder after a week and other subfolders after some other amount of time. With slightly fancier programming, probably in Perl, it's also straightforward to delete the oldest files from a Maildir until the user is under quota. The elegance of the Maildir design makes this all much easier than with mboxes because nothing has to be locked or rewritten, and the cleanup can proceed safely while mail deliveries are going on.

Backing Up and Restoring Your Mail Queue

The bad news about backing up and restoring your mail queue in */var/qmail/queue* is that it's nearly impossible. The good news is that it's rarely necessary.

The filenames in qmail's queue directory are numbers that depend on the inode number of the file containing the text of the message. Backup and restore programs don't restore files using the same inodes that the files used when they were backed up, which means that if you back up the queue and then restore it, it won't work.

If you're moving your qmail queue from one disk to another, there are two general strategies. If you can run your system with both disks for a while, rename the old queue to something like */var/old-qmail*, build two copies of qmail as described in Chapter 17 (one for the old queue and one for the new one) start up both copies so that new mail goes into the new queue while mail in the old queue is eventually delivered or bounces, and then delete the old queue and its copy of qmail. The other is just to bite the bullet and move the queue. To do that, first shut down both *qmail-send* and anything that might put mail into the queue, preferably by shutting down the system to single user. Then copy the queue to */var/qmail/queue.old* on the new disk, and use Harald Hanche-Olsen's script at *http://www.qmail.org/queue-rename* to rename the files to their correct names based on their current inode numbers. You can also use the more complex *queue-fix* program for www.qmail.org, but for this purpose you don't need anything that fancy.

If your disk fails and you restore from backups, it's usually more trouble than it's worth to restore the queue. If your backup is more than a few minutes old, nearly all of the messages in the queue when it was dumped will have been delivered, and the only ones not delivered are likely to bogus addresses that will never be delivered. To clean out the queue, shut down qmail and anything that might try to queue mail, then delete any queued mail with `rm -rf /var/qmail/queue/*` (be sure to type that correctly), go to the directory where you built qmail and `make setup check` to recreate an empty queue, and then restart qmail.

A Sample Script

A Mail-to-News Gateway

This is my batch news gateway, run every five minutes from *cron*. The incoming messages to the gateway are stored in a Maildir *~alias/newsdir*, using a virtual domain setup that sends mail to the pseudo-domains *news* and *news.example.com* to *alias-news*, which is delivered by *~alias/.qmail-news-default*.

My news gateway handles news from multiple hosts on my network by the simple trick of symlinking *newsdir*, which is exported over the LAN by NFS, into *~alias* on each host, so that all the hosts store messages into the same directory. I find this easier and faster than running a copy of the gateway on each host.

The script *run* from *cron* uses *maildirserial* to select mail messages, and *tcpclient* to open an NNTP connection to the local news server, as shown in Example A-1.

Example A-1. Script called from cron to push out news

```
#!/bin/sh

exec setlock newsdir.lock \
    maildirserial -b -t 345600 newsdir alias-news- \
        tcpclient localhost 119 \
                /var/qmail/alias/newsgate alias-news-
```

The actual mail to news script is fairly long, but nearly all of it is devoted to cleaning up headers, as shown in Example A-2.

Example A-2. Mail to news gateway script

```
#!/usr/bin/perl
# -*- perl -*-
# process batched messages from maildirserial into news

use Getopt::Std;
use FileHandle;
```

Example A-2. Mail to news gateway script (continued)

```perl
# options
# -d  debug, use tty for I/O
# -s  don't use date from incoming messages
#     to avoid complaints about stale news

getopts('ds');

$linelimit = 2000; # truncate long msgs after this many lines

$| = 1;

# get prefix to strip off Delivered-To:
$prefix = shift or die "need prefix";

# read null terminated input for file names
msgloop:
while(!eof STDIN) {
    my ($from, $sender, $replyto);
    {
        local $/ = "\0";
        $fn = <STDIN>;
        chop $fn;
    }

    open(MSG, $fn) or die "cannot open '$fn'\n";

    if(<MSG> =~ m{Return-Path: <(.*)>}) {
        $sender = $1;
    } else {
        close MSG;
        print "$fn\0Dno sender address\n";
        next;
    }

    # invent fake sender since news forbids null return addrs
    $sender = "MAILER-DAEMON\@somewhere.local" if $sender eq "";

    if(<MSG> =~ m{Delivered-To: $prefix(.*)}) {
        $recip = $1;
    } else {
        close MSG;
        print "$fn\0Dno recipient address\n";
        next;
    }
    my $approve = 0;
    my $nobounce = 0;
    my ($newrecip, $domain) = ($recip =~ m{(.*)\@(.*)}); # dump domain

    # make sure sent to something@news to prevent
    #  outside mail from sneaking in
    if($domain =~ /^news/) {
        $recip = $newrecip;
```

Example A-2. Mail to news gateway script (continued)

```
    } else {
        print "$fn\0DYou cannot send mail to this address.\n";
        close MSG;
        next;
    }
    $newsgroups = lc $recip;

    # pick off approve- and nobounce- prefixes
    while(1) {
        if($newsgroups =~ /^approve-(.*)/) {
            $newsgroups = $1;
            $approve = 1;
        } elsif($newsgroups =~ /^nobounce-(.*)/) {
            $newsgroups = $1;
            $nobounce = 1;
        } else {
            last;
        }
    }
}

# slurp up the header and regularize some of the lines
    my @headers = ( );
    $from = "";
    while(<MSG>) {
        last if /^$/;

        chomp;

        # skip blank subject
        next if /^Subject:\s*$/;

        if(/^From:/io) {
            s/ MAILER-DAEMON / MAILER-DAEMON\@somewhere.local /;
            s/<MAILER-DAEMON>/<MAILER-DAEMON\@somewhere.local>/;
            s/<>/<MAILER-DAEMON\@somewhere.local>/;
            s/:\s*\(\)/: <MAILER-DAEMON\@somewhere.local>/;
            s/<postmaster>/<postmaster\@somewhere.local>/;
        }
        if(/^\s/) {
            s/^\s+//;
            $_ = pop(@headers) . " " . $_;
            push @headers, $_;
        } else {
            s/:(\S)/: $1/;                    # force a space after the colon
            push @headers, $_;
        }
        $subject = $1 if /^Subject: *(.*)/ois;
        print STDERR "found subject $subject\n" if /^Subject: *(.*)/ois;
        $from = $1 if /^From: +(.*)/ois;
        $replyto = $1 if /^Reply-To: +(.*)/ois;
        $sender = $1 if /^Sender: +(.*)/ois;
    }
```

Example A-2. Mail to news gateway script (continued)

```
# figure out who it's from
    $from = $replyto if $replyto;
    $from = $sender unless $from;

    $from =~ s/\s+$//;
    $subject =~ s/\s+$//;

# now strip out the crud
    if( $from =~ /<(.*)>/s) {
        $from = $1;
    } else {
        $from =~ s'\s*\(([^)]*)\)\s*''sg; # strip comments
    }

# check for bogus addresses
    unless ( $from =~ m/.*\@.*\.[a-z]{2,8}$/io ) {
        print "$fn\0ZInvalid return address '$from', discarded\n";
        close MSG;
        next msgloop;
    }

    # start up an NNRP session on open tcp socket
    startnews();

# tell news server we're going to post something
    print NOUT "post\r\n";
    $l = <NIN>;
    $l =~ s/\r?\n$//;
    unless($l =~ /^340 /) {
        print "$fn\0ZCannot post $l\n";
        close MSG;
        next;
    }

# now send the nessage headers, cleaning up as we go
    print NOUT "Newsgroups: $newsgroups\r\n";
    print NOUT "Approved: news-to-mail\r\n" if $approve;
    unless($subject) {
        print NOUT "Subject: (no subject)\r\n";
    }

    $didmsgid = 0;
    $diddate = 0;
    $didcte = 0;
    $didmv = 0;
    $diddate = 0;
    $didsubject = 0;
    $didreply = 0;
    $didfrom = 0;
    $didref = 0;
    $didcc = 0;
```

```
    $didto = 0;

    foreach $_ (@headers) {

        next if /^(Newsgroups|Sender|Status|Received|Approved|nntp\S+):/io;
        next if /^(Via|X-Mailer|Path|Return-Path|Distribution|X-Status|Xref):/io;
        next if /^(Apparently-To|X-Trace|X-Complaints-To):/io;

    # inews freaks on long headers
        $_ = substr($_, 0, 500) if length($_) > 500;

    # really freaks on long references

        # lose blank subject
        next if m/^Subject:\s*$/io;

        # some headers can only appear once
        next if m/^date:/io && $diddate++;
        next if m/^Content-Transfer-Encoding:/io && $didcte++;
        next if m/^Mime-Version:/io && $didmv++;
        next if m/^Date:/io && $diddate++;
        next if m/^Subject:/io && $didsubject++;
        next if m/^From:/io && $didfrom++;
        next if m/^Reply-To:/io && $didreply++;
        next if m/^References:/io && $didref++;
        if(m/^Cc:/io) {
            print NOUT "X-" if $didcc++;
        }
        if(m/^To:/io) {
            print NOUT "X-" if $didto++;
        }

    # turn Date: into X-Date: if -s
        print NOUT "X-" if $opt_s and /^(Date):/io ;
        print NOUT "X-Old-" if /^(Sender|x-complaints):/io ;

    # only one message ID, and it has to be a good one
        if(/^Message-ID:/io) {
            # if bad msgid, let it gen a new one
            next unless /^Message-ID: +<(.*@[^@ ]+)>$/io;
            next if $didmsgid;
            $didmsgid = 1;
        }
        print NOUT "$_\r\n";
    }
    print NOUT "From: $sender\r\n" unless $didfrom;
    print NOUT "Subject: [probably spam, from $sender]\r\n" unless $didsubject;

# end of header
    print NOUT "\r\n";

    my $didbody = 0;
```

Example A-2. Mail to news gateway script (continued)

```perl
# copy the body, split overlong lines
    my $linecount = 0;
    while(<MSG>) {
        if(++$linecount > $linelimit) {
            print NOUT "\r\n[ message too long, truncated ]\r\n";
            last;
        }
        chomp;
        s/^\./../;
        while(m/^(.{500})(.+)$/) {
            print NOUT "$1\r\n";
            $_ = "+ $2";
        }
        print NOUT "$_\r\n";
        $didbody++;
    }
    print NOUT "[empty message]\r\n" unless $didbody;
    close MSG;

# end of message, see if the server liked it and report back
    print NOUT ".\r\n";
    $l = <NIN>;
    $l =~ s/\r?\n$//;
    if($l =~ /^240 /) {
        print "$fn\0Kposted to $newsgroups\n";
    } elsif($nobounce) {
        print "$fn\0Kfailed to $newsgroups (ignored) $l\n";
    } elsif($l =~ /^441 435 /) {
        print "$fn\0D$l\n";          # perm fail, duplicate
    } else {
        print "$fn\0Z$l\n";          # temp fail, anything else
    }
# done with this message
}

# end news session
stopnews( );

exit 0;

################################################################

sub startnews {
    my ($fn) = $_;
    my $l;

    return if $newsstarted;

    if($opt_d) {
        open(NIN, "</dev/tty");
        open(NOUT, ">/dev/tty");
    } else {
```

```
        open(NIN, "<&=6");
        open(NOUT, ">&=7");
    }
    autoflush NOUT 1;

    # wait for prompt
    $l = <NIN>;
    $l =~ s/\r?\n$//;
    unless( $l =~ /^200 /) {
        print "$fn\0Z$l\n";
        exit;
    }

    print NOUT "mode reader\r\n";
    $l = <NIN>;
    $l =~ s/\r?\n$//;
    unless( $l =~ /^200 /) {
        print "$fn\0Z$l\n";
        exit;
    }

    $newsstarted = 1;
}

sub stopnews {
    return unless $newsstarted;

    print NOUT "quit\r\n";
}
```

Online Qmail Resources

Qmail is well supported by its online community of users. Here are some places to look.

Web Sites

There are several excellent sources of qmail information online.

http://cr.yp.to
> Dan Bernstein's web site, the official source for qmail and all of his ad-on packages.

http://www.qmail.org
> Russ Nelson's qmail resource site, intended to have links to all of the other resources on the Web.

http://qmail.gurus.com
> The author's companion site for this book, containing scripts, updates and corrections, links to other resources, and ordering info for more copies.

http://www.lifewithqmail.org
> Dave Sill's *Life with qmail*, an online guide to setting up and using qmail. It offers specific advice about where to install qmail, and where to put all of the files and directories that qmail needs. This is by far the most widely used setup and the one that qmail experts are the most familiar with, so it's the one you should use. The file and directory locations used in this book are consistent with these.

http://www.lifewithqmail.org/ldap/
> Henning Brauer's *Life with qmail-ldap*, a guide to setting up *qmail-ldap*. Indispensable for *qmail-ldap* users.

http://www.ezmlm.org
> The home page for the ezmlm-idx mailing list manager, with software and documentation.

http://tinydns.org

Russ Nelson's site for Dan Bernstein's *djbdns*, a DNS package that relates to BIND roughly as qmail relates to sendmail. Not required for qmail, but if you're setting up a DNS server along with your mail server, it's probably the software you want to use.

Mailing Lists

The qmail community has a variety of mailing lists. While it's possible to get excellent advice on them, the givers of advice can be rather impatient with questions from people who appear not to have checked the list archive to see if their question has been asked and answered a dozen times before, or who ask questions without giving enough detail to provide a useful answer. So be sure to read a list's archives both to look for your question and to get the tone of the list before asking.

Needless to say, all the lists about qmail are maintained in ezmlm or ezmlm-idx so that you subscribe to any of them by writing to the list address with *-subscribe* appended and then respond to the challenge. For anti-spam purposes, Dan Bernstein's lists at list.cr.yp.to also use a program called *qsecretary* that sends a confirmation challenge each time you send something to the list.

The qmail list qmail@list.cr.yp.to

A discussion list about qmail is maintained. Archives are available at *http://www.ornl.gov/lists/mailing-lists/qmail*.

The qmail announcement list qmailannounce@list.cr.yp.to

Announcements about new versions of qmail. Very low volume.

The ezmlm list ezmlm@list.cr.yp.to

Discussions about ezmlm and ezmlm-idx. Partial archive at *http://madhaus.utcs.utoronto.ca/ezmlm/archive/maillist.html*.

Index

We'd like to hear your suggestions for improving our indexes. Send email to *index@oreilly.com*.

D

daemons
  defined, 28
  SMTP
    configuring, 35
    principles of operation, 70
  supervise, 28
  svscan, running, 29
  troubleshooting
    empty logs, 203
    no progress, 203
    no start/crash conditions, 202
databases
  SQL, vpopmail and, 155
  users
    address mapping, 177
    advisability of using, 178
    changing subaddress separator
      character, 206
    creating, 178–180
    creating mail-only accounts, 181
    POP toaster and, 181
    principles of operation, 180
databytes control file, 44
Date header (rewriting), 66
debugging gateway program, 136
DEFAULT environment variable, 113
defaultdomain control file, 30, 43
  masquerading hostnames, 56
defaulthost control file, 30, 44
  masquerading hostnames, 56
delivery
  ~alias mailbox, 48
  avoiding remote server crashes, 205
  bulk mail handling, 175
  dialup connections, advice about, 206
  to ezmlm, 172
  local mail
    addresses, 107
    bounce handling, 117
    bounce handling, double
      bounces, 119
    bounce handling, triple bounces, 119
    mailboxes and, 111
    problem prevention techniques, 110
    qmail file selection, 108
    user identification, 107
  location options, 27
  mailing list handling, 175
  to mailing lists, 164
  parallel, limit command and, 32
  procmail, configuring as delivery
    agent, 40
  remote
    failure error messages, 123
    secondary MX servers, 122
    TCP failure handling, 122
  sendmail local mail, configuration, 55
  testing, 33
  troubleshooting slow delivery, 201
  user database, 116
  utilities, 114
  vpopmail bulletins, 154
delivery time filtering tools, 102
denial-of-service attacks, preventing with
    limit command, 36
deny rules, spam and virus filtering, 94
dialup connections
  delivery advice, 206
  serialmail, 125
    implementing, 126
directories
  log, 32
  POP server, configuration, 142
  supervise, creating, 32
discussion lists, mail sorting
    considerations, 86
DNS (Domain Name System)
  virtual domains, 128
DNS (Domain Name System)
  black lists spam and virus filtering, 93
  purpose of, 4
DNSBL, 93
DNSWL, 93
domains
  addresses, 4
  domain-wide bulletin delivery
    (vpopmail), 154
  qmail compared to sendmail, 57
  remote, 57
  routing, uucp hosts, 58
  virtual
    address aliases, 138
    configuring vpopmail, 149
    creating batched gateways, 134–137
    customized bounce messages, 206
    defined, 127
    ezmlm lists, 171
    management, 11
    mapping addresses with
      fastforward, 129

About the Author

John R. Levine, founder of Taughannock Networks (*http://taugh.com*), writes, speaks, and consults on email, the Internet, and other computer topics. He has written over 20 technical books and is the coauthor of *lex & yacc* (O'Reilly). He's deeply involved in Internet email in general and spam issues in particular as cochair of the Internet Research Task Force's Anti-Spam Research Group (*http://asrg.sp.am*) and a board member of the Coalition Against Unsolicited Commercial Email (*http://www.cauce.org*).

He lives and works in the tiny village of Trumansburg, New York (*http://www.trumansburg.ny.us*) where he reports that being the municipal sewer commissioner is a much cleaner job than dealing with spammers.

Colophon

Our look is the result of reader comments, our own experimentation, and feedback from distribution channels. Distinctive covers complement our distinctive approach to technical topics, breathing personality and life into potentially dry subjects.

The animal on the cover of *qmail* is a tawny owl. Generally, it's dark brown and streaked with black and buff, but occasionally, it is grey. The tawny owl is the most common owl in Britain, and its distribution extends from Europe to North Africa and eastward to Iran and western Siberia. It is also found in India, southern China, Korea, and Taiwan.

The tawny owl does not built its own nest, rather it nests in natural holes and in the abandoned nests of crows, magpies, and even the nests of buzzards. It remains within its nesting territory all year round and pairbonds last for life. The female tawny owl will stay with her nestlings while the male gathers food. While the male hunts for rabbits, moles, mice, shrews, and other rodents, the female defends her territory passionately with threatening behavior and erratic flying. Occasionally, a human is attacked; in Britain, at least two people are known to have lost an eye, including Eric Hosking, the famous bird photographer.

The tawny owl is best known for its distinctive song. The normal song of the male owl announces territory, courtship, and food. The song begins with a drawn out hooo and then is followed by a pause before the male owl abruptly sings out ha, followed immediately by huhuhuhooo. Occasionally, the female tawny owl makes a similar hooting sound in response to the male's call. However, unlike the clear, resonant sound of the male song, the female's song possesses a wailing quality of wowowhooo. The duet that is performed between the two has led to a myriad of names for the tawny owl, including Billy hooter and Jenny howlet.

Sarah Sherman was the production editor and the copyeditor for *qmail*. Genevieve d'Entremont was the proofreader. Reg Aubry and Mary Anne Weeks Mayo provided quality control. Tom Dinse wrote the index.

Emma Colby designed the cover of this book, based on a series design by Edie Freedman. The cover image is a 19th-century engraving from the Dover Pictorial Archive. Emma Colby produced the cover layout with QuarkXPress 4.1 using Adobe's ITC Garamond font.

David Futato designed the interior layout. This book was converted by Joe Wizda to FrameMaker 5.5.6 with a format conversion tool created by Erik Ray, Jason McIntosh, Neil Walls, and Mike Sierra that uses Perl and XML technologies. The text font is Linotype Birka; the heading font is Adobe Myriad Condensed; and the code font is LucasFont's TheSans Mono Condensed. The illustrations that appear in the book were produced by Robert Romano and Jessamyn Read using Macromedia FreeHand 9 and Adobe Photoshop 6. This colophon was written by Sarah Sherman.

Related Titles Available from O'Reilly

Networking

802.11 Security

802.11 Wireless Networks: The Definitive Guide

BGP

Building Wireless Community Networks, *2nd Edition*

Cisco IOS Access Lists

Cisco IOS in a Nutshell

Designing Large-Scale LANs

DNS & BIND Cookbook

DNS & BIND, *4th Edition*

Essential SNMP

Hardening Cisco Routers

Internet Core Protocols

IP Routing

IPv6 Essentials

LDAP System Administration

Managing NFS and NIS, *2nd Edtion*

Network Troubleshooting Tools

Networking CD Bookshelf, *Version 2.0*

Postfix: The Definitive Guide

Practical VoIP Using Vocal

RADIUS

Samba Pocket Reference, *2nd Edition*

sendmail, *3rd Edition*

sendmail Cookbook

Solaris 8 Administrator's Guide

TCP/IP Network Administration, *3rd Edition*

Unix Backup and Recovery

Using Samba, *2nd Edition*

Using SANs and NAS

Keep in touch with O'Reilly

1. Download examples from our books

To find example files for a book, go to:

www.oreilly.com/catalog

select the book, and follow the "Examples" link.

2. Register your O'Reilly books

Register your book at *register.oreilly.com*

Why register your books?
Once you've registered your O'Reilly books you can:

- Win O'Reilly books, T-shirts or discount coupons in our monthly drawing.
- Get special offers available only to registered O'Reilly customers.
- Get catalogs announcing new books (US and UK only).
- Get email notification of new editions of the O'Reilly books you own.

3. Join our email lists

Sign up to get topic-specific email announcements of new books and conferences, special offers, and O'Reilly Network technology newsletters at:

elists.oreilly.com

It's easy to customize your free elists subscription so you'll get exactly the O'Reilly news you want.

4. Get the latest news, tips, and tools

www.oreilly.com

- "Top 100 Sites on the Web"—PC Magazine
- CIO Magazine's Web Business 50 Awards

Our web site contains a library of comprehensive product information (including book excerpts and tables of contents), downloadable software, background articles, interviews with technology leaders, links to relevant sites, book cover art, and more.

5. Work for O'Reilly

Check out our web site for current employment opportunities:

jobs.oreilly.com

6. Contact us

O'Reilly & Associates
1005 Gravenstein Hwy North
Sebastopol, CA 95472 USA

TEL: 707-827-7000 or 800-998-9938
        (6am to 5pm PST)

FAX: 707-829-0104

order@oreilly.com
For answers to problems regarding your order or our products. To place a book order online, visit:

www.oreilly.com/order_new

catalog@oreilly.com
To request a copy of our latest catalog.

booktech@oreilly.com
For book content technical questions or corrections.

corporate@oreilly.com
For educational, library, government, and corporate sales.

proposals@oreilly.com
To submit new book proposals to our editors and product managers.

international@oreilly.com
For information about our international distributors or translation queries. For a list of our distributors outside of North America check out:

international.oreilly.com/distributors.html

adoption@oreilly.com
For information about academic use of O'Reilly books, visit:

academic.oreilly.com

O'REILLY®

Our books are available at most retail and online bookstores.
To order direct: 1-800-998-9938 • *order@oreilly.com* • *www.oreilly.com*
Online editions of most O'Reilly titles are available by subscription at *safari.oreilly.com*